T.J. Rohleder

15 RULES OF MARKETING

Do Them or "Die!"

TABLE OF CONTENTS:

Introduction:

By T.J. Rohleder

15 Powerful Marketing Secrets That Will Increase Your Sales and Profits!

Congratulations on your decision to read this book. This separates you from all of the other entrepreneurs and small businesspeople who 'claim' they want to make more money, but won't take the time to study a book that can help them do it.

Yes, so many people want the MAJOR BENEFITS of being in business without going through all of the time, work, and effort to get them. This is true in all aspects of life. People want THE VERY BEST RESULTS, but don't want to pay the price to get them. **And that's sad because business has SO MANY GREAT REWARDS TO OFFER!** It can lead to a life of complete and total freedom and fulfillment. And finding all of the ways and means to make more money can be a great deal of fun!

So what's the secret? That's simple: Just become A GREAT MARKETER. This is the key to dramatically increasing your sales and profits. It's the secret that gives you a MAJOR UNFAIR ADVANTAGE over all of your competitors... And once you get good at marketing yourself and your business, you'll discover that...

THIS IS THE GREATEST GAME ON EARTH!

Not only can learning how to become a great marketer make you a lot of money, but it's also VERY REWARDING and a lot of fun!

5

Marketing is made up of **all the things you do to ATTRACT and RETAIN the largest number of the very best prospective buyers** in your market. That's it. It sounds simple because it is! Of course, like everything else that's most worthwhile, IT'S NOT EASY. This is especially true in today's overcrowded and over-hyped marketplace. But tell me ANY GAME that's easy and I'll show you one boring game that you don't want to play!

Anyway, the fact that learning how to become a great marketer is difficult is THE #1 REASON why none of your competitors will EVER do it. Remember that. Think deeply about that. Then consider this fact: **your ability to ATTRACT and RETAIN the very best customers in your marketplace is the key to making all the money you've ever dreamed of making.** Sure, there's a learning curve you must go through and it can be a bit painful. But that's THE PRICE you must continually pay to get really good at ANYTHING you want badly enough. And I promise, when you get good at all of the things you have to do to MARKET YOURSELF AND YOUR BUSINESS, you'll have a major unfair advantage over all of the people and companies who are also trying to do business with the same prospects and customers that you're trying to attract and retain.

So please **let this be your #1 FOCUS** as you go through this book. Have fun reading and thinking about all of the powerful ideas and strategies I'm about to share with you.

Here's What You'll Discover In This Book

This book gives you 15 of my most powerful marketing secrets that I've used to generate millions of dollars in my own small business. These secrets will dramatically INCREASE YOUR SALES AND PROFITS! You can use them to get ALL of the very best prospective buyers in your marketplace will practically stand in line with money in hand and beg you to take it!

HOW'S THAT for a great visual!

As you know, every business exists to serve its marketplace. And yet, how many entrepreneurs and business owners are TOTALLY FOCUSED on their marketing? And how many of your competitors are constantly seeking the very best ways to give their best prospects and customers the major benefits they want more than anything else and are not getting from anyone else? Very few, IF ANY!!! But you can and WILL when you simply do the things that I tell you about in this book. So study this book and discover the powerful marketing secrets you can use to completely TRANSFORM YOUR BUSINESS. As you'll see, **these 15 little-known methods give you a very real 'unfair advantage' over the other people and companies who are trying to do business with the same people you're after.** I'll go over all the details in this book. I sincerely hope you'll use these powerful marketing methods to attract and retain the very best prospects and customers.

And to reward you for purchasing this book, I have…

A great FREE business-building gift for you!

Yes, I have a gift waiting for you that can DRAMATICALLY INCREASE YOUR SALES AND PROFITS! Here's what it's all about: I spent TEN FULL YEARS writing down all of the greatest marketing and success secrets I discovered during that time period. Each day, I took a few notes and, at the end of a decade, I had a GIANT LIST of 6,159 powerful secrets! This list is ALMOST 1,000 PAGES of hard core money-making ideas and strategies!** **Best of all, this massive collection is now YOURS ABSOLUTELY**

FREE! Just go to: www.6159FreeSecrets.com and get it NOW! As you'll see, this complete collection of 6,159 of my greatest marketing and success secrets, far more valuable than those you can buy from others for $495 to $997, is absolutely **FREE.** No cost, no obligation.

Why am I giving away this GIANT COLLECTION of secrets, that took ONE DECADE to discover and compile, FOR FREE? That's simple: I believe many of the people who receive these 6,159 secrets in this huge 955 page PDF document will want to obtain some of our other books and audio programs and participate in our special COACHING PROGRAMS. However, you are NOT obligated to buy anything—now or ever.

I know you're serious about making more money or you wouldn't be reading this. So go to: www.6159FreeSecrets.com and get this complete collection of 6,159 of my greatest marketing and success secrets right now! **You'll get this GREAT FREE GIFT in the next few minutes, just for letting me add you to my Client mailing list,** and I'll stay in CLOSE TOUCH with you... and do all I can to help you make even more money with my proven marketing strategies and methods.

So with all this said, let's begin...

** WARNING: This complete collection of 6,159 marketing and success secrets contains MANY CONTROVERSIAL ideas and methods. Also, it was originally written for MY EYES ONLY and for a few VERY CLOSE FRIENDS. Therefore, the language is X-RATED in some places [I got VERY EXCITED when I wrote many of these ideas and used VERY FOUL LANGUAGE to get my ideas across!] so 'IF' you are EASILY OFFENDED or do NOT want to read anything OFFENSIVE, then please do both of us a favor and DO NOT go to my website and download this FREE gift. THANK YOU for your understanding.

Just One Good Idea...

Although you might perceive otherwise, given the standard Madison Avenue way of doing things, marketing isn't really about throwing huge amounts of money at something and then finding out later that it didn't work. You want to do the opposite: put small amounts of money to the test, cautiously building them into larger amounts. **It's all about seeing how many ideas you can come up with and testing on a small scale, in order to see which ones work the best. Then you take those winning ideas and see how far you can roll them out.** By rolling them out, I simply mean that you need to see how more mailing lists you can run, assuming you're using Direct-Response Marketing (as I would certainly recommend). If you're in space advertising, how many more space ads you can do? If you're doing pay-per-click Internet advertising, how many more clicks can you buy?

There are plenty of people out there running small sums up into substantial piles of cash, and you can do it too. **All it takes is commitment and plenty of repetition.** That's one of the reasons you're going to hear me say some of the same things repeatedly throughout this chapter and throughout this book. If you're really committed to mastering marketing, **repetition isn't a bad thing.** Sure, I tend to teach a lot of the same principles over and over again — but those are the fundamental principles that can make you millions of dollars. So every time you read something you've read three or four or a dozen times, get excited about that, and let it become a part of your permanent thinking process. Remember: I'm out there practicing what I preach every single day, using these same tips, tricks, and strategies to build my own fortune. I happen to believe that part of doing that is freely sharing these things, so that you can make your own fortune.

Now, I realize you can't use everything I'm telling you here; some of these points might not apply to you, and some you might not need to pursue, depending on your business and goals. But I firmly believe something that Russ von Hoelscher told me twenty years ago: **"All it takes is one good idea to make a million dollars."** Sure enough, since that time, we've had several good ideas that have generated many millions of dollars for us. I don't say that to brag on how much we've made; I'm telling you that to explain how well these marketing principals work. A single idea really *can* help you make a million, and that's the theme of this chapter. I happen to think that it's wonderful to know that at any given time, all it takes is one really good idea to become wealthy. **Of course, you may have to come up with 10 or 12 ideas, or even 20 or 30 or more, to find that one idea.** That's fine; if you're testing those ideas in a small way, you're not risking any big dollars; and when you do find that winner, it more than makes up for not only the small amount of money you had to shell out to do the testing, but for the emotional factor and the time element that it takes to test new ideas.

Believe it: you're just one idea away from huge success. Think of rock bands who toil for years; they play small, local shows occasionally for their buddies and family members, or maybe they have a gig at the night club doing cover songs. They may be really good musicians, but they haven't been discovered yet. Then they have a hit, and someone discovers them — and that same CD that they couldn't move becomes an instant hit that everybody wants. They go platinum and launch their careers. They've been plodding along and putting in their dues for years; but suddenly, that one hit — that one idea — makes them a million bucks. Writers can do the same thing; they might have written several books, and then all of a sudden, for whatever reason, one has all the right ingredients and they become an overnight twenty-year success story. **Well, the same thing can happen in business.**

All it takes is one idea to make a million dollars, and you never know when it's going to hit. **That's why I believe that you should have a pen and paper handy when reading this book, so you can take lots of notes.** You never know; maybe your one idea will occur to you while you're reading today. Or maybe your one idea has already happened, and you missed it because you didn't write it down. Fortunately, ideas pop up all the time; and just because you missed an idea once doesn't mean you won't have a new one. You've just got to pay attention. You've got to be in tune to the ideas that flow through you and all around you. My closest colleagues and I joke from time to time about how we have too many ideas, but that's because we're conditioned to find them. We're like drug-sniffing dogs, except that we sniff out ideas We've gotten more than we can handle because we've done the necessary things mentally, psychologically, to prepare ourselves to receive those ideas.

They're not all million-dollar ideas; in fact, most aren't. But by working through ideas and paying attention to them when they come, and developing them as they warrant it, you'll eventually hit a few that make you a lot of money. **You have to be in the right frame of mind, maintaining the right mindset and the right knowledge, so that you can seek out those ideas and find the best ones.** Ideas only happen when you've got the ability to grasp them and benefit from them. Like I mentioned before, you have to sniff them out sometimes — but they're everywhere. Maybe other people can't see them, but once you know what you're looking for, you can; and often, the perfect million-dollar idea isn't one discrete idea. **It's actually a combination of several or many *different* ideas, even a recombination of what's already gone before.** Even when you test something and it doesn't quite work, it's not a good idea to dismiss it completely; often we'll take certain elements of failed ideas and incorporate them into newer ideas and test those, eventually finding the right combination that works. It's like a safe. Let's say you've got four or five different numbers that need to be in just the right sequence; you know the numbers are right, but they're not going to work if you don't put them together properly. When you do, the tumblers click, you open it up, and there's a pile of money for the taking.

Earlier I mentioned the twenty-year overnight success story — and it's so common, especially in the entertainment business, that it's not even funny. **If you want to make millions of dollars, you just have to hang in there.** Stick with it. Don't give up; just keep going at it, keep thinking, and keep hatching out those ideas. Sure, some will go over like lead balloons; that's unavoidable. But some may very well pull you straight up into the sky. Just one good idea, one *killer* idea, can make you a millionaire. You see this fact presented over and over again. If you look at famous success stories and well-known companies, you can usually find that kernel of a really great idea that someone presented to the market — whereupon they were rewarded with a fantastic amount of money. It's happening even faster with the Internet; look at companies like eBay or Google. In a very short amount of time, they went from literally nothing to multi-billion-dollar companies, from just the kernel of a good idea. **That's one of the things that really excites me about being self-employed these days: that if you can find that one killer idea and run with it, you can make a lot of money**

very quickly.

People ask, "Well, how do I come up with that one idea?" What I usually tell them to do is to come up with as many ideas as possible. Sometimes people think and think and think, and they come up with just one idea. They throw it out there in the market, and maybe nothing happens. Maybe it's a complete failure, and they don't make any money. As a result, they say, "If this whole concept of making millions with one idea is so great, why didn't I make money with this idea I thought was great?" Well, maybe it *was* great — and maybe it wasn't. **The way to be sure you come up with great ideas is to come up with a large number of ideas.**

Another part of this strategy is to **put those ideas into action very quickly.** One of the challenges that I think we face as a society is this idea that it's bad to fail. People don't want to fall on their faces; they only want to succeed, so they never try anything. This is a terrible mistake. If you read the biographies of some of the most successful people in the world, you'll discover that they didn't become instant overnight successes. In many cases, it took them years, usually decades. to become successful — because they kept trying one thing after another and failing repeatedly. **Failure isn't a bad thing, as long as you don't give up! If you really want to succeed, you have to take that risk.** All business is calculated risk, after all — so be willing to fail forward and fail *quickly.*

If I knew that my 100th idea was going to make me a multimillionaire. I wouldn't tentatively try my first idea and then balk on the second one. If I knew I was going to take ninety-nine failures to get to that hundredth success, then I'd go through all those failures as quickly as possible, one right after another. So instead of being tentative about trying things because you're afraid to fail, **just recognize that you *are* going to fail — but not every time.** You're going to do some things that won't work; you'll end up wasting some money, time, and effort. Well, fine. When you do that, you're going to get yourself closer to those ideas that are going to be successful, and *they're* going to make you some money. **Instead of being fearful of failure,** *fail fast!* **Fail forward.** Move ahead and try as many things as possible. Over time, you're going to learn from your failures, and you'll eventually hit upon that idea that's going to make you a fortune.

So don't spend all your time crafting this one little idea, trying to make it perfect for months or years before putting it out in the market to see if it works. What if it doesn't? *Get something going now!* **Get it out there and see if it works. If it does, great! If not, move on to the next thing, and then the next thing.** That's what my colleagues and I do. We just throw things against the wall and we see what sticks. Eventually we'll get that homerun. But you know what? Even if that homerun turns out to be a multimillion dollar idea (and yes, we've had 'em), we keep moving forward, because we realize that there are *more* great ideas out there.

Our colleague Chris Hollinger likes to say that **massive action is the key to all success,** and I agree with him. That's what gives us our purpose, our passion, and our excitement for being in this business, and I'd suggest you do the same. Come up with a lot of ideas and put them into action very quickly. Be willing to fail forward, learning from your mistakes, and be willing to do whatever it takes to get to that one winning idea that can make you a lot of money very quickly. Don't let the word, or the concept, of failure stop you. The only real failure is finally when somebody says "I'm done. I'm never going to try again." **As long as you're moving forward, as long as you're trying to sharpen your skills, you'll continue to learn.** Stay in the game, stay deeply committed, and eventually you'll find those few ideas that can turn everything around for you.

One of my favorite success stories is that of Ray Kroc, a salesman who didn't know how to say die. At 52 years of age, his business was failing. He'd had some good years, but the market was changing, and his business was drying up. He only had one real customer left: a manufacturer that made something called a multi-mixer that mixed as many as eight different milkshakes at one time. Well, one of his distributors had a client, this little tiny restaurant in San Bernardino, California, that was owned by a couple of brothers named McDonald. He noticed that they were buying more multi-mixers than 12 or 13 other accounts put together — simply because they kept wearing them out. This little place called McDonald's had great shakes for a great price, so they always needed new multi-mixers, and they always wanted to make sure they had a back-up.

Ray's business was suffering, and he knew he had to do something. He took a look at the account, and decided he had to find out what in the world this company was doing with all these multi-mixers. So he flew out there and visited at lunchtime — and saw that the place had huge lines of customers. That's why they were wearing out their multi-mixers. **But unlike the owners, he looked at that restaurant and saw the future.** Eventually he partnered with the McDonald brothers so that they could start franchising McDonald's restaurants throughout the nation. He figured that hey, if he could get a McDonald's in every city in the United States, he'd sell a tremendous number of multi-mixers! As you can see, even then he didn't quite have his idea right — but he eventually refined it, and Ray's bright idea evolved into a multinational corporation that became so much more than just a scheme for selling milkshake mixers. At 52 years of age, you'd think that most salespeople would be more focused on retiring, but look at what he did. **He just kept hanging in there.** If you study his success prior to that, you'll see that he really paid his dues. You're probably paying your dues right now, just like Ray Kroc. So don't give up! Success is out there waiting for you, if you just don't give up. All it takes is one hit to make a lot of money.

Here's an example of that. I grew up in a little town called Great Bend, Kansas. It's an oil field town. When I was 17 years old, I worked at an oil field supply store, and I got to know these oil field guys who were my customers. They were all just regular guys too, the most average kind of guys you can imagine, and yet some of them were multimillionaires. A couple of them just told me that the oil business is pretty damn simple. You drill ten holes. Nine of them might be what they call dry holes, which means they produce little or no oil at all; but that 10th hole, it's a gusher. That 10th hole could make money for decades. That's the whole oil business in a nutshell. It's definitely affected by the demand of the market and price fluctuations, of course; but if they drill 10 holes, **they're just looking for one winner. We do the same in the Direct-Response business.** We're constantly trying to test 10 different things as fast as we can, knowing that just one of those things might really be the winner that makes us money for years.

Here's another example. Do you know what the biggest difference is between an amateur photographer who takes a few pictures of his family, and someone who sells photos to *Time* magazine or the *New York Times*? **Besides education, of course, it's persistence — and the knowledge that only a few of their pictures will be good enough to be used.** A professional photographer will snap hundreds or even thousands of photos to find the few pictures they're looking for. They're not terribly concerned with what each individual picture looks like, because when they take enough photos, they know they'll find the few that turn out to be the exact shot they want. If they're working on a photo spread for a magazine and they need, oh, a dozen photos at most, they'll take a thousand to get those few pictures that they really like, the ones that bring out the subject in the best light. On the other hand, the everyday individual taking pictures snaps a few shots and calls it good. Later, they may hold them up or put them up on their computer and look at them side-by-side and say, "Yeah, all right, we'll go with this one," and that's that.

The same kind of thing separates the million-dollar entrepreneur from the part-time entrepreneur. It's generally not their knowledge; it's not their background; and it's not their history. **It's usually the number of ideas they're working on and processing at any given time.** Since you maximize your income by maximizing your idea output, that means that you've got to constantly be looking for new and different ideas. Most people just don't have enough ideas. Most people struggle to find ideas. Worse, they haven't mastered the art of getting those ideas by processing them.

The thing to keep in mind is that **you don't want to kill an idea too early, and you also don't want to try to limit yourself to only the very best ideas.** If you spend all of your time worrying about finding that one idea that's going to make you a million dollars, you'll miss all the little ideas that it takes to get there. Even if an idea doesn't have the potential that you feel it requires to become a million-dollar idea, it can still earn you some money — and in combination with one or more other ideas, it can evolve into a million-dollar idea.

So as you work through your ideas, remember that at least in the beginning, there is no bad idea. Write down every idea that comes to you, even if you think it's a stinker, because you never know. **Keep a journal of ideas.** That's where most of your products, services, new ideas for making money, and joint venture opportunities will come from. That idea journal is invaluable, because, as you well know, it's easy to lose an idea if you don't write it down. That's what happens to most people — they don't hook their ideas with a pencil and pin 'em down.

Ideas pass across their desk or their brain, and then they're out the door and on to something else — and that idea never had a chance to take shape. So you've got to get them down on paper.

Chris Lakey and I have taken to using little digital voice recorders to record ideas. They're smaller than cell phones, less than an inch thick and just a few inches long. If you keep one in your pocket all the time, you can use it to record all your ideas instead of having to write them down. These little things can hold up 72 hours of audio; and when you need to put them in your computer, you just connect it to the USB with a cord and it'll dump all those audio files into a folder. Then you've got a recorded history of your ideas. From there, you can work through the ideas and figure out which ones you can turn into workable ideas for new products, new services, new programs and new opportunities and profits. **You see, the key is in the quantity, not just the quality — though you do end up with the quality ideas by paring down the rest to what really matters.** You'll get there if you start by just jotting down all your ideas, and keeping a flowing journal or an audio file of all the ideas that cross your mind. You've got to be that idea sniffer, constantly on the lookout. And here's something else to remember: Once you get into a groove, your mind will naturally filter your ideas for you. **That's part of why goals work.** Even at a subconscious level, your brain will pay attention to the things you really, really want.

Now, let's talk about what you need to do once you've had one of those million-dollar ideas. **The most important thing is to get it out there to the market.** After all, if nobody knows about it, nobody's going to buy it. Money's not made just by hatching out great ideas. It's made by selling things: products, services, opportunities. And before you can really sell anything, **you need to be 110% sold yourself on what you're selling.** That's really the key, you know. If you're excited and passionate about your idea, the way you're going to sell other people isn't by cajoling them, it isn't by hyping them up, it isn't by trying too hard to sell them; it's simply by transferring your level of emotion about the idea to them. That's what really sells them.

And that's a key point that I want to make, because a lot of people say, "I've got an idea, but I just really don't know how to sell it." What they're really saying is, "I don't know the 14 steps to sell something. I don't understand the sales process," or "I don't understand copywriting." They're convinced that there's this complicated process that they don't understand, so they can't sell their idea — **when in reality, if you have something you're passionate about, you can have poor salesmanship and copywriting skills and** *still* **effectively sell it, based simply on your enthusiasm.** I often tell those who are reticent about their copywriting skills, "Look, you've got a hot product that your market wants. You're excited about it, because you know it works, so you're going to find it a lot easier to sell that type of product to your market with poor copywriting skills than if you had the world's best copywriting skills but you had a product you weren't excited about, you weren't interested in, and you weren't passionate about." Do that, and you're just trying to basically shove it off onto your market.

Now, I do tell people that good copywriting skills are important — because they really are critical! — and I would certainly spend a lot of time, effort, and energy honing them. But they aren't everything. It's more important to have something that you're passionate about, that you're excited about, that you *know* delivers results and that you know is going to connect with your marketplace. **So start there, understanding that once you have that hot idea we've been talking about, the next step is selling yourself on it.**

When I go through my own idea journal, that's what I look for. **When it's time to come up with that next idea, I always**

go for those ideas that I'm personally excited about, the ones that I know my marketplace is going to be equally or more excited about. That's how I choose the ideas that I decide to sell. Then I just have to find a way to transfer the emotion that I have for it to my market — and again, that might be in written copy and sales copy, or it could be on an online video. It could be during a teleseminar. If I speak at a live event, it could be from the stage. The whole point is to transfer emotion that I have for the product to my prospect, getting them excited about it, getting them *passionate* about it. **When they have that same emotion about it that I have, in many cases they take out their wallet and buy.**

I think some people look at selling the way a car salesman does: that you're really doing some dirty deals, and you're trying to figure out some way to get the people to buy something that they don't want or need. That's not how it should be at all. You should be coming up with a great idea that you're excited about, that you know your prospects are going to be excited about, and finding ways to transfer that emotion to your marketplace. That's one of the reasons we've generated millions of dollars of income over the years here at M.O.R.E., Inc.: **we've focused on things we've been passionate about.**

Let me re-emphasize that you don't have to figure everything out from the very beginning. **In fact, in marketing, you often have to figure things out as you go along.** A couple of years ago, Chris Lakey and I came up with an idea that's extremely long-term and very powerful — and it's very complicated. It involves lots of different challenges and problems, so we're figuring it out as we go. We know this idea is capable of generating tens of millions of dollars. We know it's long-term. We're excited about it, and we're making money with it right now, working it hard as it exists — and yet we realize that our best strategies for handling this idea are going to come down the road. **This is something we're not going to just figure out all at once.** Our big years are still ahead.

Too many people want to get everything right *first*. They want everything to be perfect; they want to already have figured everything out before they even get started. Those people are really hurting themselves, for several reasons. **First, if you want everything to be perfect from the outset, you'll never get started — because things will never be perfect. Second, you simply learn more through movement than through meditation.** That was something the late, great Gary Halbert used to say, and I like that. You learn more through action, through getting out there. There's another quote that says, essentially, that **action contains its own form of magic and genius and power.** When you get out there and you're excited about your ideas, you don't necessarily know how you're going to put everything together. You may have the haziest of ideas of how you're going to pull it all off — but if you're deeply committed to doing it, there's great power in that. **Your enthusiasm will keep you in the game.**

So many people ask us, "Just tell me how to make millions of dollars in the fastest period of time!" Well, guess what? That's what I'm doing here. **You have to realize that it won't happen overnight** — overnight riches only happen in fairy tales or with the occasional lottery winner, or maybe if you choose your parents right and inherit a bundle. Well... there *is* one other option. At one time, we were working with a marketing guy named Luther Brock — he's retired now. But whenever somebody asked him how to make a lot of money quickly, he'd just say, "Go into the porno business!" He would say it sarcastically, of course, because most people don't want to get into the porno business. His point was, it's not just about making money; **it's about making money by doing something you really enjoy, that you're really enthusiastic about, that you**

21

really love the most. We have the power to fall in love with certain things. We can't love every aspect of our businesses, and yet we have the power within ourselves, if we chose to tap into it, to fall in love with the most important aspects of our businesses and get passionate about them. I'm talking about love in all its best aspects. It's something that really connects us to our businesses, something we feel at a deep emotional level, something that does make us excited and engenders other positive emotions.

So if you've got a great idea and aren't yet certain how you're going to market it, hang in there! Don't think that you have to have everything figured out from the word go. You can cross the bridges as you get to them. **As long as you have a general idea of how you're going to do things, you can get started, and then you'll figure it out as you proceed.** Enthusiasm for a project can go a long way. It can drive you through the difficult times as you're working on a promotion, working on a sales letter, or otherwise trying to take something from an idea to its logical end: where you've got the entire promotion ready, and later, when you've got money in hand and you've delivered the product or the service that you've created through that enthusiasm and excitement.

Even when you're not sure of how you're going to proceed, if you're excited about what you're doing and you're spending a certain level of emotional energy working on the project, it can really carry you. That's why when we get a brand new idea, we won't always just write the idea down and wait for it all to come to fruition; while the idea is fresh, while we're still thinking it through and still excited about it and the energy is flowing, we may write some sales copy based on the idea. **We'll spend some time at the computer fleshing out the basic idea,** writing a headline, maybe blocking out what we think the offer might look like. Then we save that whole file — and maybe it doesn't go any further. Maybe we just spent an hour learning to write better sales copy or headlines.

The truth is, sometimes ideas don't make it very far, or they end up being impractical or unworkable for some reason. It's hard to tell that when they first come to mind — but that happens to be when the enthusiasm is at its highest level, **so it's a good idea to put some energy into getting some thoughts down on paper while you're at your peak of excitement.** You can set it aside for a little bit and come back and see if that idea is going to work, if it's going to be something you can run with. That initial energy can help you focus later on, moving you through the difficult times where the copy isn't quite coming as well as it should and the ideas aren't flowing as well as they might. **Enthusiasm is important in all levels of marketing; a great acronym for the last four letters in the word enthusiasm, in fact, is *I am sold myself*.** Keep that in mind! Everybody knows that a good sales rep is enthusiastic. Even when a sales rep is new at their job and doesn't really know anything about the company's customers or products, they can do very well if they're enthusiastic. Enthusiasm is being sold yourself. That's the foundation of every good, worthwhile promotion.

Enthusiastic yet? Are you feeling that energy running through you? Are you pumped up and excited? Well, here's something that'll get you up there even higher, if you'll take it to heart. We call these the *Three Simple Words That Can Make You Into a Lifelong Millionaire*. These three simple words are: *perception is everything*! I think that's the basis of most of life, actually. Perception: in terms of what we can accomplish, in terms of what people want, in terms of who people think we are and who we *actually* are. Edward DeRopp says that man inhabits a world of delusion; basically, we walk around every single day, day after day, in a little world of our own creation.

It's all based on our own perception of reality: the things that we see, the things that happen to us, or what we believe happens to us. **In most cases, things aren't intrinsically good or bad; it's how we perceive those things that matters.**

If you're thinking, "What does that have to do with business, and selling, and making a million dollars?" here's how: **the way people perceive you makes them decide whether or not to do business with you.** It's all about their perception of how easy it is to use your product, how quickly they can get results, and the size of the results. Remember, I'm talking about perception; the reality doesn't matter as much as their *perception* of reality does.

So whenever you're developing and marketing your ideas, **you always need to be focused on the perception you're offering.** What kind of concept are you putting out there for your customers to hold on to? What kind of story are you telling your customers? What kind of facts are you providing? You have the power to shape the perception of yourself, your company, your products and services, so you can't just blindly throw your ideas out there and say, "Okay, this is what I've got," and bare everything, letting people pick and chose what they want to believe about your company. **You need to formulate your sales message to give yourself the best opportunity to make the most sales.**

There are many different ways you can do that. As I mentioned in the last chapter, one of the things that I recommend is that you pick up a book by Robert Cialdini called *Influence: the Psychology of Persuasion* before you get too heavily into marketing. **Cialdini talks about creating and building perception in prospect's minds, so that you enhance your ability to make sales.** Cialdini says that there are 13 basic perceptions that all people have as part of human nature that make them want a specific product, service, or opportunity as opposed to a similar one offered by another company. I've already told you about the cookie experiment, which demonstrated the value of using scarcity as a marketing principle. People simply value scarce resources much more than plentiful ones; so you can create a different perception of a product just by making it scarcer.

As you can see, it's possible to use psychology in a very basic way to create perception — and scarcity isn't the only way to do this. That's why I recommended picking up Cialdini's book; because once you understand that you can create perception and mold the perceptions of yourself, your company, and your product, that gives you additional marketing power. **That lets you take a little seed of an idea and give it the best opportunity to become a multi-million dollar idea.** Now, to be perfectly honest, I *don't* believe that an idea necessarily has a million dollars in it, no matter how good it is. **It might have a million-dollar** *potential,* **but that's stored energy.** To get the maximum amount of profit out of that idea, you have to do certain things to bring the product to the market, to make it connect with the marketplace, to sell it and to tweak the perception of it so that people really want it.

This is one way to translate your excitement for an idea to your prospects. **By shaping the perception of that product, and maybe even of yourself, people can come to value the product and you more.** They connect with you more, and they really do want that product more. So if you want to make the largest amount of money from your idea, you've got to think all of these things through and figure out how to alter certain perceptions that your prospective buyers have, so that they view everything that you're selling in the most favorable of all lights.

I've told this story before, but it's worth telling again. Early on, when we first got started, there were all of these get-rich-quick ads in the moneymaking magazines — ads where people were standing in front of nice mansions, or getting out of limousines or other fancy cars. Well, my wife Eileen and I didn't live in a mansion at that time, and we didn't have fancy cars; but we thought that in order to have our own full-page ad, we had to go and have a picture taken in front of somebody else's mansion, and go rent a limo, and do whatever else it took to lead people to believe we were absurdly wealthy. That's what the people were doing in the other ads: they were manipulating perception to make it look like they were wildly successful, whether it was true or not.

We said something to Russ von Hoelscher about that and he told us, "Guys, if you do that, you're out of the business in a few years — because that's what everybody else is doing. And besides, that's not who you are. You're just an average couple from the Midwest, like the American Gothic image. **Why not just be yourselves? That's the part that people will connect to: who you are, the fact that there's really nothing all that special about you. It will greatly inspire and motivate them."** And sure enough, that's been our unique selling position all along now! We've kept it to just being ourselves — and it *does* separate us from those other people who try to be something other than what they are. There's nothing wrong with tweaking perceptions, folks. Just don't tweak them so much that you distort reality completely out of recognition.

You've got to find reasonable ways to position yourself and your products. **It's all about psychology, and it's all about influencing certain things that people have within them that causes them to value one thing over another.** Scarcity is a good way to do it, and so is comparing your product to others; but there are many other ways, as Cialdini points out in his book. Another good book on the subject is *Maximum Influence: The 12 Universal Laws of Power Persuasion* by Kurt W. Mortensen. That's a book that Chris and I have studied a great deal.

Again, it all comes down to putting everything in the most favorable light, and it has a lot to do with understanding what the best prospective buyers in your market want and value the most. **Again: in marketing, as in life, perception is reality.** Think about when you meet someone for the first time, the perception they have of you face-to-face. Maybe you become a friend to them; if so, that perception is their reality. If they perceive you as being snotty and standoffish, that's probably the way you'll seem to that person forever. **It's very hard to change that initial perception.** This is just as true when selling and crafting offers. You can use that to your advantage, because if you can get the perception you're trying to create, if you can get your customers to see things the way you want them to see them by changing their perception or getting them to perceive something to be a certain way, you've gone a long way towards making that sale.

That's not to say that you're lying to people; let me emphasize that. **It's not being deceitful.** Some people might say, "Well, if you try to get people to perceive something a certain way, you must be lying — or you must be trying to get them to see something that's not really there." But that's not what getting your customers to perceive your offer properly is about! Again, **you're just putting it in the best light.** It's about presenting the benefits that you want them to see. It's about showing them the good side, all the best reasons why they should be doing business with you, why they should respond to this particular offer right away.

So you want to make sure that you use your sales copy to present a story, the right story, the kind of story you want to tell your customers, so that they see your product as being the ultimate solution for what they're looking for to ease their pain. That's critical. **In all selling, no matter what the product or service, you have to convince your customer that they're**

hurting, and that they need your solution. Now, hurting may mean many different things in different contexts. It could be that they're hurting financially and need your business opportunity. Maybe they're hurting by being overweight, and so they need your diet solution. They could be drowning in debt, so that they need your debt counseling solution. They could even be in physical pain; that's why headache pills sell so well. Ultimately, you've got to get people to recognize the pain they're in because they don't have your solution. **You want them to perceive that buying your product is the only way they're going to receive relief from their pain.**

So you've got to build your customer's perception around that goal. Perception is based largely on that first impression; **what people perceive in their mind to be true is their truth, and that will be the truth that they stick with.** You need them to perceive those things that you want them to perceive, and you need to do that as quickly as possible, so that they can begin to see themselves receiving the benefits of your offer.

And remember: people don't want cheap stuff. **They want things that they perceive as being very valuable and very expensive for a dirt-cheap price.** That may sound like splitting hairs, but it's important. Part of the whole perception thing is to build up the perceived value of what you're selling, so the price looks small by comparison to the money that you ask for in exchange for it.

Let's finish up this chapter with one final point — and it's a pretty short one. This is just kind of a marketing life lesson, because we talked about getting ideas; we talked about selling; and we talked about creating the perceptions required to effectively sell your products. This is simply a valuable warning that I believe can save you a lot of time, money, and energy. **It's just this:** *it's always easier to get into something than out of it.* Think about that. Whenever you're looking at your idea and getting excited, step back a bit and think ahead. Visualize what it's going to take for you to put it together, what the process will be like, what the business will look like in six months, a year, two years, five years out. It doesn't hurt to do that, and you may find that it doesn't temper your enthusiasm one bit. In any case, you have to ask yourself: **"Is it worth all the time, money, effort, and energy to put that idea out there, in terms of the results?"**

You can't tell for sure, of course, but this is one way to keep from getting cut off at the knees. Many times I've had a great, multi-million dollar idea — and I've jumped face-first into a hole. Then I realize that I want to extricate myself from it, and so I start the process .. but it always takes longer to get out than in. Sometimes it takes much, much longer to extricate yourself than you think. So before you commit all that time, money, energy — anything — to an idea, **really analyze it closely, and decide if this is something you really want to get into.** Because again, it's easy to get excited about the potential money you can make, and then fail to sit down and analyze the amount of effort required. This brings up opportunity cost, too: what other ideas might be able to make the same amount of money with less energy, and less time, that you could be doing instead?

One reason many entrepreneurs are self-employed is not just to make a lot of money, but also to have a lot of time as well. **We don't get into this business just to work 80 hours a week or more and be filthy rich, but not have time to enjoy it.** There are certain ideas that can make you a lot of money, and make you very successful and fill up your bank account — **but can really rob you of your time and your life.** That's why I think it's important to weigh whether your great idea is worth all you'll have to put in it. This is a factor that a lot of us don't realize going into the business, which is another reason I wanted to point it out now. We've learned it the hard way by taking on any and every idea, and then dealing with the consequences later on.

Nowadays, I always look at the potential challenges involved with an idea. **Do I have an exit strategy, in case there's a downside?** What is that exit strategy? How quickly can I get out? You should always analyze the potential downside and challenges you may to face along the way, before you jump headfirst into anything. **I think it all comes down to knowing yourself.** The more you know yourself and what you value the most in life, and what you *don't* value, the easier the decision will be. There are several examples of different things that I almost got involved with, ideas that I was disappointed with at the time because they didn't work out. Now, I look back and I say to myself, "Thank God!"

Here's an example: about six years ago, I was approached by a couple of people about getting involved in a business opportunity with them. We got excited about it. We saw the potential to make lots of money — but one of the reasons they wanted to take me and another guy on as partners was because they were already fighting amongst themselves. They wanted us to get involved in the deal because they thought that *maybe* that would be a way of easing the war between them. It was potentially a multi-multi-million dollar deal—and yet, it would have cost me so many frustrations, so many headaches, and so many hassles. We'd probably all be in court right now, right this very minute. And then there was another deal back in the summer of 2007. I approached a couple of guys on this business opportunity that I wanted so much, and they turned me down—and I was so disappointed. Now I look at them and at the whole situation, and I'm relieved they did, because I realize now some of the things I would have had to do that I didn't know about at the time.

I also know myself enough now to make better decisions. I know that I value my independence—that's the most important thing to me. Twice in the last several years,

I've been ready to join an opportunity... and stalled. Both times, I had the paperwork already filled out, ready to be faxed in—and both times there was something that stopped me right before the fax went. I swear I'm not making this up. Right before I hit the send button I'd decide not to do it, and I didn't know why at the time. I just knew that I wanted to do the deal; I saw that there was money to be made, but there was something stopping me. It took me a long time to know why I wouldn't allow myself to do it, but now I realize what it was.

It's all because I value my independence too much. I knew that if I went ahead and got involved in either opportunity, I was going to have to give up too much of my own independence. I just couldn't do that. I think making the right decision about an opportunity does come from knowing yourself, knowing what you like, knowing what you don't like, knowing what's most important to you, knowing what you're willing to do and what you're not willing to do. **Sometimes it comes from making mistakes and getting your rear end kicked a little bit.** Then you say, "Man, I'm never going to do that again." I think sometimes, unfortunately, the way to make good decisions is to make some bad decisions first, and go through the painful process of learning from them.

I feel that this concept is a great way to bookend this conversation about ideas and where they can take you. So let me repeat it: **You need to spend a lot of time thinking about where an idea is going to take you, and what your end goal is, and how you'll get out of that idea if you need to.** Maybe this is less true when you're first getting started, because you're jumping out there with nothing to lose. You can just take ideas and run with them, because you know you'll just figure out stuff later, and you just need to get the money to start coming in. That's not a bad way to go; but if you can, **you should still be a little selective,** especially once you've got something significant to lose. You should analyze the possibilities for profit and all the other things that come along with well-cultivated ideas.

Good ideas always lead somewhere, and they usually lead to obligation as well as possibility for profit. Remember that. You've got to think those things through. Think about who you'd be working with, what kind of results you'd be experiencing, and what kind of demands there would be on your time and your resources and energy. How long will this obligation be? Will this be a 30-day idea? Will it be a six-month idea? Will it be a lifetime idea? What happens if it succeeds, and does everything you hope it will do? What happens if it fails? What are your liabilities and obligations?

You can be selective in choosing the ideas that present the best opportunity with the least amount of effort. You can choose ideas that require as little of your time as possible; you can also choose ideas that require a lot of your time. **It's all determined by what you're trying to get out of that idea, and how that idea meshes with your goals.** At M.O.R.E., Inc., we've had lots of opportunities presented to us that might have made us a lot of money but didn't fit within what we were trying to accomplish for the company, and so we had to pass on those ideas—even though it hurt sometimes. But sometimes there are other factors that are more important than money that you have to consider. You've got to consider all angles.

So let's summarize: **First of all, let all the ideas flow.** Don't shoot an idea down too early. The ideas will come more freely if you let them come early and often, and if you don't spend too much time worrying about killing them. **Later comes the time for evaluation, for reflection, for looking at an idea and analyzing it and determining whether it's going to be something that you want to invest your time and resources in.** If you determine that it's one that you want to pursue, pursue it with all your passion, with all your heart, with all your emotions, with all your energy behind it, and make sure that idea has every chance to succeed. Earlier, I quoted from Edward DeRopp. Here's another great quote from Edward in his book *The Master Game*: **"Seek above all else a game worth playing, and play it as if your entire life and sanity depended on it— for it does."**

Think about that. Play to enjoy, but play to *win*.

Raking It In

What is marketing?

If you ask a thousand different marketing experts that question, you're going to get a thousand different answers — and if you ask most college business professors, you're going to walk away totally confused. Some of those guys could go on for hours, and you still wouldn't get a good clear idea of what marketing is, because all they know is books, and most of their theories apply only to Fortune 1000 and 500 companies. And in any case, if they know what marketing is, why aren't they out there doing it and getting rich?

Here at M.O.R.E., Inc., **we define marketing very simply: it's all the things you do to attract the best customers and then resell to them repeatedly for the highest possible profit per transaction.** That's it! You could put that on a single 5x7 index card, because it's such a simple explanation. Just attract and resell, looking for the highest percentage of the *best* prospective buyers who can offer you the highest profit per transaction. **Do that, and the question is not *will* you get rich, but how rich will you get?** It's all mathematics. It's about having relationships with people who love what you're doing so much that they're sold on you, and they just keep coming back.

In this chapter, you'll find that a lot of what I'm telling you will seem repetitive, for two basic reasons: **1)** Many of the subjects I'll discuss here overlap with other subjects I've discussed (and will discuss) on a very basic level, and **2)** It *is* repetitive, because I believe that repetition is an excellent way to learn. The things I re-emphasize here are the things that need to be re-emphasized. As Robert Bly likes to say, **you have to really learn the rules well before you can break them.** I think that's profound, because you can learn the basics rules of marketing in a few days — but it takes long-term study to master the science and art, if you will, that's involved. I've been in the field for decades and I'm still learning new things.

Wherever you are right now, I've been in your shoes. I realize that it's frustrating to go over the same ground repeatedly, but it's necessary. You may discover something you haven't noticed before, right under your feet. You may be a lot closer to success than you imagine, and I guarantee, if you'll keep at it and keep emphasizing the basics, it'll all come together for you. When it does, the money will start flowing in, and you'll say, "*Holy crap!* Where was all this money before?" Well, it was out there in the wallets, purses, and credit card authorizations of millions of people who have problems they need solved. **It's just a matter of you using the right methods to connect with those people and sell to them initially, and** *then* **conducting enough repeat business with them over a long enough period of time.**

My director of marketing, Chris Lakey, is a news junkie: he constantly follows the news, reading articles both online and offline. He pointed out to me an interesting statistic back in February '08: For the first time in their history, the U.S. Postal Service was cutting jobs — on the order of 40,000 positions. In a different article in the *Washington Post*, it was noted that the USPS was projecting that they would carry nine billion fewer pieces of mail in 2008 than they had in 2007. Nine billion pieces fewer! Most people wouldn't even think twice about that; they'd read those two articles, and they'd probably think, "Well, the postal service is suffering just like everybody else. I guess that's what's happening in our bad economy." Chris, of course, thought instantly of Direct-Mail, and everything he knew about Direct-Response Marketing and about mail order. Clearly, the big mailers were cutting back, if not much. But falling back to 98%, as Citibank did, and 96%, as Merrill Lynch did. really adds up. Chris connected the drop in the amount of mail sent through the postal service with the job cuts at the USPS, and started thinking about the opportunity that gives those of us who are serious Direct-Response Marketers. **Less mail is getting into people's mailboxes, so the direct-mail we send will get through to them more easily.**

The other thing that Chris was thinking of as he was reading these two articles was that **they just prove the need to specifically target the people you want to reach.** Of course, the post office serves all kinds of people, and they're cutting jobs, and that's a separate issue; but why are all these billions of pieces not getting mailed by all these companies? Well, under normal circumstances, Citibank is probably flooding the market, hoping that enough of their credit card offers stick; apparently that's not working as well as they like, so they're cutting back. But we're in the business of targeting smaller groups of customers, people that have proven that they want to spend money on the kinds of products and services we have to offer. If you'll stick to these proven formulas of target marketing — first finding a group of people that have a common interest and then creating products and services that give those people what they want — you don't have to be afraid of getting through. **Now, of course you want to test, but you can be confident in using the mail to deliver your message to a group of clients, because you're specifically targeting your message to a certain marketplace.**

You don't have to be fazed by the fact that the Post Office cut 40,000 jobs. You don't have to be fazed by the fact that there were nine billion fewer pieces of mail out there in 2008. You can be confident in going to your marketplace with your message, because you know you sell the exact kinds of products and services they want. Don't believe all the bad news — because one person's bad news can be another person's good news. **The drop in mail volume is a real opportunity to people like us.** Sure, everybody's focused on the Internet these days, and the Internet is great — but it has many weaknesses that the Internet marketing gurus will never tell you, because then you wouldn't buy their courses.

The biggest weakness, of course, is that we're all inundated with email. We go online and there are a hundred email messages — and we ignore most of them. Either we only answer the ones that are from people that we know and trust and want to hear from, with the occasional marketing message thrown in — or we delete all the marketing messages, period. So how do you get through to people if they're deleting your emails? That's no way to build a fortune.

But that's exactly what we've done, and what we're still doing. There aren't really a lot of secrets to doing that; in fact, there may only be five, ten, or twenty really good, hot secrets. All the other stuff is details, and figuring out how to implement those big secrets. I really do think that if you can find out the key secrets to making huge amounts of money and put them in action, you can literally go from zero to riches in a short time. **And that's what we brought to the table in this chapter: another handful of the best of the best marketing tricks and secrets that can have the biggest impact on your bottom line.**

So I'll jump right in with one of the biggest. In fact, I think that if you really lock this into your brain and you truly get it, if you really understand it, you're going to be able to make money for yourself for many years to come. You're going to have total financial security. Now, let me mention a quick example before I reveal the secret; it's one I've mentioned already, in fact. Let's say you work in a Home Depot and someone comes up to you and says, "I'm looking for a drill." So you take them to the drills and ask, "What do you really want? What are you really looking for?" And they tell you, "I want a Makita 18-volt compact lithium ion cordless ½" driver drill kit." Well, that may be what they're *telling* you they want. But what do they *really* want? Do they *really* want that drill? No! ***What they want is a hole!*** That's why they've come to get the drill. The drill is really a tool to get the result they want.

This is one of those things that I warned you I'd be re-emphasizing, because it's so very, very important. If you can internalize this at a deep level, you're going to make a whole pile of money. *People want results.* **We don't care how we get those results.** We don't really want the manuals and the courses and the pills and the potions and the lotions; all of those are just the *tools* to get us a result. We want to be happier. We want to thinner. We want to be better looking. We want to be richer. We want to be more successful. *We want, we want, we want!* We want results! What you need to do is identify a group of people, also known as a niche, who all want the same results, and cater to their wants. Again, as I emphasized in Chapter 3, **their wants matter more than their needs.** Does that sound cynical? Sure it does. But it's the truth.

For example, I just mentioned that people want to be thinner. That's a niche: a group of people who are interested in weight loss. It's a big niche, but what you have to do is understand that these people all want the same thing. There are a lot of companies serving that particular market, and they're helping people get their results by using different tools. Those can be books, reports, courses, live events, hypnotherapy, acupuncture, and programs like Weight Watchers and Jenny Craig. Those are all tools that help people achieve the results they want.

What you should always be focused on is finding a group of people who have a very strong desire to achieve a particular result — whether, again, that's happiness, losing weight, being in better shape, living longer, having more retirement money... whatever it is — and you to need to give those people what they want. That might sound incredibly simple, but it's the key to riches. **You just sell them the tools that they can use to achieve that result,** whether the tools are products, services, or training. Let me extend that, and make this even more powerful for you. Not only do people want results, but **they want their results as quickly as possible, as easily as possible.** You can give somebody a book on how to lose 100 pounds, and you can show them how to do that through strenuous exercise and a diet of bark and twigs and everything that tastes bad — and in three years they'll lose that 100 pounds. They won't be happy about going that route, though. They're going to get the results they ultimately want, but they're not going to be excited about the *way* they're getting it.

What they'd rather have is a magic pill they can pop every single night right before they go to bed — a magic pill that tastes good, slides down easily, and gets rid of that weight in about three days. Now, they'd *prefer* for it to be gone in 24 hours or less, but three days sounds a little bit more realistic, doesn't it? That's really the key. **People want their results, and they want them fast and easy — and the faster and easier you can help them get their results,** *the more money you're going to make.* If you had that tasty magic pill that could help people lose 100 pounds in a couple of days, and all they had to do was take it every night without exercising or changing their diet, you'd be a multimillionaire in no time. That's why there are companies out there generating hundreds of millions of dollars selling weight loss pills and potions. That's why the Acai berry spam is flooding your email: because millions of people want that result, and they want it fast and easy.

One of the things that I would have you do as a new entrepreneur is to look closely at the group of people you're focused on, look at the result they want, and find a way to help them get that result fast and easy, in the exact way that they want it. They want the minimum amount of effort, the minimum amount of time, sometimes the minimum amount of money. That said, you'll find that if you can give people a magic pill that makes them *not* have to change their behaviors, *not* have to do anything different, but still get the results they want very quickly and easily — well, some will be willing to pay a lot of money for it: hundreds, even thousands of dollars. That's the overall formula for getting rich very quickly, and it's not just true with the weight loss market. **It's true in all markets. Everybody wants the result, but nobody really wants to pay the price to get it — at least in terms of changing themselves.** But they may very well pay you big money to develop the products and services that do it all for them.

I attend a lot of marketing seminars, and I've discovered that almost every one of the presenters that I see include, as part of their close, **an offer for some sort of done-for-you services** for the first 20-30 people who meet them when they get off the stage. Of course when people hear that, they all make a mad dash to the presenter. You have to kind of dumb things down a little bit. You have to realize that this is a trend here; I see it more and more. People are just so lazy nowadays it's not even funny. That's not a judgment; it's just an observation. I'm lazy too, in some ways. **We only have so much time and *we want it all*, so we're all looking for shortcuts.**

I used to keep a quote from Gene Schwartz, one of the greatest copywriters who ever lived, up on my wall. It's tattooed

41

on my brain. What Gene said is **what people really want is a miracle** — and when I read that and realized that Gene had made many millions of dollars, it connected. I hope it resonates with you. **Once you've found out what people in your market are looking for, make them the biggest, boldest promise possible, and then dumb it down. Simplify it.** Remember that when it comes to getting people to take action, don't even think of the people that you write to as people at all. Think about them as if they were greedy dogs and write to them *then*. Again, that's not a judgment call — it's recognition of reality. **People are greedy.** They want it all, and you've got to be able to promise them they'll get it. If you don't, somebody else will. **The one who gets the money is the one who makes the biggest, boldest promise and then can back it up — or provide the perception that they can back it up.**

I like the analogy of the drill versus the hole, because it really sums up the difference between selling a feature and selling a benefit. **You have to sell benefits, not features.** The only reason a normal person would want to buy a drill is to get a hole. So you've got to give people what they *really* want — and to do that, you've got to find out what that is first. **You've got to know your customer base and your marketplace very well.** That means you've got to do research and brain sweat and figure out what those true wants are. Not what they *say* they want — what they *really* want.

It would be handy if you could get into their wallets or checkbooks and find out what they're spending their money on. Absent that possibility, you need to use other means to determine what they're buying. Hopefully you're doing Direct-Mail, and can rent mailing lists of people that you know have purchased other things. **You can rent lists that are very targeted,** providing you with information about people who have bought products or services that are similar to the kind you're selling, and you can create products based around what they're buying. You can get pretty specific when it comes to mailing lists and demographic or psychographic information, such that you're *really* targeting in to a specific small segment, a niche marketplace of people who all have very similar buying patterns. **You *know* that if you're selling something similar to what the company was selling when they got that person to buy, then at least you've got an opportunity to sell them something they want.**

Once you know that someone is interested in what you have to sell, then you at least know you're in the ballpark in terms of reaching the right person. We often have people ask questions about where they should advertise. Occasionally, we'll have someone tell us that they'd like to avoid business opportunity magazines, even though they're selling business opportunities, because they're just jam-packed with ads for biz opps. Instead, they'd rather advertise in the local newspaper where there are no other biz opp ads. Well, you don't want to advertise where there's nobody else advertising! **You want to advertise where there are all kinds of other ads, because you know that those ads are reaching people interested in the product you sell.** They're interested in making money, after all; that's why they're reading that magazine. That's what makes it a good place to advertise. To do otherwise would be like deciding to open a fast food restaurant, and instead of putting it downtown where all the other fast food restaurants are, you decide to put yours three miles outside of town where there is *nobody*. There's no other competition, and maybe you'd think that would be the best place to go — if any hungry people pass, you're the only joint around! But of course, you soon go out of business.

You want to be where everybody else is. If you're selling a business opportunity, that means you want to be advertising where others are advertising the same kinds of products and services, because they're reaching that marketplace. **In Direct-Mail it means renting mailing lists that already have proven to be full of people who have bought the same kinds of products and services that you sell.** Remember, it's all about giving people what they want. And don't expect to make a fortune right away. Many people believe that they're going to get rich on only one product and soon retire. **But the reality of marketing is you're probably going to lose money on that first sale** — that is, what's usually known as a "front end" sale. Rarely does any company, even a big one, actually make a significant profit on the front end; you're lucky if you can break even.

The key to making a lot of money long-term is on what we call the "back end" — all the other sales you can make to a person once you hook them with that front end sale and start building a beneficial relationship with them. So when people come to me and say, "Okay, what hot product is really going make me a lot of money?" what I normally say is, **"Look, don't work too much on your front end. Don't focus entirely on that first piece of the pie."** Unfortunately, a lot of people think they need to focus 100% of their attention on that first product — and normally it's a $25 book or a $50 course, or something low-priced like that. In many cases they think that's going to be the be all and end all; they're going to make a million dollars off that deal.

In reality, acquiring a new customer can be incredibly expensive. The fact is, most companies go in the hole to generate a new customer. Sure, you may make $50,000 selling products to new customers — but it may take you $100,000 to make those sales! That's the glory of the back end. Again, the back end is simply all those products, services, books, courses, and whatever else you sell to new customers after the first purchase. **The front end generates leads or first-time buyers. Every additional sale after that is the back end. And that's**

where the money is, because you've already invested the money to generate that new customer. When you make back end sales, *you get that money back* and start making a profit.

People really dig themselves into a hole when they focus all their attention on creating just one product only. What usually ends up happening is that they launch the product and, if they're lucky, they break even — but in most cases they lose money. Then they look around at the marketing landscape and say, "How in the heck is everybody else making money? I've got my full-page ad out there. I'm selling this product on the Internet and I'm doing just what everybody else is doing, but I'm not making any money. How can I survive doing what all these other people seem to be doing?"

The reality is that most of the people have a back-end system in place. It may be hidden; you might only see the front-end marketing — that Direct-Mail piece, that full-page ad, the infomercial, whatever it is — that sells the front end. But the back end is there, or the ads wouldn't continue to be successful. **In fact, a lot of the companies that have been around long-term have multiple back end products.** They have more expensive products. They have live events. They have coaching. They have continuity products. They have all sorts of different things that they're going back and selling to their customers again and again. I've done it myself for many years, and I guarantee I wouldn't have been around these last couple of decades if I hadn't been able to go back to my customer list over and over again, selling them new products and services and opportunities. If I'd spent 100% of my time going out with brand new products, I would have dug myself into a hole that I'd still be trying to get myself out of.

No matter what you're selling, you always need to have this thought in your mind: **"What am I going to sell my customer next?"** And then you either develop or license that product, service or opportunity, whatever you need to do. Once you've got that in hand, you need to ask, "Okay, what's the next thing and the next thing and the next thing?" **You *always* need to be thinking about what you're going to sell your customers next.** Look at a company like Pizza Hut. What are they selling? Pizza! How are they going to sell you the next pizza, that back end pizza? They bring you back in by selling you *different types of pizza*. "Hey! Guess what? We're taking the cheese off the top and we're sticking it in the crust!" Or "We're making it into squares!" or "We're selling 'em for five bucks!" They do all sorts of different things to get you coming back to them over and over again. They're always offering you new things.

I want you to get this idea out your head that you're going to find that one perfect product that's going to generate such a big pile of cash that you'll be able to retire forever. It can happen, but it's rare. **A better concept is to find something that will generate customers and leads.** Sure, try to break even on it, but even if you lose a little money, that's fine. What you need is a plan, a system, for selling them that second product and then that third product, fourth product, fifth product and on and on and on. **Where does that end? It doesn't!** This is a business. Once you get those customers in, you need to constantly be promoting new products, services, and opportunities to them. That's how you generate long-term lifetime income: by creating a list, by building up customer relationships, and then going back to them over and over, month after month, year after year to generate those profits. Once you've already invested in acquiring that customer and building up a relationship with them, **it takes very little money to go back to them with a Direct-Mail piece or an email blast and sell them your next product.** Now you're keeping more of that next sale as profit.

I understand that there used to be a time when you could

actually get rich on just one product. That's more or less a fantasy now, just like my big dream of having a million people send me a dollar. A dollar is nothing; just about everybody in the U.S. could give me a dollar, even most 7- or 8-year-old kids. It wouldn't hurt them; it would just be one measly dollar, for crying out loud. It'd be no big deal. And you know, I still wish that they would do that! I've thought about the *Give T.J. a Dollar* campaign a lot. And I think I could do it now. In fact, I *know* I could do it, without any doubt. I could get a million people, as early as two months from now, to grab $1 out of their purse or their wallet and mail it to me. I *know* I can do it!

So take note! This is a great idea here I'm going to share with you. If you want a million people to give you $1, it's simple. All you need is about $10,000,000 to launch that campaign. If I did this, I could make a big deal about how I'm going to do something for them, or how I'm going to put their dollar to use. *I know* I could get a million people to give me a dollar. But that's probably all; it would probably end right there. That's the punch line: **it costs money to make money.** Everybody's heard that before; it's a cliché, but it's still true. **Just as it's true that you generally lose money on the front end.** That was an old argument that my wife and I used to have when she ran the company: I used to tell her over and over again, "Honey, it's not losing money. *It's an investment towards future profit.*" I must have said that a million times in the fourteen years she ran M.O.R.E., Inc. And it's true, if you're doing your job right.

It's ultimately about relationships. People do business with you once, they find out they like you and what you're selling, and they like what you're doing. You've got a product line to match the market. They come back and buy additional related items. Everybody is always saying, "Well, what do we resell to the customers?" It's simple: **you sell more of the same,**

with a new twist. Earlier I used the Pizza Hut analogy. I mean, come on, how many ways can you make a damned pizza? And yet they're always finding *some* way to do something with the cheese, something with the crust, something with the sauce. They're coming up with all these weird names; and what's in a name? **But people are addicted to new things, and they have to feed that addiction!**

A while back I was working on some website copy and I wanted to get it done, so I was really focused on it. Then all of the sudden the TV stopped playing this show my wife was watching for some breaking news — and of course I had to stop what I was doing, sit there like a fool, and watch the breaking news because I'm addicted to new things, just like everybody else. Since you've got to give your customers what they want, and what they want is new stuff, you have to provide just that. If not, they're going to buy it from somebody else — so you're actually losing money that could and should be yours.

Ideas for new products abound. Like most entrepreneurs, I can come up with all kinds of ideas for products and all kinds of niche marketplaces that I can serve with different products. Every time I read a magazine or a book or watch a TV show or drive down the highway and see a billboard, I see ideas. I start thinking, "Man, I could create a product that that marketplace would need, and I probably could make some decent money selling that product —" and then I stop, give myself a shake, and realize that **just because I could sell that product, that doesn't mean I could continue in that vein.** In most cases, there's no long-term business there, because I don't want to be in that business. I just like to be an entrepreneur. It's a fun game to be in.

The point is that the product itself should NOT be your focus. Once again, your focus should always be the marketplace. You need to flip that focus around to the group of customers you want to sell to. **If you focus on the marketplace instead of the**

product, you'll always be able to develop additional products and services to sell to those customers. If you start with the product, you pigeonhole yourself. You get stuck where you have one product, and then what are you going to do after that?

Now, of course you do have to have that one product to start with. **So if you're just getting started, get your first product out of the way.** Develop it, then get out there and sell it. **Again, you always have to focus on what's next.** What else is coming up? What else can you sell to those people? What are you going to do once you've sold that product? Most likely, if you make a profit on your first sale, it's going to be a small profit, so you've got to think about a back end. You've got to think about what's going to be next in your funnel. What else do you have coming down the pipeline? What else can you sell to those people? If you'll focus on the marketplace and serving them, then the products and services will come. **As you expand and develop your relationship with that marketplace, you'll come up with ideas for new products, all geared toward that marketplace you're already serving.** I think that's where people get trapped. They focus too much on the product, when they need to be focused on the prospects and the clients that they're trying to serve. You use that focus to develop projects, not only to sell the first time, but as part of an ongoing strategy for continuing to sell more and more products. The market always comes first.

Here's a point Jeff Gardner tells me he learned early on — not right away, but early enough to make a difference in the amount of money he was making in his business. When Jeff first got started selling information products, he sold inexpensive things like $5 reports and $20 books; the most expensive thing he ever sold was right under $50. And he really thought he was going to make a million selling this type of stuff! Fortunately, he soon realized that it was going to be a long time before he made it, because you've got to sell a lot of low-dollar items before you hit $1,000,000. That's 20,000 copies alone of a $50 product — and that's just to get the gross sales, not the net. Believe me, it costs a lot of money in advertising and promotion to make 20,000 sales.

So Jeff decided he needed to do something different, and took a look at what other marketers were doing. He saw that other people weren't selling just these low-cost items: they were selling products for $200, $500, $1,000, $2,000, $5,000 and in some cases even $10,000 and more. So Jeff started trying that himself. He was a little worried that people weren't going to buy a $200 product from him, so he offered a $97 product to his list — and a lot of people bought it. In fact, about the same number of people who bought the low-cost items bought the $97 one. So then he moved up slowly from there. He went out to his list with the $197 product, and people bought it. And then for a long time, the highest he would ever go was $497. By then, Jeff was making a lot of money, mostly by selling high end products that had a very high markup. In fact, they had an 8-10 times markup, which basically means that if he was selling something for $500, he wanted his cost to fulfill that product to be about $50. Once Jeff got beyond that mental block of $500, he went up to $1,000 products — and his income jumped incredibly, because he still had a lot of people on his list who were willing to pay $1,000 for a product, a course, or information. He continued to push that envelope, and now he regularly sells $2,000 products. He's also had a life seminar that sold for $6,000 a seat.

If you really want to make an incredible amount of money, you need to make sure that you have high-end products in the mix, because it's going to be very difficult to make millions of dollars selling low-end products. And believe me, you've got people on any list who are willing to pay more money for some products. Now, I *will* tell you that you're going to get fewer people buying a top-dollar product, but guess what? It doesn't take very many of those sales for you to make a lot of money very quickly. **Do the math.** What does it take to make $1,000,000 if you've got a $1,000 product? You need only 1,000 sales. You only need 100 sales of a $10,000 product to make a $1,000,000, versus the earlier numbers, where you have to make 20,000 sales of a $50 product. So you're much more likely to reach $1,000,000 with a high-dollar product than you are trying to get there with a $10, $20, or $50 product. Unfortunately, a lot of people are still stuck in this idea of having a catalog of low-dollar products, thinking they're just going to make it up in volume. **But the smart way to do it instead is to always keep creating higher and higher-priced products, services, opportunities, and turnkey deals, and going at your list with those offers.** I assure you, you're going to discover that a certain percentage of your list is going to want to buy those high end products.

Another benefit of doing that is that I really believe that you create a better customer. If you're only selling $50 products to your customer list, you're building a list of people who only buy $50 products. If you start pushing your list and sell them $500 products, or $1,000 or $2,000 products, some of those people are going to flush out of the system — but some won't, and they're going to become better customers who are willing to pay you lots of money. Then you can go back to those people again and again, and you'll find that some of them will be willing to pay even more for a good product.

Jeff still hasn't pushed past that $6,000 seminar price, but he and I have marketing friends who sell products right now for $8,000, $12,000, and even up to $20,000 or more — and there are people in their mailing lists who are willing to pay those prices. At M.O.R.E., Inc., we have a few products that sell that high. **Those high-dollar products are the ones that really add**

the profit to the bottom line. All these little $5, $10, $20 or $50 deals bring in customers, but the profit is in the high-dollar, back-end items. So if you want to generate the maximum amount of money, you have to break through any mental block that you might have that tells you that you can't sell high-end products. **Push yourself to do it, testing carefully.** Just about every time I've pushed myself to sell more expensive stuff, I've expanded my bottom line, increasing the amount of money my business has made.

A lot of people have never figured this out. It took me a while, too. I started my first business, a carpet cleaning business, in 1985, and my whole deal was, "Hey, I've got the cheapest prices of any carpet cleaning company around!" That's what I advertised as my unique selling point... and it was stupid. On the very first date that my wife and I went on, she told me that I should raise my prices. I was afraid to raise my prices. The only way I knew how to get business was by charging *low* prices. Of course, then I'd go in there and try to upsell; every job, I'd go in to do a couple rooms of carpet and walk out after doing the whole house and all the furniture, and getting all their neighbors' and friends' names. So I was doing a couple of things right.

But look: **oversaturation in the marketplace is the real issue.** We're living in a society where there are so many people trying to compete — so many of them sharp marketers, too. And then the bills — they just keep growing and getting bigger. Everything costs more than you think it will. For all of those reasons, and the fact that you need to reward yourself — so that you'll stay in there, doing all the things necessary to stay in business — you've got to charge high prices. **There's one big reason why people don't do it: it's a dirty, filthy, nasty, four-letter word.** It's an F four-letter word, but it's not the F-word that some people might think it is. **It's the word *fear*!** Fear is what stops people from doing it.

I remember the first time we sold an expensive seminar. If it hadn't been for our joint venture partners in Kansas City, the Anton brothers, there is no way on God's green earth we would have ever tried to sell a $5,000 seminar. I didn't have enough courage to do it on my own; I had to have business partners who were saying, "Now calm down, T.J., calm down, calm down." I was afraid that if you charged $5,000, nobody would come — when in fact we had over a hundred people in the room! Once we got past the first one, it was easier. Six months later we had our second one, and this time we did it without the Anton brothers. **You've got to get past that fear.**

The more money people spend, the better customers they are, and that's the gospel truth. If I had $1,000 for every customer who was a total pain in the rear but bought almost nothing, I'd have a pile of money ten feet tall. There are some really nasty ones that take all the joy and pleasure out of business, and then you go back and look in their buying records to see what their buying history is and find that they've hardly bought anything from you. In fact, recently we even had an angry "customer" who called us up, raising all kinds of Cain — and then we looked into the database, and he hadn't even bought anything! He was just a lead, somebody who bit on one of our free offers.

Now, that's the case only in a general sense. Not everybody who doesn't spend much money is a problem, but often they are. On the flip side of that is the fact **the least amount of problems come from those who spend the most money with you.** That's a good argument right there for increasing your prices. Think about it just from a logistical standpoint: **you're dealing with fewer customers in order to make the same amount of money.** If you have 1,000 people give you $10, you have 1,000 people to deal with. If you have 10 people give you $1,000, you have 10 people to deal with — and I say "deal with" in the most pleasant and positive way. It's the same dollar amount in the end, but with many fewer customers. **You can build an entire business around premium prices, have fewer customers to work with, and have better relationships with them because, traditionally, they're of a higher quality.**

Most people's prices are way too low. All they have to do is bump that price up a little to see an increase in profits, with very little drop-off in sales. **Usually, the value is high enough that it's simple to justify a higher price.** They've just got to have the guts to go out there and ask for it. Most people are willing to pay more, as long as you've built value in and you have a good solid guarantee.

I'm going to finish this chapter up with what I call "the icing on the Get Rich cake." Personally, it's something I wish I would have done earlier — and everybody that I've talked to who has implemented this concept admits the same thing. If you're online and haven't really gotten started yet, the perfect time to start this is immediately. **Basically, it's the concept of creating continuity or residual income.** This is income that you get month after month, year after year, from making one sale.

I'll give you a couple of examples, but first let me explain that a little more. **You spend the money advertising and marketing a product or service one time, but you get paid on that sale over and over again automatically.** This can be something like a service; website hosting, for example. You go to a website host, you buy the service, then you're charged for it every single month, month after month. Your cable bill is the same way; so is your electric bill. That's why these companies are huge — because you sign up with them one time, but then they charge you over and over again, year after year.

Once you've got thousands, tens of thousands or even *hundreds* of thousands of people paying you a monthly fee over and over again, you're banking some serious money. **Plus it offers a lot of financial security, because you know what to expect next month.** If you've got a thousand people paying you $25 a month, you know that next month you've got $25,000 in the bank automatically. Now, of course you're going to have some attrition; some people are going to drop out, just like they do with any service or product. But of course you're always adding people to the mix, too. **As long as you're always adding an equal or greater number, you're building those profits over and over again.**

Another reason why I say continuity is so important is that it gets you out of this process of always, *always* having to create that next best thing. It doesn't mean you're completely out of that loop, **but it gives you time away from your business, a little more freedom,** because at least some of the bills are paid next month. **You already know that money's going to be there whether or not you come up with another product.** You've got a little bit of foundational money, a cushion for those times you have personal or family issues to deal with, or you want a vacation.

And here's yet another reason why I really like continuity: the sales process happens once. You do the pitch and spend the money once to get that customer in, so they're paying you for months or years. Even if you're using a solid customer list, offering new products means you have to go back to them over and over again, going through that exact same process of selling them that next product. There's still a process of contacting them, of them saying yes or no, of them ordering, and then of you shipping out the order. You'll still have to do this to some extent with continuity, but the repetition is so much less. **You sell them on your product once, and they pay you repeatedly.** It can be a very simple process of your database auto-charging their credit card or their checking account — and if it's electronically delivered information, you don't have to do anything else. **It's a lot less expensive than pushing the back end products repeatedly;** it's a lot less hassle, and it gives your business the stability of an ongoing cash flow instead of always having to ship new things out to your customers.

One of the things that Jeff Gardner offers, for example, is web hosting; his company helps people keep their websites up and running. In addition, they have a membership site where people pay $25-$30 a month to have access. They also have a monthly newsletter. In the past he's done monthly audio newsletters where he's just basically recorded himself talking for an hour, and then sent that out to customers. Now he has a 12-page print newsletter — but again, that's charged every single month at $19.95 per month. That continues until the customer tells him to stop.

There are a lot of different ways you can have continuity products that pay you a residual income, even if you're in the informational market field. It really is an important part of a company's product mix to have some sort of continuity offer, if not multiple continuity offers, so that you can start to build up that ongoing cash flow and create some stability in your business. **If you study the most successful companies in any field, you'll find that a high percentage of them are dealing in continuity.** For example, my best friend has a pest control business. The unique thing about pest control is that those companies are readily bought and sold all the time — sold for high amounts of money, and sold very, very quickly. That's a little secret about that industry. Pest control is sold on a contractual monthly, bi-monthly, or quarterly basis. It's continuity-based. People will gladly pay that repetitive fee to get rid of the bugs and keep them away. Continuity is just such a great way to make money! Instead of starting over every month and fighting to pay your bills, you've got something in place that will ensure that those bills get paid. **The money comes in automatically.**

The strategy of starting over again constantly reminds me of one of my top ten favorite movies. It's a Ron Howard movie called *The Paper,* with Michael Keaton. It's one day in the life of a newspaper… a struggling newspaper, by the way. One day; that's all it is, just one day. One of the things Michael Keaton says is, "We've got to start all over again the next day and we have to do it *all over again* the next day." That's how most businesses are; they're just working their butts off. It's a very painful process. **Well, you don't have to do that once you've got residual income in place.** Why should you miss out on the opportunity to have automatic money coming in month after month? Your bills come in month after month, don't they? Why should you have to worry about how you're going to meet those bills?

As consumers, we're used to paying our electric bill every month. We pay our cell phone bill every month. We've got our cable bill, or the mortgage, or the rent. We're paying that car payment. We've got this payment and that payment, and it's all coming out every month. Some of it comes on our credit card; some of it comes on our checking account; for some of it, we write checks. We've got money out all over the place on a monthly basis. The same is true for all those other consumers out there: **they're very accustomed to paying monthly for various products and services, so it's an easy add-on to whatever you're already selling.** If you've already got a $100, $200, $500, or $1,000 to $5,000 sale, whatever it might be, it's simple to step people up to a monthly payment just by adding it on to your order form and telling people there's a monthly surcharge.

What do you do with that monthly charge? Well, it could be for a newsletter; it could be for website hosting; it could be for a small coaching program. You can come up with all kinds of reasons why you have a monthly fee. Maybe it could be for affiliate support, if you've got a business opportunity. That monthly fee could be as little as $5-10 bucks; it can be as much as $100 or more. Some people have coaching programs where they're charging people a $1,000 a month. You can do all those kinds of things, and **it's an easy thing to get people to go from making an initial sale to making a monthly sale.** People are used to making monthly payments; they're comfortable with doing it. And here's the great thing about it: people usually forget about the bill. They're not that concerned about it; it's not like they get their bill every month and they're dreading it.

You know, people are pretty much creatures of comfort and habit. They do the same things over and over again — like in the movie *Groundhog Day* with Bill Murray. Every day is a lot like the day that preceded it; that's just the way people are. They're comfortable with shelling out $30 or a $100 a month, so that makes it easier for us as marketers.

Now, I have people come up to me and say, "Yes, I've heard that before; I've heard that multiple times. But how are you implementing that in your own life and your own business?" Well, people want new stuff, remember? **The trick, and the challenge, is realizing that they want it before they've already implemented the old tried-and-true stuff that's worked every single time.** So yeah, you've heard it. That's why I keep telling it to you. That's why other people keep telling it to you, because it works, and it works every time — but you've got to implement it. **So before you go out and find the next new thing, the next hottest thing, the next big breakthrough, put these into action first.** You've got to work these pointers to get them to work for you. Just hearing them, however many times, isn't going to do anything; hearing them once, and actually putting them into action, is going to be much more powerful than hearing them 40 times and doing nothing.

Big Time, Obscene Profits

My colleague Chris Hollinger, a great marketer in his own right, was recently listening to a radio show and he heard a phrase that we marketers absolutely hate to hear: "obscene profits." That's why I've named this chapter "Big Time, Obscene Profits" instead of just "Big Time Profits." When real entrepreneurs hear that phrase, it makes our stomachs turn. We see companies being accused of making obscene profits, but how much is obscene, exactly? When we go to school, we're taught that if we want to be successful we need to study, to learn, to be productive citizens. **But then, if we go out and actually become extremely successful, we may get labeled as making obscene profits.**

I firmly believe that just about everyone of normal intelligence in America can do well monetarily. You don't have to be a genius; **you just have to be smart enough to surround yourself with people who are smarter than you, which is my secret.** But the thing is, with some people it's not a popular to make bold statements that anybody in America can start with little or no money and make however much that they want to make. They frown on that because they don't want to give people unrealistic hopes. They think poor people will always be poor, and they're always going to need help from the government. You see, phrases like "obscene profits" derive from a class warfare mentality that stems from a belief that there are certain people who will always be rich and keep getting richer, and others who will be poor and always keep getting poorer. It's not necessarily true. Lots of people who are rich become poor, and lots of people who are poor become rich. **We live in America, where everybody really *does* have the same opportunity.** You can be what you want to be, with very few restrictions; and most of those are artificial and mental anyway. I think a lot of people have a sort of split mentality where, on the one hand, they want people to make it good... but they don't want other people to make it *too* good.

On MSN.com, they offer an MSN Money site where they post articles about business and finance. You see articles all over that site, and all over the Internet in general, about how to either how to get rich or retire with a healthy nest egg and never worry about money. You see them on the TV news as well. But you also see politicians telling you that we need to hate the super-rich, and that the CEOs of big corporations make too much money. We need to tax the rich more, because they don't need all that money anyway. **So you've got this internal struggle, where many people can't reconcile the fact that they want to make a lot of money with their general dislike of rich people.** They don't want to be seen as obscenely rich.

Well, you know what? There really is no such thing as "obscenely rich," because no matter how much money you make, someone will think you're obscenely rich. Consider the fact that the teeming billions in Africa and Asia who live on less than $1,000 a year probably think the average American salary of $30,000-40,000 is outrageously obscene. But that's an artificial differentiation; there's no line drawn where people say, "Now, it's okay if you make up to $100,000 a year, but no one really needs any more than that. So if you make anything over $100,000, you make too much." **What matters is what you do with the money** you have, not so much as how much you make.

Obscenely rich, I think, is a term that comes from this distrustful mentality of anyone who is wealthier than *you*. It's a popular catchphrase that doesn't really apply to the real world, because you can be as wealthy as you want to be. Some people live very comfortably on $100,000 a year, and other people would starve on $100,000 a year because of their lifestyle is very lavish. So while society says one thing, in reality, you've got the ability to make as little or as much money as you want.

In this chapter, I'll let you in on some secrets that will let you do just that.

Lead Generation

One of the keys of business success is learning the secret of lead generation, **which is basically anything you can do to get a prospect to raise their hand and want to know more about what you're selling.** At that point you're a guest, not a pest.

Think about some of the sales calls that you may receive. Let's say you're sitting down at your dinner table, and all of a sudden the phone rings, and it's some guy with a local life insurance or financial planning company wanting to set up an appointment to show you how his planning services can change your life forever. That's what we call a cold calling situation, and most people are annoyed by such calls. **But with a proper system in place, where you can have people calling *you* wanting more information, that reverses the whole table.** That puts you in a better selling position for your business.

But in most businesses that this strategy is directly applicable to, you don't just want people to raise their hands. **You want to qualify that prospect and make them more**

likely to become a customer. I'm going to share with you a couple of specific ways that I use to help qualify the people I hope to eventually turn into new customers: specifically, I'm going to share an online method, and I'm going to share a direct-response method.

Online, you can drive people to a website using any number of basic advertising methods: Pay-Per-Click, banner ads, direct-mail pieces, postcards, or space ads in newspapers or other publications, or opportunity magazines. Once someone is at my website, I'm going to share with them some information that's very bold, that grabs their attention; and I'm also going to have a direct call to action. **At this point, I'm going to make them jump through some hoops, and I'm going to want to start extracting information from them.** For example, one site my colleague Chris Hollinger was using recently has them watch a video. Okay, they've jumped through **Hoop 1.**

Hoop 2 is to gets them to click through to another page. There's another video there with more information. It's very graphic and designed to get their attention. For **Hoop 3,** Chris has that lead jump to a lead capture page, which collects basic contact information. But remember, at this point he wants to qualify them even more; so when that lead ultimately ends up in his email box, he has other information to go on that further qualifies them. And some of the questions that he asks them on this lead page are: How much time do you have to give to a new business venture? How much money are you looking to spend to build this business?

If you look at this situation, here's how it goes. Chris has somehow contacted the leads by various advertising methods, he's driven them to a site, and he's had them jump through a few hoops and ultimately leave him some information. Now, he has their name, their email address, and their contact information all right there; but he also has some key information that qualifies that prospect. That's the time they have to spend, the money they have to spend, and their level of interest. **In essence, they've qualified themselves at this point.** So now, when they get an email back, they're also probably going to get a phone call from Chris. **At that point they're receptive to his message;** in a sense, they're out there waving their hand back and forth, saying, "Chris, I want to know more about this." **By doing it this way he probably ends up with fewer leads, but they're far more highly qualified, which means, ultimately, that he's going to have a better chance of closing each of them.** It's not good enough just to generate a lead. He wants to generate *highly qualified* leads — people who really want the information he has to share.

You can use direct-mail the same way. You should start by looking at the product, the service, or the opportunity that you have to offer, and then spend a lot of time analyzing the people who comprise your target audience. **One of the best ways to start qualifying prospects is to have a good relationship with a list broker,** because you can go them and identify specific traits and demographics of the market you want to hit, and they'll find the right marketing list for you. For example, I can go to my list broker find a big list of people who suffer from heartburn. Then I can write a headline that goes right to their source of pain, something like, "Does thinking about retirement turn your heartburn into a raging inferno?" In other words, I'll craft something I can use to capture that specific market. Having a good relationship with a list broker can help you qualify prospects right from the beginning.

In the direct-mail piece itself, you have to present an offer that really blows their mind. As you're writing, **you need to make some very bold statements and promises in that to get their attention.** If you don't, it's just going to pass by in the heap of mail that people get every day anyway. So create those bold headlines, but back them up with meaningful, passionate, and logical arguments. Be specific enough so they ultimately want to follow your call to action, which is to send off for some more information. But still, you want to go ahead and further qualify these folks, just like you would with the online version. **And nothing qualifies people more than spending their own money.**

Many of us use what we call a five- or ten-dollar hand-raiser. This is basically a call to action, saying, "If you like what you heard here, then go ahead and send me $5, and I'll going to send you the complete packet of information." You've probably seen this format used in the past. **Again, you might not generate a ton of prospects, but those you *do* generate will be highly qualified.** They've sent you that five or ten dollars, and they get a fantastic back-end package that includes a nice, long-form sales letter that sells something much more profitable.

So with every product, service, or opportunity that you have, spend some quality time to generate a qualified lead, and you'll turn a significant percentage of those into big-time profits. **Basically, we're trying to filter and screen.** Think of it as panning for gold, where you're trying to sift through all this rock and mud so you can find those few gold nuggets. **Understanding your market is the most important thing:** the people you're trying to target, what's most important to them, the best possible benefits you can provide, and more. You have to ask yourself some tough questions in the beginning. As Abraham Lincoln was once quoted as saying, "If I had three hours to chop down a tree, I'd spend the first hour sharpening the ax." **So you really think things through in the beginning, and strategize as much as you can.** It's a process of testing and finding out what works best, and really understanding what you're trying to accomplish.

We have a $4,985 package we're trying to sell to business

owners. We'll start with the nation first and then, if we're successful, we'll broaden out to the world. There are millions of business owners out there, and not all of them are interested in the coaching programs that we're selling. **But you have to begin with the end in mind;** that's some of the best advice I can give anyone when it comes to lead generation. Our end in mind is this big package that we want to sell to these business owners. So how do we sell the largest amount of these packages? Well, one of the strategies we're using is a radical one. First, we're trying to sell them a $749 package. If that doesn't work, we'll try to sell them a $495 package — and we might even test a $295 package. **The only purpose of that smaller package is to bring us the highest qualified prospects, so we can convert 20-30 % of those people over to the $5,000 package.** And if we're able to pull it off... well, again, there are millions of business owners out there, and all we need to do is make 10,000 sales every year times $5,000 to get $50,000,000 a year. That may not happen, but it's fun to play with numbers like that, and to look at how much money you can make when things go right for you.

Most marketers start out realizing that they need to make a lot of sales. **Their fatal flaw is that they think the best way to do it is to go straight for the sale.** The thought process goes something like this: "I've got a $1,000 product. I have a mailing list of people who could be interested in my product. I've targeted the list. So what I'm going to do is mail 1,000 sales letters out to get that $1,000 sale." They feel that their best change to make a sale is to directly mail that $1,000 offer to their thousand-piece mailing list that they rented to buy their $1,000 product.

And that's absolutely the wrong way to think. Instead of trying to get all those people to buy your $1,000 offer, **why not just focus on say, the 5-10% who are going to be the most**

likely to buy it? You do that through lead generation. Maybe you ask for five or ten bucks; maybe you ask for more. We've had offers that ask for $20 as a lead generation amount. And we even do some where it's absolutely free — there's no cost or obligation. You just raise your hand and you'll get the Special Report for free.

The point is that you do something to narrow the field, to get people to raise their hands and express interest in what you have to offer. **By doing that, you end up with a group of people much more likely to buy from you.** That's something a lot of marketers just don't figure out... ever. They never learn the strategy of extracting bigger profits from smaller numbers of people. And, of course, you want the most people to sell to as possible. Common sense tells you the more people that you have to sell to, the more money you can make. So you need the highest possible number of qualified leads.

You can actually lose money by under-qualifying. Here's what I mean. Some people are scared to ask for money to get a lead, because they're afraid they'll get too few. **But in most cases, you can actually earn more money by having a smaller group of better qualified leads.** You figure out exactly where that boiling point is by testing different prices. You should test free leads, you should test a $5 lead, maybe even just a $1 lead. That's been successful for us in the past on certain promotions. Maybe just ask them for $5, $10, or $20. As I've mentioned, we've tested offers where we've asked for $750-$795 as a lead for a $5,000 package. You always want to test, and you always want to do something to get people to raise their hand, take a small step, jump through a small hoop to get themselves qualified before you go on to attempt to make that larger sale. **If you'll qualify your leads, you'll have a much better chance of making more money *and* keeping more of the money you're making,** because you're not wasting it on dead and unresponsive leads.

I know there have been many times early in my career — and I'm sure most marketers can say the same — when I put an offer out there, generated a bunch of leads, and I thought, "Oh man, this is going to be absolutely awesome!" And then I spent so much time, energy, and money going through that whole big pile of leads — and made hardly any sales in the end. That's why *qualified* lead generation is so key here.

Make More Money by Doing Less Work

This tip flows directly from the topic I was discussing previously, lead generation, and it's absurdly simple. **To make more money with less work, you have to keep selling to the people who have purchased from you before.** I see marketers and retailers make the same mistake repeatedly — and I'm sure I did the same at the beginning. They make a new sale, and because they have all this apparatus in place to make a sale, they then move on and make another new sale... forgetting that the real riches are in consistently re-selling to your best customers.

Your existing customers are the best pre-qualified prospects you'll ever get. They're ideal for testing any new offer you have, because if your best customers don't bite, then no one will. This is what the best marketers in the world do, and of course you want to be one of those people, right? **So learn how to consistently make good, solid back-end offers to your existing customer base.** That maximizes your profits, because it's such a highly pre-qualified group. You may have heard the term "the gold is in the list," and that's especially true in our field. **Look at every sal as an opportunity to build a relationship that will lead to another sale down the road.**

Here's a great analogy, courtesy of Chris Hollinger. Every day when Chris drops his daughter off at school, he goes to a little restaurant right down the road and gets a cup of coffee and maybe some breakfast. Now, there are plenty of places he could choose from, but he chooses to go to this restaurant every time. They've built a relationship with Chris. They know what he likes, and he keeps coming back because they take good care of him and have invested time in building that relationship. Your business needs to be the same way. **You need to consistently make good, solid offers to your regulars.**

There are a few key things you should keep in mind when re-selling to your customer list, of course. Obviously, it can get to be a lot of work, because **the first key is that you have to maintain a good list.** And yeah, we've got computers, but still it takes some time to segment that list so you know what lead generation piece a particular customer responded to, what they bought, and how much did they spent. That's how you get to know who your best customers are.

Another key to re-selling customers is this: **absolutely, positively don't prejudge anything unless you know the facts.** What I mean by that is, I've seen marketers go through their list and just arbitrarily delete someone's name because they said, "Oh, they'll never buy." But ask yourself: "Why *won't* they buy?" It's a 100% guarantee that if you don't make this offer to them, they're not going to buy. Now, obviously you do go through your list and decide who you're going to make this offer to, but don't just arbitrarily prejudge anybody. **Make them the offer and let *them* decide.** Ultimately, you may be doing them a big favor by making them the offer; and I can tell you from experience that the flipside is that often it will come back to you if you *don't* make them the offer. They may be offended by you not giving them that opportunity to even see it, particularly if it's gone on and made other people a lot of money and they're missing out. Don't prejudge anybody when it comes to making those offers to your best customers. Get it out there and let *them* decide whether or not it's is right for them.

**You need to make your best customers feel special...
because they** *are* **special.** You want to give them the first chance
to see this opportunity, because it's so hot. **Do that, and you'll
make big-time profits easily.** You know, everybody thinks that
making money is a numbers game — and at some level they're
right. I just told you that if we end making 10,000 sales every
year at $4,985 a pop, we'll make about $50,000,000 a year. And
here's an example I read about Steve Jobs a while back: When
Apple released their iPhones, they sold over a million in the first
10 weeks at $600 each. Well, do the math: that's over
$600,000,000 in their first 10 weeks! Talk about your obscene
profits! By now they've exceeded the billion-dollar mark.

So yes, at some level it *is* a numbers game. But more
importantly, **it's a relationship game.** I think that the restaurant
analogy I used earlier is especially apt here, because anyone
with half a brain knows that, except for extreme examples, most
restaurants could never make it unless they have regular
customers who come again and again. **People who buy from
you repeatedly have developed a relationship with you;** that's
why if they won't go crazy over something, then you'd better
just scrap the idea — because if they're not excited by it, first-
time buyers won't be either.

**When you cultivate those relationships and keep going
back to the people who trust you and what you have to offer,
you've created your own money machine.** Too many people
don't realize that they could be selling more stuff to their
customers. I used to sit around and worry, "Oh my God, we're
making our customers too many offers. They're going to get
upset with us and they're going to go away!" But now that I've
got some experience under my belt, **the only thing I worry
about is not getting** *enough* **offers out there to our best
customers... because they really are insatiable.** Given a good,

69

solid offer that's useful to them, they'll continue to buy. And consider this: **all you need is for a small percentage of your customers to buy from you on any current offer to make the whole thing extremely profitable.** If they don't buy from you this time, then next month, when you make them another offer, some of them might buy. That's the secret we've used to make millions of dollars.

Which brings up another point: **not all of your customers buy from you every single time.** Depending on your marketplace, you might have some people buy everything you offer because they're loyal customers; they like you and trust you, and they know that you're going to provide good value. **But keep in mind that even in a very successful direct-mail campaign, you might have only 5-20% of those you mail to actually buy.** The next time, you again mail to 100% of your customers — and 5-20% of them buy that time, too. Some of the same people might buy each time, but you're likely to attract a different section of your list the second time. Just because you mail to all your customers frequently doesn't mean that all of them are buying every time; **the idea is to get them to buy consistently over time.**

And keep in mind that continuing to do business with your existing clients doesn't mean the situation is exclusive; it's not like a good marriage. Your clients also do business with your competitors, they spend money on gas, food, and groceries, and they spend money buying jeans at the department store. There's all kinds of money being spent by your clients, and they'll continue spending it. **What you want to do is make sure they're spending as much money as possible on you.** Since they *will* continue spending, no matter what, they might as well be spending money on all the related products and services that you have, or that you can develop or purchase the rights to.

Let me reiterate: **existing clients are a great source of**

revenue, and most people forget that. They spend too much time worrying about bringing in new clients, and too little thinking about what they're going to do to enhance the relationship with existing clients. That's a fatal mistake. **You should *always* spend most of your time offering more products and service to your existing clients** and, really, you should see new customer acquisition as something you just have to do for the life of your business, to keep the pool of clients from drying up. It shouldn't be what you focus most of your energy on.

And again, **don't prejudge** who will buy from you or how much they'll buy; I think a lot of people make this mistake. It could be that you've got a group of clients who've already spent a lot of money; if you've got expensive products, maybe this segment has already spent upwards of $10,000-20,000, which puts them above that magic threshold where you think, "Surely they're not going to spend any more money." Wrong; get that out of your head! **The people who have spent the most money with you in the past are the ones who are most likely to spend more money with you in the future.**

Don't prejudge people in the other direction, either. Maybe they've never bought from you before, but they continue to request information. **As long as you're qualifying people properly during your lead-generation process, don't assume someone will never buy just because they haven't so far.** Chris Lakey tried selling cars for a year and hated it. But one of the things they taught in the car business is not to pre-qualify or prejudge the people who come onto the lot looking for a car especially based on appearance. Some of the people he saw wore dirty blue jeans that looked like they hadn't washed them in... well, maybe years. They smelled funny, and they looked like there was no way they could afford to buy a car from you; and you didn't want to bother trying to sell them one, because if you went out there on the lot with them, they'd take hours of your time and you wouldn't have a deal. If you don't have a deal you don't earn commission, and that's not a good thing. **So you start to** *want* **to prejudge people.** However, some of those people are farmers; they've been busy in the field all day. They didn't have time to take a shower because they've been working, and as soon as they get done buying a car they're going back to the field. That's especially true where I live, because we live in and are surrounded by farming communities.

So you don't prejudge people about anything, because you never know who your customer is going to be. **Some of the most successful people in America are unassuming and look average.** You wouldn't look at them and think that they're worth millions, or that that they could afford to live in all the McMansions you see going up everywhere. They don't look like they could afford a Pinto, let alone a Cadillac. But they can. **These people quietly live very successful lives.** If you prejudge them, you've definitely cut them out of consideration, and there's no way they can become your customer.

There are all kinds of books that have been written about successful people, like *The Millionaire Next Door,* and *The Millionaire Mind*, that caution against prejudging people. Sometimes, the people who walk around wearing fancy suits, eating in fancy restaurants, are drowning in debt up to their eyeballs. But the backbone of America's successful entrepreneurial system isn't necessarily made up of folks you could pick out in a crowd and say, "That person right there is successful." Put them in a lineup and you'd probably pick the wrong people every time. They don't have fancy lifestyles, even though they could. A lot of them are just average people, just as a lot of those guys driving the fancy cars and wearing the nice suits are a paycheck away from being homeless.

A Framework for Success

Next up, I've got a framework for a successful sales organization that I want to share. **These are 10 easy things that you can do *right now* to quadruple your profits, and ruthless marketing takes into account each of these key areas.** Very briefly, they are:

1. Giving people what they want.

2. Developing products/services that appeal to a specific market.

3. Making sure those items have the largest profit margin possible.

4. Developing marketing systems that identify the right prospect and communicate the right message to them.

5. Reaching and selling to those people as fast as possible for the largest profit.

6. Re-selling to them as often as possible to squeeze the largest amount of money out of them.

7. Creating sales messages that build strong bonds with your customers.

8. Positioning yourself so that you can seem unique.

9. Creating offensive marketing strategies that allow you to control the selling process.

10. Making specific offers to your customers on an ongoing basis; that is, taking them by the hand and compelling them to come to you, instead of waiting for

them to somehow gravitate to you on their own.

I chose to provide this framework for two reasons: I believe most of the points are self-explanatory, and because I've seen too many new marketers stall out and crumble because they didn't know what to do next. **Business is a never-ending game.** If you return to and address each item on this list regularly, you'll always be improving your business and focusing on it. You're always asking yourself, "Okay, what can I make better? What can I do to position myself so that I seem more unique?" **You can use your answers to create marketing strategies that will allow you to control the selling process.**

Another reason I wanted to share this with you is that **you can use this guide as your business grows.** Maybe someday you'll need to hire employees, or maybe you have them already. If you have this framework, you can bring people into specific areas and say, "Okay, this is the part of this framework that I want you to focus on," and then show them in detail how they can do that. **This allows you to focus on what makes you the most money.**

Basically, these ten items give you a blueprint for a super successful sales organization of any size or complexity. It could just be a mom-and-pop operation or something with lots of infrastructure and employees, but the framework will keep you focused. Here's another quote attributed to Abraham Lincoln: "Good things come to those who wait, but only what's left over from those who hustle." I guarantee you, if you're focusing on these ten aspects of your business, you're always going to have something to do, and you're going to be hustling. It's always there for you to look at and apply to your business.

In the end, the basics of making as much money as you want are so simple. **It all boils down to developing the right kinds of products and services for the market that you're**

aggressively going after. You're continuing to look for newer and better kinds of things to offer those people, and trying to get enough people to re-buy from you often enough, at a large enough profit per transaction, to make good money. Do that, and the question is not, "Will you get rich?" It's only, "How rich will you get, and when will you get that money?" Because that's really as simple as it is. **Having a checklist like this simplifies things greatly, especially when you're just getting started.** There are so many different variables to consider, so sometimes it can be overwhelming to start thinking about all the things that you *could* do or exactly what you *should* do. Instead, just focus on a system, like this one, that you can put into place and follow religiously, no matter what business you're in or product or service you sell. It really can help take you to the next level, because you've taken things from broad general concepts to a specific ABC process that you can follow. And that's a good place to be.

Speaking of Focus...

One of the points I often make to my clients is this: "You must put as much of your time, attention, energy, passion, and skills into the specific areas that bring your business the largest profits. Focus. Identify these areas and put everything into these activities." **By focusing on those things that make you the most profit, you don't waste time on all the details.** I especially want to drive that message home for those of you that who think they have to do everything.

So how do you develop this focus? **One way is to develop relationships with various business entities that can handle the details that aren't directly related to your marketing.** If you're doing direct-mail, that would include relationships with people like printers. You need a quality printer; someone you can send a job to, and have confidence that it's going to get

75

done to your satisfaction. If you live in any halfway decent market at all, there are business entities out there that can handle complete turnkey mailings. Having someone who can handle those details will free you up to focus on your marketing and those other things that make you the most money. Another type of relationship to develop, of course, would be with people who can handle advertising for you. **One of the cheapest and least expensive ways to start generating leads is by putting nice little space ads in publications around the country.** Identify people you can call who can place those ads quickly, so that task doesn't gobble up a lot of your time. You're developing relationships with these people and setting up systems simultaneously.

Another great relationship to develop is one with a fulfillment house. Many entrepreneurs, like my friend Chris Hollinger and his wife, work from home. Instead of concentrating on having to make sure all these packages are going daily out the way they're supposed to, they can call the guy at their fulfillment house, and boom, it's done. Again, building that kind of relationship helps you to stay focused on what makes you the most money. Even if it's just you and the kitchen table, you have to realize that at some point, you might need to hire (at least temporarily) some help to keep you out of the day-to-day grind. **Do that, delegate everything else, and it will keep that money flowing.** Now, having said that, I'll be the first to admit that I'm guilty of getting bogged down in what I term the day-to-day operations of my business. When this happens I end up working "in" my business and not "on" my business. Subsequently, my profits drop off, because I'm concentrating on the wrong things and not delegating them.

Simply being mindful of this principle will help you avoid the pitfalls of getting stuck in what I call the "minutia" of business. All that stuff that has to be done, but it's not directly connected to your marketing and making money, so it can and should be delegated. **The easiest way to do that is to set up those systems and outsource it.** Ultimately, your overhead is going to be lower than you expect. **Keep that cash flowing,** because again, no business ever went out of business by making too much money... unless of course they got shut down by the government, which can and has happened.

There are so many small businesspeople out there who are working too hard. They come home really tired every night, and the stress and the pressure and the strain are just killing them. It's making them old before their time, and it's robbing them of all of their zest and enthusiasm. And yet their businesses are struggling. Why? Because they're not focusing as they should. They're wearing all the hats in their businesses; they're trying to do everything. If you ask them very specifically what they did today to make bring in more money for their company, they really wouldn't have a good answer for you. Now, I've been one of those people myself, so I don't want to try to pretend for a second that I've got this thing nailed, because I don't. It's something you struggle with. Everybody's got to struggle with it. **But the key, again, is to stay focused on whatever's most important** — and when you can, to narrow that focus even further, to only those things that are of the utmost importance.

There are *so* many ways you can outsource the less profitable parts of your operation. Don't ever fall into the trap of trying to do it all yourself, like many business owners do! They feel like they're the best person to do whatever it is that they're trying to do, that only they can do it the best, that no one else can do it quite like they can, and no one else has as good a system as they have. So they get stuck trying to do everything — whereas there are other people who can do what they need done, and some have developed systems that allow them to do it better than anyone else.

One thing you should always control is your marketing, as long as you *understand* marketing. Now, there are certainly beginning stages when you're just trying to figure things out, when there are good reasons to let someone else help you with marketing. There are benefits to services like the Direct-Response Network when you're just getting started. **Once you have a good understanding of marketing, you shouldn't let other people do that.** But things like fulfilling your products and mailing sales letters should certainly be hired out. I've sat at home in the evening and stuffed envelopes, and it's not fun; it takes a long time, and it's tedious work. Well, there are machines at mailing houses that can do 10,000 envelopes an hour. How many can *you* do an hour when you're sitting in front of the TV? You look up and watch the show for a minute, and you get stuck.

So don't get stuck in this mindset that you have to do it all yourself. Most of it comes from control issues, and some of it comes from money issues — that is, you're worried about spending money, you get shortsighted, and you start thinking that you need to do it all yourself. And yes, it does cost a little money to outsource. **But think about how much faster you could get things done.** Let's say you have 5,000 pieces of direct-mail you want to mail out. A mailing house can get it all out the door in a day, while you might take you a week or two just to get all the envelopes printed. Then you've got to fold the letters, get them in the envelope, hand-address the envelopes, and attach the postage. This is time consuming. **You should be spending your time marketing.**

There are people that can do all kinds of other things for you, too, from designing your letterhead to putting your website online to creating your logo. Again, there are services like elance.com, which we use periodically when we need things like this done. There's all kinds of professionals trolling the site ready to do anything, from data entry work to graphic design, website creation, writing, and more. If you don't want to go the Internet route, you can go to local colleges and companies that can do all those things.

This is a point that's often overlooked. **A lot of marketers have this do-it-all mentality,** where they want to take care of everything themselves... and often that gets them in trouble, because they end up spending too much time doing things that just don't matter in the end, and just don't bring in sales.

Become a Good Storyteller

Stories sell, especially before-and-after stories. Today, many of us have short attention spans, and stories help to grab the prospect's attention. That's why you must create powerful stories that captivate your prospects and your customers. Now, **what I'm talking about here are stories about you, your company, or your products or services.** Choose your stories carefully. Not only must they *be* real, they must *sound* real. **They have to be believable, and they also have to be highly emotional.** There needs to be some drama there, some special secrets, some perceived benefit or a promise to the reader. Stories help you make the sale when nothing else will.

The best stories to use in your sales material are before-and-after testimonials. This is a powerful sales method, because the story tells about the problem, then introduces the solution, and finally shows the great life-changing benefit. **The reader puts himself or herself into the story and is sold.** So when you're writing copy, long-form sales letters in particular, and you need to add something to draw people in, use a story. Stories help you reach the constant barrage of demands for your customer's attention and capture their competition. **They cut through the clutter and help your message get through, enabling you to**

connect with your prospect. It engages them and transports their mind to the place where you can weave your message into their reality. Ultimately, they have to experience a moment of clarity where they can see themselves experiencing success.

People tell me I have a great rags-to-riches story, and I certainly use it a lot in my marketing. But stories don't necessarily have to be about you, your company, or your product, specifically. They can be fictional. They can be situational. **They can be written to make a point, or to highlight the pain that you know your prospect is suffering.** Here's an example of a story that my colleague Chris Hollinger recently used in a sales letter:

<u>Always Rising to Meet the Challenge</u>

Today we are faced with a myriad of potential disasters, be it terrorists, natural disasters, recession, inflation, or taxation. We face these things daily. While we must acknowledge that there are dark clouds on the horizon, it is vital that we not lose sight of our most important and endearing national trait — our sense of optimism about the future, and our conviction that we can change it for the better. By taking steps to secure your financial future with me today, we are in essence becoming an agent of social change. Providing prosperity for yourself and the ones you love is more than the American Dream. Today your success makes our country stronger. Join me and see how much success we can spread.

Now, here's some information about me that I wanted to share with you so you'll know who I am and what I'm all about. My wife Kim and I live with our daughter, Milayna, here in Wichita, Kansas. We were both born and raised in small towns here in the rolling hills of Kansas. It's here where we learned the value of shooting straight with folks, and the hardships and rewards of integrity. Five years ago we started our own business, and soon became so busy that I literally was coming home from teaching and coaching and then working until two in the morning. Obviously I could not do both, so I told my fellow teachers and my principal that I was leaving to concentrate on my new business full-time. Many of my colleagues could not believe it, because not only was I giving up a tenured position with benefits, but I had just recently recovered from a very rare form of cancer. They were literally floored when I told them of my plans.

Since then, Kim and I have created a life that allows us the freedom to raise our daughter with all the love and attention to detail that being able to set our own schedule gives. I've been honored to be a speaker at seminars around the country, from Florida to San Diego. Last year I spoke at four very special seminars. All were recorded, and the information my colleagues and I presented is yours free by joining me on my next conference call. If you had attended all four seminars, you would have paid over $19,000. Join me on my next call, and they're yours free.

And that's the end of Chris' story. **You can see how he weaved quite a few themes into one little story.** It's a good example of a story that basically goes back to those key points I discussed earlier, using all parts of his personal story, including one that a lot of people wouldn't have enough courage to use — his struggle with cancer, and his rise above it. That was one of the concerns that many of his colleagues had when he first left teaching, because he had a job with all these benefits and health insurance, and he'd just recovered from that rare form of cancer.

Things were honestly up in the air as to whether or not it was going to come back, and I guess you're always in that boat when you've been diagnosed with cancer. That was one of the things that made their jaws drop. **Not only could they not imagine stepping out and starting up a whole new business at that point in Chris' career, they couldn't see him doing it after going through that whole ordeal with cancer.** But that story resonates with people. It takes a lot of courage to do something like telling your story, and talking about some of the struggles that you've gone through.

Stories really do sell. **They help you to connect, and they help put your prospect into that sales vacuum where your message is receptive.** Therefore, if you want to jazz up your sales messages and bring in more money, weave stories into them to make them more compelling.

Earlier, I mentioned my own story. It's an important part of our marketing — telling the story about how for years, my wife Eileen and I struggled for every single penny that we made. We *knew* that there was a way to make millions of dollars. We *knew* that other people had done it. And yet, we kept trying one plan after another, and nothing was working. All of our friends and family told us how absolutely insane we were, and they begged us to quit sending for all of these plans and programs! **And yet, we continued to believe there was a way to do it, and finally we sent away for a couple of good programs. We combined them and made millions.** It sounds good, and yet it's the God's honest truth — that's exactly what happened. Our clients have heard that story for years, and it resonates, because many of them have been sending away for the same types of plans and programs. Many of them have friends and family who have begged for them just to give up on their dreams. And yet, they don't want to do that any more than Eileen and I did. **We finally found a way to make millions of dollars — and so they know**

that they can do it too! If we can do it, they can do it. Our story is our connection with the people we want to do business with. It adds all those personal dimensions, it creates the relationships and the bonds with people, and they remember it. Our story is powerful. It's emotional.

So I hope that you will have the courage to take a page out of our playbook and **just be open and be honest with people that you want to do business with.** Tell them things that are very personal about who you are, and help them want to do more business with you. **Try to blend stories around whatever you're selling.** Stories are obviously very powerful when told in the right way and used for the right purpose. In the Bible, Jesus spoke in parables to get his points across; and in fact, people have been using stories all throughout history to do the same. And while I'm not telling you to lie to your customers — never do that — in some cases, the story doesn't have to be true. You can use a fictitious story to illustrate a point, as Aesop did with his fables. It's important to distinguish between the two so that you're not coming across as misrepresenting yourself or a product; **so tell people whether you're telling a real story or a fable.**

I realize that this might be difficult for you. Too many people are afraid to share anything about themselves with their customers; they'd rather not be personal, not put themselves out there. **But people are emotional beings, and we like to hear stories; we identify with stories.** If you're writing to a prospect that you know is like you and would identify with a story about you, you should be unafraid to tell it. Spend some time writing it out, even outside of a sales letter. **Get it on paper, keep it in the file, work on it, perfect it, hone it.** Make additions or subtractions as you go and as you find the time to work on it, and you'll soon have a story that you can weave into your sales material. You can use it, too, when you do personal selling, or if you talk to people on the phone or do presentations from a stage.

People can identify with and appreciate you if you're honest in this fashion (remember the power of honesty?). Oftentimes, people try to *hide* behind their company. They want people to think that they're perfect, that they're not human. And yet, we're all human, and everybody knows that; so why hide it? Why not just tell people a little about who you are and where you came from? This is especially important to the degree that it helps you tell people why they should do business with you; it involves a little more rapport-building, which is always good.

In addition to stories about yourself, **you can tell stories about your product.** Let's say you have a great product you discovered; you can tell the story about how you went to a remote jungle in Africa and came back with this cure for this disease, how all you have to do is eat this special fruit that you discovered and all your worries are gone; those kinds of things. **You can learn great storytelling by reading catalogs.** Some catalogs, like J. Pederson and Brookstone, have very good copywriters who do a lot of explaining about the thought processes behind the product or a story. That helps draw you in, and shows you why that product is good.

It should go without saying that how you word your story can determine its impact. You could tell the same story multiple ways; one way might be a boring, dry way, while you could say the same thing in another way so that it comes across as emotional, tugging at the heartstrings. **So take your story and learn how to write it in such a way that it draws on people's emotions, and storytelling can be a big sales tool.**

Appealing to the Prospect

In this section, I'm going to re-emphasize a truth that I think too many would-be entrepreneurs miss completely: **it's all about the *prospect*, not the product.** In a larger sense, it's all about the market. **The market is comprised of prospects with similar wants, needs, and desires, with desire being very important.** I've seen marketers fall in love with a product that was indeed needed, but not desired (and I'll be the first to admit that I've done this also). Then the marketer didn't do a very good job of creating desire for the product, and was dismayed when the market rejected their product. To avoid this, you want to really focus on and understand your market and your prospect. **You really need to know what the prospect and the market *really* want.** You need to know exactly who your ideal prospect is; you need to know what they love, what they fear, and what they want most. **And you *absolutely* need to know what in their life is causing them the most pain,** because as I've told you more than once, pain is very important when it comes to this form of marketing. Once you know these things, you need to have the intestinal fortitude to, in essence, jab a red-hot poker into the prospect's heart and twist it as hard as you can so that they can feel the worst imaginable pain (I'm speaking metaphorically here, of course, within the realm of your marketing). **And *then* you can craft a message that's intended to create incredible desire for your product, service, or opportunity.**

Here's a proven way to do that, using your knowledge of the prospect's wants, needs, and desires and what causes them pain: **Start by identifying the biggest selling points of your product. Then find a way to put your prospect in as much pain as possible.** You've got to make them feel it! You really stick that red-hot poker into their deepest fear and twist, and then add some rock salt and grind it in. **Once your prospect is properly painful, you give them the most logical solution to relieve their pain, heavily dosed with your main selling points.** People will do almost anything to avoid pain. This simple tidbit of information has produced billions of dollars in sales, and continues to profit savvy marketers worldwide every day.

So you use these emotional factors to first create pain, and then offer them the solution to that pain. In some ways, it's a terrible, terrible metaphor, this idea of peeling back the scab and pouring salt in there. But it goes back to the last thing we talked about, with the stories. Once you visualize this analogy, you'll never forget it — which is another purpose of telling stories, by the way. People remember stories. **And people will always do more to avoid pain than they will to gain pleasure; that's Psychology101, and, after all, marketing is just math and psychology.** So *you're* the one that has to put people in pain. *You've* got to make them see that not having what you're offering them will be potentially painful — that they're going to miss out on something very, very special — and you've got to make it real.

Given the number of competitors who are after the prospects you're after, you need to wake up and understand this, and know in your gut why people buy what they buy. That's much more important than the products themselves. When we tell people that products don't matter, **what we're really saying is that the *market* is more important, and that you've got to match the products to the marketplace.**

Sometimes — again, to illustrate the point you use a story, and in this case it's an analogy — it's salt in a wound. It burns in your mind, because everybody knows how that feels; or if you don't, you can guess. Again, we're coming at this from the premise that you have a solution to their pain. You're not just being mean and rubbing in the pain like a bully on the playground. **You're identifying their pain because you have a solution; and in order to make the solution real, you must first remind them of the degree of their pain.** It's the reminder that brings out the desire for your solution, which is what makes people want your product — because your product cleans the salt away and heals the wound.

Going back to the original point, you have a much better opportunity for profit if you stop focusing so much on the products and start focusing more on the prospects. **It doesn't matter what you sell so much as who you sell to. Your marketplace really determines what you sell.** Too many people go into business thinking otherwise; they have an idea for a product, and from that idea comes the product development. After it's is developed, they sit in their office, admiring their little work of art. Then they start thinking, "Okay, now that I've got this product, who am I going to sell it to?" They struggle, then, with trying to find a marketplace for the product they just created. **Well, you should never have to find a marketplace for your product, because you** *start* **with the marketplace, and then you find the product the marketplace wants.**

People will always buy what they want, and they'll always buy more of what they're already spending money on. If you can identify a group of people who are spending money on certain kinds of products and services, then you can come along and offer a newer, better, faster, more convenient product or service that fills those same wants in a better way, and you can make a profit. *It starts with the marketplace.* Never get that out of your head. Write it down. Hang in on your wall. Put it next to your bathroom mirror. Stick it someplace in your car, maybe, where you can look at it every day. The marketplace *always* comes before the product. Always, always, always. **If you'll remember that, you'll never struggle for what to sell.** You'll only struggle figuring out what the marketplace wants. Let the product follow the marketplace, and you can create a never-ending stream of products and services to offer to that marketplace once you've identified it. And once you've identified one marketplace, there's nothing to keep you from identifying others that you can tap into with other products and services.

I would look for markets that are very, very rabid. Not long ago, Chris Lakey and I were looking at a rather large market that we wanted to sell our products and services to. It turns out it was a fragmented market and, what's even more, the people in that market weren't really excited about the types of things we wanted to sell anyway. We knew that because there was such an absence of good, strong competitors. That was the one telltale sign, having done a little bit of research. **What you're looking for are places where other people are already making a ton of money!** I know it sounds like common sense, and yet so many people want to be the pioneers. They go out there and fall in love with these products, or they fall in love with a group of people they want to sell something to. They see a lack of competition, and don't even realize that it's because the market they want to sell to isn't crazy about the types of things that they offer. **You always go in the areas where other people are making a lot of money, and design your initial products and services to be very similar to what other people are selling right now.** The time to be creative, the time to be the pioneer, the time to go out there and experiment, is when you already have millions in the bank — or however else you define being financially secure. That's when you can test your other ideas and experiment with markets where there's an absence of competitors.

On TV once, I saw a little special documentary about Simon Cowell, the guy who started American Idol. Obviously, he's a music guy. One of the things they mentioned was the fact that in the mid- to late-1990s, he noticed that people all over the world were going crazy about these humongous professional wrestlers like The Rock and Stone Cold Steve Austin. He saw that people were already making a lot of money with that market, and there was a lot of interest and desire connected with these wrestlers, so he convinced them to cut their own albums. And even though the music was horrible, that was one of his first big breaks. He sold literally millions of recordings of professional wrestlers doing their best to be singers. The market was rabid for these guys; **he just gave them another product and, in turn, made millions of dollars.** And then he kept expanding and expanding, looking for other unique areas to excel in.

Simon Cowell was filling a demand that wrestling fans had; he was able to get on the other side of the cash register and understand his market at a deep level. That's part of what getting on the other side of the cash register means. Stop thinking like a consumer; start thinking like a marketer. **Start looking at what other people are doing, and ask yourself how you can do things that are similar.**

Now, that anecdote on the previous page is part of Simon Cowell's story. If you don't have your own yet, start working on it; sit down and write a little about who you are, and why people could identify — or would want to identify — with you and your story. And don't write your story as it is, necessarily; maybe you haven't achieved success yet, and at the moment your story is all about struggle. **Go ahead and write your story as if you've gone ahead and found success, because you eventually will if you keep working at it.** When you get there your story can be already written — all you need to do is work in the details.

Dispelling the Marketing Fog

To start off this Rule, I want to take you back about 60 years ago, for just a moment. If you're older than 50ish, you might remember this: London, Friday, December 5, 1952. That date might not mean much to you, but it's well-remembered across the pond, because it's the date of a huge catastrophe. It was a cold winter, and on December 5, everybody was burning coal in their fireplaces to heat their homes. Due to the extreme cold, the smoke from the coal fires was trapped in the city, and it combined with the natural moisture in the air to create this huge fog. The fog set in thick. At that time, it wasn't that uncommon for there to be a fog over London, so people didn't think too much of it; but by December 7, the fog was so thick that visibility fell to just about a foot. People could literally hold their hand a foot in front of their face and not see it. They couldn't see their shoes.

Hundreds of people died the first day from respiratory distress due to the smog. Within four days, something like 4,000 people had died; the smog had choked the life out of them. They couldn't breathe, and couldn't see to go anywhere. Ambulances stopped running because of the lack of visibility. Business, theaters, concerts, and the like shut down. In the subsequent coming weeks and months, another 8,000 people or so died because of the effects of the December 1952 fog; many survivors of the actual event later developed lung conditions or pneumonia, or had complications from those, so as many 12,000 people died from this unnaturally thick fog.

Of course, that was a tragic event, and a horrible situation; but I think it offers a good analogy to marketing in many instances. **Marketers sometimes sit in this kind of fog; we feel like we have a little information, yet it's indistinct and hard to see.** We can't really see the connections, and we don't know which way is up or down. We're all confused, and without the right help — without someone grabbing us and showing us which way we're going — we're like those people in London in 1952. We just can't see more than a foot in front of our faces and we're destined to fail. **We need some help and we need someone to show us the right way.**

That's what we do with the Direct-Response Network, and that's what I'll present in this chapter. **The idea is to hopefully lift that fog, at least briefly.** If you've been sitting around feeling confused, not really sure where to turn, what to do, or which direction to go, hopefully these strategies will help lift the fog you've been experiencing, help you come out of the haze, and reveal a clear direction to start you down your road to success.

The Minnow and the Whale

Here's a fundamental truth of life: you can't catch a whale by using a minnow as bait. Now, think about that. **If you want something big to happen, as in making big sales and big profits, you've got to do big things!** Bill Glazer, a marketing expert who's a real hero of mine, puts it a bit differently: he says that most businesspeople are trying to shoot an elephant using a BB gun.

Now, here's where the fog analogy comes into play. Most

businesspeople are so deluded in their expectations, it's almost as if they're in a fog. **They simply don't realize the high level of forces working against them on a daily basis.** Some of these forces include increased competition, lower profit margins, and consumers who are more and more demanding all of the time. There used to be that phrase that went, "The customer is king." Well, these days, customers are more like dictators than kings. There's a growing skepticism in the marketplace, and that's not going away; it's only going to get worse. **People also have a tremendous amount of apathy towards most marketing messages.** They've learned how to tune them out because of the information overload problem; they feel too overwhelmed to listen to everything, and don't want to learn anything anymore.

There's hostility against advertisers. Everybody hits the "mute" button when a commercial comes on the TV, and there's a strong resistance to all sales messages. **The average consumer today is more educated than ever, and is very cynical, too.** They're on guard constantly; they don't believe a word that you say. And yet, most businesspeople are so "fogged in" that they think that all they have to do is run a few ads or a few TV spots, or drop a few postcards in the mail, and people are going to automatically rush to them. That's a real delusion.

This is one of the big reasons we teach Direct-Mail Marketing (DRM) as the most effective way of doing business, compared with the ad agency methods of advertising. As a small business especially, ad agencies push you to just put your name in the Yellow Pages so that if anybody needs you, they'll find you. Or the businessperson might think, "I'm only going to use word of mouth, and if people want me, they know where I'm at." This all comes back to the quote a mentioned earlier, which is attributed to P.T. Barnum: "You can't catch a whale by using a minnow as bait." Now, I used to fish a lot when I was younger, and I know that you always match your bait to whatever fish you're trying to catch. When you're after little fish, you need a tiny hook and little bit of worm or a piece of corn, because otherwise the fishes can't get the hook in their mouth. And there are other times when you want to try to catch huge catfish, so you use larger hooks with bigger bait. Now, maybe you first catch little fish so you can use them to catch the larger fish. Someone who didn't know better might ask you, "Why are you using such a big fish for bait? You're only going to catch a big fish." Well, duh — that's what you want to do! **You're being** *selective*. If the fish is too small you don't want it, so you do your best to arrange things so they can't take the bait. The only way to catch a whale is to use a giant hook and a substantial bait. **The point here is that you have to match the tackle and bait to whatever you're trying to catch.**

In business, you're trying to catch the best possible customers, folks who will spend the largest amount of money for the longest amount of time; so minnows are out. That also means using the right bait — if your target market has no interest in what you're offering, you're probably not going to catch their attention. And if you're using the using the wrong advertising, you're not going to catch them, either. **You have to have to present the right offer (the bait) with the right advertising in the appropriate medium (the tackle).**

The unfortunate reality with most business owners is that when they start a business, all they do is buy themselves a job — and admittedly, they're usually good at what they do. Let's say they're a dry cleaner; well, they're probably really good at cleaning clothes, and can get a stain out like nobody's business. **But it's just as likely that they have no clue how to market their business, and no interest in learning how to do so.** And so all they are is a good dry cleaner. Similarly, someone who has a local clothing store may be really good at measuring you and helping you pick out just the right suit for that special occasion, but they have no clue or interest in learning how to market their business and attract more customers. The two traits often go hand in hand, but what good is a new business that you just start without the ability to advertise and bring in new customers, and continue to resell to the customers you have?

So you have to keep alert to the marketing opportunities, and you have to keep current, because of the problems I've already mentioned: the increased competition, the lower profit margins, customer apathy, and consumers who are savvier than they used to be. The Internet has continuously crept more and more into our lives. These days you can buy a refrigerator with an Internet connection built right into them, so it will keep track of your groceries and tell you when you need to go to the store. You can go virtually anywhere the world, and handheld devices keep the Internet at your fingertips. **The Internet is making people smarter consumers because they can research on the world wide web,** find out more about the products, and find out whether they should shop with you or the competition. **They're more educated these days, and demand better service.**

Even 10 years ago, if you were going to buy a new car you had to do a lot of digging to find out what the dealer paid for it. Today it's easy to go on the Internet, pick out the car you want, and know exactly what the dealer bought that car from the factory for. **That means that as a consumer, you have the ability to go in and demand a price.** You can say, "I think that on this particular car, a good profit for you is $150," and they would say, "How do you know how much profit we're making?" You tell them, "I know that you paid this much from the factory, so I'm going to pay you *this* much, and that should leave you a profit of $150." The Internet gives you increased knowledge of the market at a low cost. **As a consumer, that's great; as a**

marketer, it puts you at a disadvantage.

Plus, again, there's a lot of doubt in the marketplace in general. **People aren't as trusting *or* as trustworthy as they used to be, so that means there's more questioning.** Apathy shoots you down; it's so easy to zap forward on your DVR or TiVo and skip the commercials altogether. Many people turn off the radio or change the channel during commercials, if they even listen to a radio anymore. Since people have grown used to just tuning out the sales message, **you've got to do something to stand up and make them pay attention.** People are overloaded with information, and they lead such busy lives these days. If they've got a family, they probably have a kid going this direction one night and a kid going another direction another night. They've got soccer practice, football practice, baseball practice, basketball practice, choir, and school programs in the evening. All these things go on, and they take up people's time. Because people are so overloaded, not only with information but with busy schedules, **you've got to cut through the clutter.**

In general, too, people are resistant to sales messages. **They don't want to be sold — but it's clear that they not only want to buy things, they *love* to buy.** If you look at the numbers, even in a bad economy, you'll see that people will still spend their money. People want to buy the things they want to buy. But they don't want to be sold, so you have to break through that reluctance and deliver a sales message that makes them want what you offer. **At the same time, you want them to feel they're making the choice to buy from you, not that they're being pressured into buying something.** They want to feel like they're making the buying decision.

That's where direct-mail comes in; it's part of this whole strategy of using the right bait to catch the right fish. With direct-mail, you can either compile or rent a mailing list of people who are interested in what you have to offer, contact them, and use the method of qualifying leads I talked about in the last chapter to deal specifically with people who you *know* are interested in your offer. **In fact, they asked you to make your pitch.** You can use direct-mail strategies through classified advertising or display advertising; even small businesses can use Yellow Page advertising effectively this way, by getting people to raise their hand and say they're interested in what you have or by getting them to call a phone number, visit a website, or whatever so that you can capture that lead, get them to give you their contact information so that you can present them with your sales message, and give them an opportunity to buy what you're selling. **If you'll do that the right way, you'll cut through that fog.**

The fog analogy is a good one for another reason: Not only are most businesspeople absolutely blind to all the changing market forces that result in more customer cynicism and sales resistance, **they also have a tendency to think people are excited about their product or service just because they are.** Nothing could be further from the truth. It's a mistake that entrepreneurs make all the time, since they love what they're selling. Well, that doesn't necessarily mean other people love it or are even interested in it. And this whole idea that things just sell themselves is one of the biggest lies I've ever heard. It may have been true 200 years ago, but it ain't true today. *Nothing* **sells itself.** Whenever you start hearing somebody try to pitch you on something that sells itself, they're either lying to you or they're deluded themselves — in which case you're still being lied to in an indirect way.

Now, I don't want you to think that any of this is negative, because it's not negative at all. **This is *reality*.** There are certain forces out there that are working against all of us, but that's no reason for you to put your tail between your legs and tell yourself that you can't go out there and make a lot of money. On the contrary, **there's never been a time in history for the average person, someone who has no special knowledge, no special skills, no special abilities, to go out there and make millions!** In fact, with today's technology, including Federal Express and other distribution systems, Internet technologies, modern personal computers and cellular technologies and all of the future technology that will continue to evolve, you have more power than ever before — if you choose to use it. **And you can't delude yourself; you've got to get rid of the fog.**

Here's one quick strategy we're using right now. We have a plan to go out there and dominate a much larger market than the one we've been reaching until now. Well, any fool can have a big goal. Just because you want to go out and make millions of dollars doesn't mean you're going to do it. **But it all starts with a goal, and that leads to a plan.** Here's our plan: we've got a $5,000 package, and we're willing to spend up to $4,000 just to make every $5,000 sale. Now, think about that. We're willing to make a gross profit of only $1,000 on every $5,000 package that we sell. Why? Because **#1,** it has residual income associated with it. And then, **#2,** there's a lifetime customer value that's attached to it too. That lets us be so much more aggressive with all of our marketing. We can do things that most of our competitors would be scared to death to do. We can be aggressive, we can be bold, we can go out there and spend more money. We can have a bigger presence in the marketplace. In so doing, we'll make sales that our competitors would never have made. We'll get new customers that our competitors would have never been able to reach, because we're going to be able to do so much more. **And that's been our strategy in general: to be as aggressive as possible, to be willing to spend as much money on every new sale as we can — because we realize that the profits are to be made from repeat purchases.** Now, it's not about trying to suck money out of people; you have to get them the first time before you can get them again and again, and every time thereafter you have to give them tremendous value, or they're going to go away. **It's about serving people in the highest way possible, about making them so happy that they're glad to buy from you repeatedly.** Having an aggressive marketing strategy lets you go out there and willingly spend more money in your new customer acquisition, and with the subsequent purchases or offers that you make to your established customer base.

Nine Mistakes to Avoid

Instead of talking about positives as I usually do, this particular strategy illuminates **dangerous errors that entrepreneurs often make.** That's because I think it's helpful, sometimes, to discuss the things that you can do wrong as well as right, so you know what to avoid. Here are the nine mistakes I see all too often, and what you have to do to keep them from grounding you:

1. **No focus.** The list of prospects is of primary importance, and you need to home in on highly qualified prospects and get to know them in the most intimate way possible.

2. **No compelling offer.** You need something to get people to take action now; otherwise, they have no reason to respond to or to buy from you.

3. **No deadline.** You've got to build urgency into your offer. The more urgency you have, the higher your response rate will be.

4. **A lack of testimonials.** You should *always* remember that what other people say about you is much more important than what you say about yourself. A lack of testimonials is a detriment to your marketing.

5. **No way to measure results**. The only thing that counts in any business is return on investment. Know your numbers. Don't get hung up on response rates, because you can't put them in the bank.

6. **No follow-up**. Most people give up way too soon; 82% of sales happen after the first follow-up. You need a plan to follow-up with your leads to try to convert them to sales.

7. **Trying to be cute and funny using non-direct-response, Madison Avenue advertising**. Don't be cute and funny. Try to make the sale.

8. **Bad copy**. Having a bad sales letter can kill your sales rate. Learn to write.

9. **Too much reliance in one medium**. You need to diversify. Advertise in more than one medium.

As I've indicated above, **what you need to do is the exact opposite of these nine mistakes.** Regarding the first one, which is lack of focus, everybody's heard the little cliché that says, "If everybody is your customer, then nobody is your customer." I think people tend to discount all clichés in general, but they're clichés for a reason, aren't they? Often, there's a lot of truth in them. So ask yourself: **who, exactly, are you trying to reach?** That's the most important thing. **The market comes first,** as we tell people again and again when they come to our marketing workshops. And when we say "market," we're simply talking about a group of people who have some strong commonality that causes them to buy the type of products and services you sell. Who are those people? Where can you reach them?

Next, what must you say to those people in order to get their attention and get their interest? **Most people just don't** have a compelling offer; but to really tear up the sales floor, you've got to do something to get people to take action *now*. **You have to prove to them that what you have is much more valuable than the money you're asking them to give up in return.** If there's not a strong reason to take action right away, most people won't. Think about those TV infomercials where they say, "You'll get this and this and this... But wait, there's more! You'll also get this and this and this and this! And, for the first 50 people who call in now, you'll also get this and this, too!" and they just keep stacking it up. Some of those infomercials have a time clock, and that time clock starts winding down. That's something that creates a sense of urgency.

Which folds into number three on our list: no deadlines. **You have to build a deadline into your offer, and give a good reason why you're not just lying to them about it.** You don't want to lie to people; we're not talking about lying for a living here. But we *are* talking about doing things to dramatize your offer, to give people more reasons to go ahead and do what you want them to do.

Our fourth item is a **lack of testimonials,** which I've already talked about in detail in the last chapter; you've got to have clear, honest testimonials to get other people to buy. Number five — **no measurement of results.** All that matters is how much money you spend versus how much money you make. This goes back to an earlier topic, where I discussed how everybody wants to try to catch a whale by using a minnow as bait; that is, most people are trying to spend as little as they can in order to make each sale. In one sense that's smart, because you don't want to be spendthrift; on the other hand, offering up big bait does give you a competitive advantage. I mentioned the strategy that we're involved with at M.O.R.E., Inc., where we're happy to spend up to $4,000 in order to get that $5,000 sale. We're willing to be aggressive, because it's all about return on investment. **You've got to know what you're numbers are, and you can't get hung up on response rates.** People may say, "Well, I only got a half of a 1% response rate." That doesn't mean anything to us. **The only thing we care about is how much money you spend versus how much you make — and even then it sometimes takes a while to close the gap.**

Not to brag, but there was a time not too long ago when we were bringing in almost $2,000,000 a month. We had a promotion where we were spending huge sums of money just to get the initial sale — I'm talking about *huge* sums of money. **The truth is, we were going negative to get the first sale, but then we had a nice big, fat upgrade attached to the first sale — plus we had continuity revenue, too.** We were just rolling in money while that promotion lasted, and it was great. That's the general type of thinking you need to adhere to.

Number six: **no follow-up. Most marketers give up way too soon.** That would be like asking your girlfriend one time if she wants to marry you. If she says no once, what, are you just going to shut up? Not likely! You're going to keep asking her again and again until, ideally, she finally says yes. The same is true in business. And then number seven — trying to be cute and funny. There was recently a promotion in our market that a bunch of people were involved in, but those people were never likely to make any money, because they were using cartoons as part of their message. **You can't be cute. You can't be funny.**

Number eight: **bad copy. You've got to write great ad copy, or you'll absolutely kill your own ability to make money.** Now, learning to be a great copywriter is a skill that anybody can learn, and it's one of the greatest marketing skills, if not *the* greatest marketing skill, that you can acquire. All it takes is learning how to put words on paper in a way that causes people to send money to you. If you can accomplish that, it's the most amazing feeling that you'll ever experience in your life —

and it's within your reach. The importance of writing copy can't be over-emphasized, and in fact I've written whole books about it. Of all these items you should avoid, bad sales copy is the worst. **As a marketer, writing good sales copy is one of the most important things you can learn, because it sets the foundation for everything else.** Not only will you learn to write copy that's compelling, you'll learn how to handle follow-ups and other important aspects of the business. If you can write great sales copy, you'll be using Direct-Response Marketing, which means #5 will come into play, **where you'll be able to measure your results — because you'll have specific offers that go out, and you'll know the results you got from that particular advertising.** It all starts with great sales copy, and each of the items in this list can be backed with an understanding of writing great sales copy. You should enhance your education on that front at all times. There's always more to learn, always more to study when it comes to being a great sales copywriter. **School is never out for the pro.**

Finally, number nine: **you do have to mix it up.** I love direct-mail, but we're also using space advertising as well as some major Internet marketing. **So you don't want to put all your eggs in one basket.** Think of it like a chair; you need to have at least four different legs before the chair will be really solid.

The Importance of Advertising

Remember P. T. Barnum? He's the man who said that you can't catch a whale by using a minnow as bait. I've got several books about Barnum; in my opinion, he was a great man. Recently, I was going through one of my favorite Barnum biographies and I found this quote. It's great wisdom, and there's a lot to talk about here: "In a typical year (1877), the cost of advertising and publicity for Barnum's circus came to over $100,000." You could do a lot with $100,000 back in 1877; in today's money, that's probably equivalent to about ten million. **But that was almost one-third of his total expenses!** Think about that. Almost *one-third* of his total expenses went into advertising and publicity.

   The lesson here is that you have to keep pumping your revenue back into the areas that make you the most money. Discipline yourself to do this on a consistent basis. People often tend to try to get by on the cheap with advertising; and certainly, if you only have a limited budget, you want to do it as little as possible. But even so, the smaller your budget, the bigger the percentage of that budget you want to put towards advertising. And always, **always put aside some portion of your income for advertising.** That's something we've taught for years, basically ever since we got started in the business. **You need to take a percentage of every dollar you bring in and put it into an advertising fund.** Maybe for you, that means opening a bank account called "Advertising" so you can stay disciplined. The percentage you put aside for advertising is up to you; maybe it's 10%, 20%, or 50%. The point is, be disciplined about putting that money aside. Then pull that money out once a month (or whatever schedule you determine) and advertise.

   This is hard to do, because people are inclined to spend every bit of what they bring in. We live like that as a society; most people are living paycheck to paycheck, with consistent expenses, and often that's what drives people to get into business for themselves. They want a better lifestyle; they want to be able to vacation and do things for themselves. What that means is that when your business starts working and you start bringing in money, you enjoy your spoils by taking a vacation or doing whatever you've been dreaming of doing. **But don't spend it all: keep putting the advertising percentage aside in a separate account and be vigilant about it, or you'll suddenly be right back where you started.**

You've got to feed your business, and the way you do that is with advertising, promotions, marketing, and those kinds of things. **Now again, the key is to keep pumping more of your revenue back into all of the areas that** *make you the most money.* There are all kinds of advertising options you could spend your money on. **Experiment with multiple methods, and keep the ones that work best.** If you find that advertising in a certain magazine does best for you, then you want to keep advertising in that magazine while testing others. If you've found that a certain mailing list has continued to work for you, you want to continue using that mailing list. And you should always test small. Test a lot of things and test consistently, but once you know that something is working and is making you a good profit, continue pumping more and more of your revenue back into that area. **Advertising isn't a cost: it's an investment towards future profits.**

Here's an example of what *not* to do with your profits. When M.O.R.E., Inc. first took off in 1988 and we were rolling in the money, one of my best friends at the time got around our business and fell in love with it. I had a chance to help him get started, and right out of the gate I showed him exactly what to do; and then, lo and behold, he started making thousands of dollars. He was so excited! He was going to build a company just like ours. Well, we had already been in business for a couple years, so we had some infrastructure built. Steve made his thousands, and then took that money and rented a nice fancy office and got all this computer equipment, spending all of the money that he'd made! **He lost his momentum, because then the cash flow dried up.** If he'd just stayed in the game and continued to reinvest his money into more advertising, and had then built it up and started putting some of it into infrastructure, he would have never lost his important momentum. But he did, and it didn't take him long. Within 90 days he had quit. He could have ended up making millions if he'd just practiced what

I've talked about.

Every day, you have to discipline yourself to take a percentage of your money and put it back into more of the things that made it for you to begin with. Period. End of story. Ignore that reality, and you're likely to fail.

Doing the Two-Step

Two-step marketing is one of the keystones of modern marketing, and it's the place that you're really going to make your money. I don't think people can hear this enough, because even entrepreneurs tend to under-value the benefits of two-step marketing. They just want to go after the sale, and they feel that asking for it right up front is the best strategy. Instead, they need to remember that two-step marketing is the safest and most profitable way to make money. It's simple. **Step One is to attract a high-qualified prospect first.** Use a great offer. Don't try to sell them too much at first; just get your hooks into them. I talked about using the right bait earlier in the chapter; find that bait, entice them, and then set the hook. Make it easy for them to buy the first time. Sell a low-priced widget. Educate them. Make them feel that they came to you and not the other way around. Sometimes that's with a low-priced sale; sometimes that's with a free lead, where you're just asking them to raise their hand and request a report. **Step Two is actually making the profitable sale.** Now it's time to bring out the big guns. You have their attention and their interest, and you're in the position to show them how you can give them what they want the most. **It's a great strategy that's responsible for billions of dollars in sales yearly.**

Two-step marketing is nothing less than the best way to make the largest amount of money as safely as possible. Let's say you're in a large, rabid marketplace ours, the opportunity market. Well, there's an estimated 30-50 million people who want to make more money and are willing to do something about it. But how in the world are you ever going to reach such a huge audience if you're not a Fortune 500 company? The short answer is: you're not. **The trick is to narrow it down as much as you can, by finding ways to get to the most serious prospects only.** For instance, we'll advertise in some of the moneymaking magazines, because that's where we'll catch the people who are really serious about making money — or they wouldn't be reading those magazines to begin with. We run small display ads or even small classified ads in those venues, pinpointing our marketing efforts by presenting our offers directly to the people we want to attract the most. We're getting them to come to us by offering them something of value for free or for a low cost. A very small group of people will probably take us up on our offer; they'll go to our website, call our toll-free number, send for the Special Report or program, or even buy whatever we're selling at low cost. **That's Step #1. When they do that, they end up on our mailing list.** Well, that cost us very little, didn't it? **With Step #2, we try to sell them an offer that's related to the one they bit on.** That's all there is to it. There are a lot of different themes you can use here, but they all involve separating the smaller group of qualified prospective buyers from the larger group of people who are less qualified. Once you do that, you can spend more money to reach that smaller group of people who you know are serious because they took the first action.

Two-step marketing is the backbone of what we've been doing here at M.O.R.E., Inc. for many years. It's become almost second nature to us, and yet a lot of businesses struggle with this concept, because it's easy to get caught up in thinking about the total universe size that you could mail or advertise to. And who wouldn't think, "Well, I know that there are 5,000,000 who either want my product or who should, because it's a great product. Everybody in this marketplace should want it." And so you start thinking, "Okay, if there are 5,000,000 people in my market, how do I reach all of them with my sales message?" Of course you could get their names and addresses and mail 5,000,000 pieces of direct-mail, or you could advertise in a magazine those people read and sell your product "off the page."

You get tempted into doing that because you think, "I want to reach everybody." But let's get real; it's true that if I ask for people to just raise their hand, there's no way everybody is going to see my sales message. But that's the wrong way of thinking. The way you want to think is: **"I really only want to focus on selling to the people who are the most interested in and most likely to buy my product."** So you use your lead generation tool, Step One, to attract the right kinds of people. Let's say of those 5,000,000, there really are only about 5,000, or even 500, that are the most likely prospects to buy your end product or service. **Therefore, you focus all your energy on selling to those few.**

It would be astronomically expensive to try to advertise to 5,000,000 people all at once. But let's say, for the sake of this example, that it costs you the exact same amount of money to reach those 5,000,000 as it did to acquire 5,000 qualified leads. You're still better off spending more money to sell to those 5,000 leads than you are spending money to advertise to all 5,000,000, because you're advertising to people who have already gone through one hoop, who have already raised their hand and said they're interested. **Dollar for dollar, you're always better off spending your money advertising to people who've already qualified themselves.**

That's why when you see infomercials on TV, the strategy isn't just to sell you what they're offering on that 30-minute spot. The real strategy is to get you to raise your hand so they can pack on the benefits. They just load them up and make it seem like you'd be the stupidest person on the planet if you didn't pick up the phone right now and order, because they're going to give you all this stuff for only two easy payments of $19.95. And then when you do call, not only do they instantly upsell you on the phone, but you also get a package in the mail. And then you get another offer and, hopefully, you buy from that, and they do some more telemarketing to you. They've got another package they're trying to sell, but they know that they can't make that sale by just having you look at their 30-minute infomercial — **so they just focus on getting you to take that initial step.**

Giving Them What They Want

You know, there are certain basics that you have to go through in this business—and sometimes your emotions aren't always your best indicator of where you are in the game. You can put in years, sometimes, just struggling as I did, and then all of the sudden things just magically come together. I've already mentioned in previous chapters what I call the "20-year overnight success story." Hopefully, you won't be one of those! **But there *is* something to be said for having to struggle for a while.**

I have a niece who is a great musician and singer; the only problem is, she's young and dumb. She's going through that deluded stage of life where she thinks the world owes her something. She was singing in front of me a couple years ago and she has a beautiful voice, just beautiful. She was talking about her desires to be world famous and have millions of adoring fans and all that, and I told her, "Amanda, here's what you need to do, hon. You need to find a band, get on the road for about five or six years, and practice every single night—**just practice. Keep getting better and better.** After five or six years on the road, maybe you'll be discovered. Then lo and behold you'll be on TV, and you'll have your multimillion-dollar record contracts, concerts, and all these adoring fans. You'll be famous." But of course that advice fell on deaf ears.

Millions of people want to get rich. If you go out on the street and ask a hundred people, "Hey, you want to be a multimillionaire?"…well, most of them would probably think that you're trying to con them or lie to them, so they'd back off real fast. But if they really believed there was some sincerity to your question, I'm sure that most would say, "Absolutely! I would love to be a multimillionaire; who wouldn't?" **And yet, when you ask them to do anything on a regular basis, to pay any kind of price necessary, they're not willing to do it.** True success often requires an investment of money as well as investment in certain actions and the willingness to do certain things—to go through a learning curve, so to speak. Most people, though, will not do *anything*. And if they do, it'll be short-lived.

When you study the lives of the people who have made it in a big way, you'll find that they all paid a price for success. Sure, there may be an exception here and there; but the problem is that everybody wants to be that exception. **The norm is that *you have to pay the price*.** With very rare exceptions—like rich heiresses and lottery winners—**the people who get rich are the people who make a habit of doing difficult things.** Sometimes those difficult things sound easy, when it fact they can be difficult. That's often (but not always!) true of this chapter's theme: *Making Money by Giving the Customers What They Want*. Not what they need, but what they *want*! Sometimes most of the difficulty lies in remembering this. You're not here to give people what you think they need. *You're here to give them what they want.* For many of us, it takes a while to crack that part of the code. That's part of the price we pay: that struggle to finally get it, the understanding of which finally opens the floodgate to real wealth.

It was like that for me, and it was like that for my colleague Jeff Gardner. He struggled for years, and it really didn't look like he was ever going to pull it off. Just like me, he had some people in his life who thought he was a little bit crazy to think that he could make millions of dollars. And yet, he's doing it now! **And part of what makes him so great is he really *does* love to help other people.** If you've seen him live at a seminar, you know it!

Jeff's story starts back when he was about 15 years old. Even before then, he knew he wanted financial freedom. He didn't know it was called that, but he knew that he wanted to make money, mainly because he saw his parents struggling all the time. They certainly weren't what you would consider poor, but you certainly didn't want to be around the table on bill night, because there was a lot of stress and a lot of unhappiness there. Well, Jeff just didn't want to live his life that way.

So Jeff tried to figure out a lot of different ways to make money, primarily by going door-to-door and selling this and that. But ultimately, he stumbled onto mail order. In mail order, it didn't matter how young Jeff was; he was able to sell things to people all over the nation — and later, all over the world. He started out selling other people's products, but eventually shifted to his own products that he'd put together. **Over time, he started making some money.** He wasn't a 20-year overnight success, but it did take him a number of years to become successful — nine, I believe.

That's because he took a shortcut by learning from other people. **He found people he could model: that is, he examined their methods, figuring out what they were doing the right way and the wrong way.** You should do the same as Jeff, and in fact you've made a good start! Instead of trying to figure it out yourself through trial and error, you're doing the easy thing by reading this book and hopefully acquiring some workable ideas you can then apply in your own business.

The other thing that really helped Jeff was his persistence—his stubbornness, if you will. He knew other people had made a lot of money working for themselves, and he was going to do it one way or another. Now, you may be thinking, "Heck, I'm very stubborn too, so I'm sure I'm going to make it," and that's great! **But you have to attach taking action to being stubborn.** If you're just stubborn, you're not going to really be super successful; but if you're *persistent*, if you take action and you're constantly getting out there, doing things, marketing, coming up with products, different marketing ideas, seeing what other people are doing and taking the best of what they're doing, putting it in your business, **then I *do* believe that you're going to shortcut your journey to success.**

That's my intention with this chapter, so let's move straight on to the first topic, which we call **How to Create Super-Selling Power That Can Make You the Fastest, Easiest Money Possible.** We all want fast, easy money, don't we? **The way to get it is to become a power-seller.** Now, I know some people think, "Wow, these people who make millions of dollars selling products and services are well-trained, skillful people," and yes, that's one way to do it. If you have to sell products that there's a lot of competition for, or even products that people really don't want, then yes, you've got to have some super-selling skills to get people to buy. But if you want an easy way to get people to buy, if you want to create an almost magical super-selling power in a very short amount of time, **here's the key: You've got to have something that the buyer wants badly, even desperately.** If that's the case, then you, the seller, has all the power. But keep that in mind: **the power isn't really in you. It's in that item that the buyer wants so badly.** That's why you have to look for the hottest possible products and services to sell.

You know, I talk to a lot of people about writing copy. People really get stressed out about writing sales letters. They're worried about things like, "How do I write a headline? How do I write an opening and a close? How do I write a guarantee?" Even starting out, they think they have to be perfect at it. They're so worried about writing the best sales copy that they'll sometimes go out and spend $10,000, $15,000, $20,000 or more hiring a professional copywriter to write their sales letters for them. **What they fail to realize is that you can sell a ton of a hot product with a poorly-written sales letter, as long as you've enthusiastic and have something that a market desperately wants.**

And conversely, I honestly believe that if you've got a product that nobody wants, it doesn't matter how great your copy is—you're probably not going to sell very many. So the key, in my opinion, isn't having the best killer sales copy. It's great to have it if you can, and you should always work to hone your skills; **but I would much rather have the best, hottest, most in-demand product than the best sales copy.** So when people are looking for products to sell to their market, or they're just getting started and they don't know what to sell, I always tell them, "Find the hottest offer. Find the hottest product, something that people are desperately going to want to buy."

If you do that, and you implement everything right, you've made the whole situation of selling so much easier... because now you're not really selling. **You're giving the buyer the opportunity to buy something they want already, which really does give you amazing super-selling power.** It's like the money just rains out of the sky. We've experienced that a few times over the years—money came faster than we could intelligently spend it. We still knew how to spend it of course, but not intelligently!

To really sell that hot item, you've got to create an irresistible offer. This starts with matching your offer to the right marketplace. **You have to begin with the end in mind,**

sometimes, and work backwards in order to create that irresistible offer. I know that that sounds a little complicated, and sure, it *is* somewhat advanced. But it's necessary, especially if what you have sells for a high ticket amount. With few exceptions, you can't just ask people who have no relationship with you to give you a lot of money, and actually expect that they'll buy in large numbers. One way you can build that sort of relationship, though, is to **work up to it by starting with lower-priced products and stair-stepping your customers to higher-dollar items.** That's one aspect of it. **The second is knowing that it's the back-end products that produce all your real profit,** so you'll want to think some of that out in advance. Because, you see, nobody gets rich by making one sale to one customer one time. **The secret is to resell to your customers over and over again;** so before you sell a single thing, you've go to think that through, in at least a general fashion.

Most businesses just sell people what they need: razor blades, socks, bread. That's one of the reasons they struggle so much. If you want to get rich, **focus on selling people what they *want*.** Now, be careful with this; sometimes what people want really badly is stuff that will put you in jail. In fact, the most profitable things in this world, it seems, are questionable or even downright illegal. Exclude those from your equation, unless you're really into living dangerously; work within the universe of things that are legal. And realize, too, that sometimes people want the craziest things. They can get typical stuff anywhere. **They're really looking for things that are different; things that are *unique*.**

So how do you figure out what people really want? **Market research, of course.** One of the things we tell people in our seminars is to find a marketplace they understand very, very well. We often talk about how to get rich in the opportunity marketplace, for example. So if you're a fan of the opportunity market and want to enter that marketplace, **you need to find the things that excite *you* the most.** You understand the market; so if things get you excited, then you know that they can get other people excited, too. Create an offer like the one that excited you, and make it irresistible. You've got to stack things up, giving people so much value that they just say *holy crap!* and jump at the chance to become a part of it. They just can't help themselves: they all just start giving you their money at once.

Generally speaking, the more someone wants something, the more money you can make selling it to them. **It's not about need; think about it.** If all people needed was transportation, they'd buy a super cheap car that gets great gas mileage. Or maybe they'd just buy a moped. All they really *need* is transportation. But what they *want* is something else again— which is why when you're a car salesman, you can sell people convertible sports cars and SUVs that will get them from Point A to Point B in style. If someone wants to buy a home and they're just filling a basic need, there are plenty of inexpensive homes on the market. You're not going to make a lot on a product like that; the real money's in selling a home that someone really wants—a high-end house that sells for many times the price of basic shelter.

It's the same way in most businesses. If you're selling what people need, you're probably making small profit margins. **If you're selling what people want, you're probably in a high profit margin business.** The greater the want, generally speaking, the more profit is available in that marketplace.

Again, the best way to know what people want is to determine what you're excited about yourself. Chris Lakey likes golf and other sports. Though he's never been in such a business, he could probably get into one fairly easily with a little basic research, since he's a consumer in that marketplace. He knows a lot about golf, he knows what makes him crazy on the golf course, and he knows the parts of the game that he struggles with. He knows the things that tend to frustrate all golfers, no matter their experience level. You may be the same; maybe *you* know your hobby very well. **Any hobby can be turned into a business if the marketplace is right—and if you offer your prospects something they want *really badly*.** The bigger the want, the more money there is to be made.

So you don't look for the biggest needs; look for the biggest, hottest wants. If you know your marketplace well enough, you can easily discern what these are. Those form the foundation for your sales success to that marketplace. They become the basis for your sales material, because you specifically address the wants people have. The bigger the want, the higher in your sales copy it should be placed. **That's why you should take a look at your competitors and determine which ones are making the most money.** Study what they're doing. Get on the other side of the cash register; think like somebody in the business, rather than a consumer, who *doesn't* think. Consumers, especially the most rabid ones, are buying for subconscious reasons; they're not really able to think in a more logical, holistic kind of way.

So many people are beating their heads against the wall because they're trying to sell people things that *they* want to sell, rather than things that the customers want to buy. That's a path to business failure! **You've always got to know where your focus is—and your focus should almost *always* be on your customer, very rarely on yourself.** You're not necessarily your customer; in fact, sometimes you and your customer are two completely different people. But if you know what they want and are willing to deliver just that, you're going to be more successful than if you decide, "Well, I only want to sell this," and try to sell it to people that don't want it. You'd be surprised how many people do that. **Sell people exactly what they *want*,** which you find by studying the hottest products in your marketplace, and you'll be a super-seller in no time.

Let's jump to a related topic: the **Magic Formula for Making Millions Selling Virtually Any Product or Service.** Now, this is a key item, and it definitely connects to my earlier topic. **The concept here is that we must find people who are very hungry for what we sell, and then feed it to them.** Finding an endless supply of hungry prospects is the golden key to becoming wealthy—and there are some markets that really do have an endless supply of new prospects coming in all the time. Here's an example: the matchmaking market. Look at companies like eHarmony.com or Match.com, companies that focus on this market and are making millions of dollars by doing so. This is a market that will always be there; there will *always* be a fresh, new supply of people looking for other people to date and, ultimately, to marry. And once they're ready to get married, they enter what's known as the wedding market. During the short period of time they're engaged, they become prospects for wedding cakes, dresses, invitations, announcements, and wedding bands. That's another market with a constant stream of fresh prospects.

The dieting market is a *great* market. There are always people who want to lose some extra weight, so in that market you're always having new people come in. You're having people drop out and come back, too. They want pills and potions and diet plans. They want to go to Weight Watchers and Jenny Craig, and are always trying new things. The business opportunity and moneymaking market, the one me and most of my colleagues are involved in, is the same way. **There will always be people who want to make more money, who want to know how to ensure their financial freedom.**

Those are both pretty general markets, but there are markets that are as specific as something like back pain. It's a niche market, though; while there are plenty of people in that market, they can be difficult to reach. After all, they don't all read one publication like *Back Pain Monthly*. Nevertheless, it's possible to reach the market—there are plenty of companies that offer pills, potions, and lotions for back pain sufferers. They know, as we do, that there will always to be people who really want relief from back pain.

Focusing on a market with a constant, never-ending stream of prospects is necessary if you want to have a strong, growing business. If you're trying to sell to a group of seven people, and once those seven people are gone that's it, then you aren't going to have a very strong business, are you? It doesn't matter if the number is seven or seven thousand; eventually the pond will dry up. So you need to focus on a market that's fresh and has lots of new prospects, and simply go out and find what they want to buy. Do your research! You might go to their seminars, events, or organizational association meetings; read their magazines; or even conduct surveys or interviews. **Find out what their common problems are, and deliver the solutions.** That's the magic formula here—but it's almost a common sense formula, really. Once you've done all that, it's easy to figure out what to sell.

Let me reiterate: **Making a lot of money in the marketing field is *not* about what you want—unless you're able to make yourself want what your market wants.** A lot of people miss this somehow. They say, "Well, I want to sell X," whatever X may be, and that's the end of the argument. They try to shove it down the throats of the people in their particular market—if they even have a market to sell it to. That's the wrong way to do it. You need a vibrant, dynamic market that new people are coming into all the time, one where the buyers are rabid for new products. **Find out the problems they want to solve, and then create or find products that solve their problems.** Deliver what *they* want, and you're going to find it a lot easier to make money than if you're delivering only what you want. And even if you do find a good market, try to home in on that one niche that's more vibrant than the others.

Let's use the opportunity market as an example. It encompasses many different segments: everything from niches where companies sell dirt-cheap, flimsy reports, to people selling a whole bunch of cheap stuff, mostly to each other, to companies that sell million-dollars franchises. Then there are the big companies like us that are selling what I think is top-notch information, and others that are just doing Internet stuff at one scale or another. Some of the niches are unique. Recently, someone handed me this business card. First he told me that he's involved in this business opportunity where they're making candles—and I had no interest, believe me. But as soon as he handed me his business card, I knew that somebody involved really understood marketing. It was a beautiful three-panel card that did a great job of selling and really got my attention. The next day, he gave me one of his candles, which I later burned as part of my morning quiet time. It's supposed to be a healthy candle, really good for you, and it really is a superior product.

Then I started studying the market niche that he's in. It *is* an opportunity, but it mostly reaches the stay-at-home mom market, a specific segment of the opportunity market. A lot of housewives want to supplement their income and have a little bit of freedom so they don't have to beg their husband for money; that's a big thing. And they want to get away from the kids for a little while, to have something else going on. They may not want to go into the work force full-time, but they want to do something that feels productive. **Well, when I started investigating, I found that with about 500 hours worth of work, you could make a go of it.** That's always the joke, you know; "Hey, I got a multimillion-dollar idea for you, and it's only going to take 500 hours worth of work!"

But the truth was, with 500 hours of work, somebody could actually put something together that's very similar to this deal. As I've pointed out, you think about the market first; in this case it was the stay-at-home mom type of market. And then you look at all of the companies selling business opportunities to that particular market, and you plan accordingly. It's got to be a large market, and it's got to be reachable. **There should be a lot of competitors already in the market, and they have to be doing well.** By the way, this company out of California doing this candle thing is publicly traded. Usually little rinky-dink companies aren't—so this should make you smell some money there somewhere.

Whatever you come up with, don't copy what the other companies are doing; but do use them as models. **A big part of marketing is differentiation, what separates you from everyone else.** These other companies should serve as your maps into new territories. Take a little from this company, a little from that one, and put them together in a new way to form something that is totally unique that will serve the marketplace.

One of the points I'd like to make here is that too often, people get caught up in worrying more about the product than they should. They focus on creating a product that sounds good to them or, for one reason or another, they come up with a product and then, after it's developed, then they think about who they should sell it to. Or they never really think about who to sell it to at all; they just invented something, and now they want to figure out who might want it. That's a huge mistake! **Find the prospects first.** Find the group of hungry people, and then offer them something to eat. That's the golden formula: Start with the marketplace. **Too many people try to do it all backwards.** Find the group of customers *first*, then make money by filling their wants—not their needs. It all starts with the prospect, not the product. **And be sure the group of people you start with is large—the bigger the better.** Sometimes you can get into a niche that's too small, where there wouldn't be the opportunity for profit because of the number of people in the niche. But you know, ideas are everywhere. There really are too many ideas and too little time, so as I pointed out in the last chapter, you have to pick and choose. That's one place where defining your marketplace, your niche, can really help you.

Let's move on to the third item on this chapter's agenda: **How to Create a Never-Ending Stream of Money By Always Doing One Simple Thing.** We're still sticking with this theme of giving customers what they want, and the idea here is to always strive to fill the deepest unfulfilled desires of your customers. How people are, deep down, is very interesting to me—how our egos work, especially. **People constantly *want* things.** We're never at a state of peace where we feel like we have everything. Maybe you want a new car, a new home, more money, better health, better looks—but you want *something*. Usually we want multiple things. What happens is that we take actions to fulfill those wants, and in most cases those actions include buying things. So if we want a new car, we'll buy that new car. If we want a new house, we'll buy a new house. If we want better health we might buy better food, eat at healthier restaurants, get a gym membership, and go to Jenny Craig. We've been conditioned as consumers to know that if we have a want, we can fulfill it by buying something. Which is great—as marketers, as business owners and entrepreneurs, you want to applaud the fact that consumers have been conditioned in that way. **When people decide to fill those wants, they're willing to pay you if you've got a product or service that will fill their wants.**

Now, the great thing about filling people's wants is that **their desire will, in many cases, be satisfied only very briefly**

by buying something. This happens a lot in the business opportunity market. Let's say somebody has the desire to make more money. They want to be filthy rich and live in a beautiful mansion, have fancy cars, and purchase everything that catches their fancy. To fulfill that desire, they might buy a course called "How to Make Money in Real Estate." They send away the $500, they get the course, and they feel like they've taken action and fulfilled that want a little—until they start going through the course, and discover they've actually got to take some real action to make their dreams come true. Well, they're busy in their lives, and so what happens is that they set that aside. They put it on their bookshelf, and then—maybe very quickly, maybe very slowly—that little voice in their head starts telling them they still want the money, that house, the trip, the vacation, and the lifestyle that was *not* fulfilled with that first purchase. So what do they do? **They make a second purchase, a third purchase, a fourth purchase and a fifth purchase—and on and on.**

It's the exact same way in the weight-loss industry: someone has that desire to lose weight, so they'll take action to try to fulfill that desire, to fill that want, and they will not get the results that they want. **Most people want instantaneous results, which is unlikely to happen.** If they get that book on "How to Have Super Abs in Eight Minutes a Day or Less" and they read through it, and they've realized, "Yeah, eight minutes a day *for the next twenty years*," but that want hasn't been fulfilled—so now they have to go out and do the next thing: buy the pills or potions, or go to Weight Watchers or to the gym. **They just keep on buying things.** That's how human beings work.

So don't worry too much about over-fulfilling their wants. What do I mean by that? Well, here's what I *don't* mean. Some people say, "Well, I don't want to give them everything, because if I fulfill this desire completely, then they're never going to buy the next thing and the next thing." No, that's absolutely not the right way to think. **Don't hold important information back; make it all available.** Here's a good example: there's a gentleman who sells books and courses on how to have more and better dates. He's got this great eBook that he sells for $20, and it's got all of his best information in it. He's had thousands of people buy that book, and you'd think that would be the last thing that they would buy from him. Well, no, they're unsatisfied. They want still more information. They feel like they've got to have more information, because certainly this simple formula can't be all it takes to get more and better dates. So what they do is buy his DVD courses; they buy his audio CDs; they go to his live events for hundreds and, in some cases, thousands of dollars. They end up having spent thousands of dollars. In fact, some of these people are on continuity programs with the guy.

It's because they have this constant desire that is very rarely completely filled. Don't be afraid to fulfill people's wants, because what's going to happen is they're going to be satisfied very briefly, and then they're going to want some more. **Understanding that at a basic level will help you generate a never-ending stream of money—just knowing that people are constantly wanting, wanting, wanting, and your job is to continue to fill that wanting.** People are insatiable, and thank goodness for that. They just can't get be satisfied. I realize that this causes some real misery in some people, but that's not our purview here. We're marketers, so we take advantage of the fact that people are obsessed with the kinds of things that we sell.

Incidentally, let me repeat something that I'll certainly say again: our consumers don't want the products themselves. They never want the products; **they want *the benefit the product brings.*** If you need a hole in something, you don't really want the drill you have to buy or borrow to make the hole; you just want the hole the drill makes. You're looking for the benefits of the drill. Well, guess what? For many products and services, the associated benefits aren't real in any way; they're just perceived. **In fact, some of the best benefits are perceived benefits. It's the fantasy in people's heads that matters**—and I'll give you an example from my own life. For years, I fantasized about having an RV and traveling all over the country; and I still do, a little, though I realize it's a fantasy. In my fantasy, one day I'll look out my window and there's a big beautiful set of mountains out there. Next week I look out my window, and there's the blue ocean. Then I'm down in the desert the next week, and then I go off to Canada and I'm in the forest. Occasionally in the past, especially when I was having problems in my life, I would, in my mind, jump in my little RV and take off; and in my mind I would be content, and life would be perfect. I wouldn't have any problems.

Then a few years back I went to an RV show. It was my first show ever, and I sat in a bunch of RVs. That's all I did—I just went from RV to RV, and I sat inside each one and I fantasized a little and tried to picture myself driving it. Somewhere along the line, I realized that's not really what I want—not at all. I don't want, for example, to have to dump the toilets and flush out the "brownwater," as they call it. That's part of the reality of an RV; and that's not what I want. It's the fantasy that I want. Now I kind of wish I hadn't gone to that RV show.

People sometimes want the perceived value more than they want the real value. For example: most people who buy into business opportunities don't really want a business. Who wants a business? Some days, I wouldn't wish a business on my worst enemy. People don't really want to have to put up with all the crap you have to deal with to have a business. No, what they want are the *perceived benefits* of the business! They want the dream to be true. They want whatever they envision a business can bring them; and generally it can, if they're willing to work hard and deal with the reality of business life. So if you're selling biz ops, you're not really lying to people; but you're not telling them the whole story, either—that sometimes, owning a business is very stressful.

People want the fantasy, and they want it to be real. They love the benefits and so they focus on those, and they just can't get enough of the dream. Pursuing that fantasy becomes an obsession; they end up buying more and more of whatever it is that promises the benefit of eventually, somehow, fulfilling this insatiability that they have. **The marketing lesson here is that the more people buy, the more they buy. It's a hunger that just can't be satiated.** If someone's in the marketplace for certain types of products, the more they get of those types of products, the more they want those and related products. The buying frenzy continues because they're buying.

And keep this in mind: you have to be right there to offer them more. The longer they go without buying, the more the hunger wanes; and over time, it goes away. Chris Lakey tells me that golf is like that for him. He notices that when he gets busy and can't golf as often, he doesn't miss it as much. That desire wanes because of his lack of participation. He's also an avid technology junkie: he always watches for the latest cell phone, and likes watching the latest high-definition televisions on the marketplace, and reading technology blogs. Now, frankly, he could get by with the old technology if he wasn't out there in the marketplace, always looking for what's new. But he is, so the more he looks, the more he sees other things that he thinks would be cool to own. It's the same thing with any business or product or marketplace: **the more someone is active in the marketplace, the more they want to own things that are related to that marketplace.** And, again, the opposite of that is true. If someone's out of the market and they haven't been active in it, that desire wanes.

So this insatiability is actually a good thing for us. Sometimes entrepreneurs are worried about competition, about prospects buying things from other people in the marketplace. Well, the fact is, people are going to spend their money in that marketplace, and if they're buying something from your competition, it means they're still feeding their hunger for those kinds of products and services, and so it means that they're still hungry. **Therefore, there's still a chance that they'll do business with you.** So don't worry about someone buying something from somebody else, especially if you have consumables or products that people tend to buy a lot.

There are obvious exceptions, of course; for example, if they buy a car, they're probably out of the auto market for a while. But most marketplaces aren't that way, so there should be no fear of them buying from the competition, because that means they're still hungry. Even if they've already bought something very similar to what you have to offer, they may very well buy from you, because **people will continue to want other types of products and services in the broader marketplace you serve.** That hunger keeps them going; the more they buy, the more they feed that hunger, and it's just an endless cycle until someone gets out of the marketplace for some reason.

Remember, too, that some markets are seasonal, so someone who's in a certain marketplace may not always be in that marketplace. **There is a season, a specific period of time, when they are hungry and are buying.** It's the same as any other market in that respect: while they're hungry, while they're in that moment, while they're interested in those types of products and services, the more they buy the more they want to buy. **It can form a continuous cycle, a type of feeding frenzy that can last a long time** and give you plenty of opportunities not only to make sales once, but to continue making those sales, and to continue serving your marketplace by offering them more of what they want and more of what you know they've already bought from you the first time.

This leads to *The Number One Mistake That Costs Inexperienced Marketers Millions in Profit.* It's a simple mistake, and I can certainly understand how people who are just getting involved in marketing would make it. It's in selling logically. **This happens quite often when people are selling something they think people need, and they try to explain why they need it.** They don't realize that people buy based on what they *want*; that is, **purchases are more likely to be based on emotions and desires than on what someone should logically need.** Oh, they may justify that purchase through logic; they may say something like, " I really need that," or "I can use that in the future because it's going to do this, this and this." It doesn't matter; the purchase is almost always based on their emotions and their desires.

Even we marketers, who ought to understand this stuff, are all blinded by our desires. **It's those things that we want that really control us.** I've already mentioned the quote by Edward DeRopp that says, "Man inhabits a world of delusion." If you were to take away the things that we attach to the facts or to products and services, you would have a whole different perception of the world. **But what happens is that people identify products or services with being healthier and happier.** We desire certain products or services because of the results they're going to give us, or how they're going to make us feel, or how they're going to change our lives or our lifestyles. If you realize that most people live in this world of delusion, then that really does give you the opportunity to make more sales.

There are ways to train yourself to see how that delusion works. If you study psychology, you can come to understand, somewhat, how the human mind works. In knowing how it works, you can you create products, marketing campaigns, and sales copy that really does generate an incredible amount of money. I've already mentioned an excellent primer on that: Robert Cialdini's *Influence: the Psychology of Persuasion*. It's a great book about the different types of persuasive methods that you can use to get people to perceive your product as the best in a particular market, especially if you have competition. Now, we're not talking about a product that people don't naturally want; **we're talking about persuading them to go ahead and buy the product they *do* want.** Remember, you should already be selling things that people want, just to make the selling process easier. With the information in Cialdini's book, you're going to have them buying it faster, and paying you more, with less hassle.

The second book that I would recommend is *The Science of Influence: How to Get Anyone to Say Yes in Eight Minutes or Less* by Kevin Hogan. Again, it's all about the psychology behind people's emotions, their desires, their thinking, and how to influence them to see you, your company and your products in a certain way, and to get them to take action.

You have to realize that we don't live in a world of reality. **We live in a world of perceptions, and unfortunately, most inexperienced marketers focus their attention and marketing on the features of a product.** Basically, what they're doing is saying, "This book is hardback. It has 237 pages. It's got a blue cover." People aren't out to buy a 237-page document with a pretty blue cover. That's incidental. They want what's between the covers: the information that a non-fiction book provides, or the thrills and excitement they can get from a novel. People don't want a thing to have the thing; **what they want is what that thing will provide, or what they perceive it's going to get them.** They want results!

Even though people buy because of the results, once they get the product, oftentimes they still don't take action. They don't do whatever additional thing they have to do to get the results they want—so they're soon back in the market again, looking for that next product that they believe is going to get them that result. **Really, this is the foundation for successful marketing — understanding that people buy based on emotions, desires, and wanting, and that they're never going to be truly satisfied.** If you spend even the smallest amount of time learning the basics of psychology, especially by reading these books I've mentioned, you're going to become a powerful marketer who can get large groups of people to give you amazingly large amounts of money.

When I was 25 years old, I had a chance to spend some good, quality time with a man who, at that time, was about 82 years old. He came to visit me and was only going to stay for about a week; but then he got sick, and so he ended up staying seven or eight weeks. It was seven or eight of the best weeks of my life, now that I think about it. We would talk for hours when he felt well enough, and we talked many times into the night, just on and on and on. He was just such a smart guy and he taught me a lot of things. One day I asked him what the perfect business was. He told me, "You know, I've seen all these companies running these small classified ads in national magazines year after year, and I've thought about it a lot. I think that's the business you should be in."

Of course, I didn't do anything with it for a few years. But then, one day, I asked him this question: "Bill, what's the most important thing you ever learned in your whole life?" And he goes, "Well, let me think about it for a few days." I forgot I'd even asked him — and then one day we're driving down the road, three or four days later, and all of the sudden he says, "I got the answer to your question. Everybody in the whole world is crazy." Of course, I thought he was kind of joking with me. But you know what? The more I understand human psychology, especially as it affects marketing, the more I realize what Bill was saying. Emotions bring out the best and the worst in people — the best *and* the worst. **People often buy for unconscious reasons, especially rabid buyers.** They're the ones who buy the most, and most often the ones that are totally obsessed. It's all about the emotions.

Back in the 19th century, there was a woman named Madame Blavatsky who was into the weirdly spiritual, and had thousands and thousands of followers. Basically, she conned a lot of people. On her deathbed, she said that **people believe what they want to believe, and they see what they want to see.** I've thought about that a lot. It's as true now as it ever was. There's a very popular book that sold millions of copies recently, and now they're doing seminars all across the county. The promoters are making a fortune. Basically, the idea behind that book is that if you just sit around and get your mind right, you can command the universe to bring money and riches and all the wealth that you want. You could just sit in your living room on your couch, even in front of the television, and you could command money to come to you. People are buying those books by the millions. I'll admit that I bought the stupid book and the audio CDs myself. *Shame on me*! The crazier the idea, sometimes, the more people gravitate to it — almost likes a child who wants to believe in fairy tales.

I talked about this earlier. **People just don't buy logically.** If we did, we'd all drive Hondas and live in cheap houses, using thrift-store furniture. We'd have no use for televisions, because that's just a waste of money. We wouldn't have two or three cell phones to our names; we might have just a home phone. We'd live very frugal, basic lives — almost like the Amish do.

The reality is that we don't live that way because we don't want to. We don't think through purchases and decide whether they're needed or not; **we buy based on emotion, and a lot of**

the reasons we buy are subconscious. We don't even know why we buy, but we do — and we buy often. We spend lots of money doing so. Imagine where our economy would be if we only bought what we needed, how little money would be spent in our marketplace. Of course, that would mean fewer jobs, because most jobs are provided by companies who sell what people want. The truth is, the world economy is driven by emotional spending. We buy what we want, and many times we buy what we want with money we should be spending on things that we *need*. Think about that one. A lot of people will go without health insurance — but they're probably eating out several times a week. They probably have a big screen high definition TV in their house, with cable or satellite dish. They probably have a couple of cell phones — and yet they're among the 47,000,000 Americans living without health insurance.

People *always* spend money on things they want over things that they need, which is why you want to be in the business of selling what people want. That assumes, of course, that you can figure out what they want. Sometimes, they themselves don't know; people don't typically think about it like that. They just know that they're buyers. And sometimes, people don't really know what they want until you sell it to them. Or they know what they want, but really don't know *why* they want it. So it's up to you to determine the psychological angles, and to figure out what they want. **Once you can figure that out, you can sell to people's emotional buying habits — and that's going to make you the big money.**

Become a P.T. Barnum of Marketing

This Rule will show you how to make people so excited they'll practically be willing to crawl over broken glass to buy your products and services. Now, I know that sounds just a little hyped; but by the time you finish reading this chapter, I honestly believe that you're going to feel like you can do exactly that.

One of the greatest copywriters of all time, Robert Collier, once pointed out that **showmanship sells.** He wasn't the first to realize that. **The fact is, in order to really succeed, you've got to put yourself out there and not be afraid to stand out.** A lot of people worry about their images, what people are going to think about them... but sometimes, the best thing you can do is commit image suicide. **By that, I mean that you need to quit worrying about what most people think, and become more concerned about the people that you're going to help, and what *they* think.**

If you want to become a literal marketing giant, **learn to be like that great marketer P.T. Barnum.** That's going to give you the competitive advantage, no matter what market or industry you're in. Now, let me tell you a little bit about old P.T., who was probably the greatest showman and promoter the world has ever known. He would go out and find out *exactly* what it was that would excite people, and once he knew that, he would give them exactly what they wanted with the greatest possible display of showmanship. **He came up with all kinds of new promotions and ideas that, in his time, were quite controversial.** Some of those concepts involved using celebrities in his marketing campaigns, having reserved seats at the theater or museums, and offering what he called matinee shows. All that is common today, but in his day it was very unusual. He stood out, right on the edge. And he wasn't afraid to be there, either.

In 1870, Barnum's circus, *The Greatest Show on Earth*, grossed ore than $400,000 in its first year. Now, $400,000 may not seem like a lot of money to some people today, but in 1870, it was an enormous fortune. And get this: P. T. Barnum wasn't the best circus owner in the world, but **he *was* a consummate showman.** If you employ showmanship, folks, you don't have to be the best at what you do. He wasn't the best owner of a museum or a theater or a ship, either, but **he was bigger than life. *He stood out.***

Here's the bottom line: **If you want to really stir people's emotions, you need to use showmanship to get them to respond.** You have two choices. You can be just like everybody else, like a little wallflower over there doing nothing, or you can be a true showman. That's what P.T. Barnum was. That's what *you* need to become if you expect to be superbly successful in this industry. **Be controversial; stir up emotion.** I'm not trying to tell you to create hatred for yourself and your product, but **what you *should* understand is that if you use showmanship, you're going to sell more of your product.** Let's face it: there's a lot of competition out there for your customer's money. Never forget that. If you can't answer the question of "Why should I give you this money and not give it to your competitor?", then you don't really deserve the business.

Let's look at sports again. It's a fact that the team that wants it most is going to win, all other things being equal. Sometimes, even if things are vastly unequal, the team that really, really wants to win will. They're not necessarily the best team, but they're out there really providing a show, offering the entertainment, doing what they do best as hard as they can. Think about those highflying basketball players. Is there really any need for them to go soaring through the air? Absolutely not! But it's all part of the show. And then there are the cheerleaders — completely unnecessary to the game. We all understand that show, obviously. And I like think back a few years to this one young boxer by the name of Cassius Clay. He transformed himself, using showmanship, into an individual who changed an entire sports industry: Muhammad Ali. I know I'll always remember listening to him. He would say things like "Float like a butterfly; sting like a bee," and make fun of Howard Cosell. *That* was showmanship. *That's* what the people wanted. It was controversial, but it got people's attention. And let's go back a little farther, to a place called Tupelo, Mississippi. There was this young truck driver there who had a guitar and a crazy name, and nobody knew him. Then one day he started to sing. He dressed crazily, did some odd dancing, became really controversial — and it wasn't long before Elvis Presley became a household name. Elvis epitomized showmanship.

So how do you apply showmanship to your marketing? Well, first of all, **you've got to grab the attention of people** by positioning yourself in front of your target market with the biggest and the boldest benefits you can offer. Then you've got to **stimulate their interest by treating the prospects as if they are already interested in what you're doing,** and he wants what you're offering. *Then* **you have to create some desire in him** by providing him with facts that he can't fail to appreciate, and must accept as beneficial to him. **Finally, you've got to help him take action by giving him specific directions.** When

137

Elvis was on that stage performing, he always told everyone that **you've always got to leave them wanting more — and that's what you've got to do as a showman.**

One of the greatest copywriters of all time was a man I've already mentioned, Gary Halbert. One example of how Gary used showmanship was to mail out a letter with a crisp, new, $1 bill attached to the top. In the sales copy he would say something like, "As you can see, I've attached a crisp new dollar bill to the top of this letter. Why have I done this? For two reasons, actually. First, since I have something that's extremely important to tell you, I needed some way to make sure this letter would catch your attention. And secondly, since this letter concerns how you can make a lot of money, I thought using a dollar bill as a financial eye catcher was especially appropriate. Here's what it's all about…" And then Gary would go on to explain the offer. That was showmanship in print. He was using something bold and daring to catch their attention, to build desire, and to bring them in to what he wanted to share with them.

Here's another really great example. Back in 1919, there was a newspaper publisher by the name of E. Haldeman-Julius. He started publishing what became known as *The Little Blue Books*. He would sell people 50 of these little books at a time for ten cents each. His showmanship involved using bold, daring, and controversial book titles — and remember that this was back in 1919, so today they're not too controversial. But he had titles like *Love Letters from a Portuguese Nun, Prostitution in the Modern World,* and *The Art of Kissing.* And when sales got bad for one book title, he'd simply employ showmanship in print by *changing* that book title. For example, when the book *Gaither's Fleece of Gold* was changed to *Quest for a Blonde Mistress*, sales jumped from 6,000 copies to 50,000 copies. By being bold, by being daring, by using showmanship in print, he sold more than 100 million books. That's a lot of dimes.

Showmanship is simply the ability to attract other people. When you can attract those people by being different, they're drawn to you; they're drawn to your sales message, to your sales copy, and as a result they buy from you. And as Elvis liked to say, always leave them wanting more. Selling is a performance, but it's also about motivation. A lot of people think that selling is persuasion, and I used to think that way, too; but really, **it's motivation.** You've got to get people in who are already persuaded. You can't try to persuade people to do what they don't want to do; **you've got to be talking to people who already have a sincere interest and desire for the kinds of products and services you sell.** So first, you attract people who are already coming to you with a strong desire for the benefits your products and services provide. And then you motivate them to take the kind of action you want them to take. To do that, you've got to give them a show.

I'm a big P.T. Barnum fan, as you've no doubt already noticed, because P.T. Barnum was a great promoter *and* a great entertainer. He knew how to get people excited, motivated, and inspired, and just like Elvis, he always made them want to come back for more. **That's what we try to do: We make our seminars fun, so people will want more.** Sure, people are there to learn things, but they want to be entertained at the same time. So you've got to give people a helluva show; you've got to make it as fun and exciting as possible, and blow it up as big as you can. **Do something that makes you stand out head and shoulders above everybody else.**

A few years back, Chris Lakey and I found out about a premium gift that some marketers we knew were giving to people who bought a $1,000 item. It's an atomic clock that picks up radio signals from Ft. Collins, Colorado, daily, resetting itself so that it keeps time to within one second of accuracy in 20 million years. It's the world's most accurate clock. Well, instead

139

of giving them away as a bonus gift with a high-dollar purchase, we started giving them away *absolutely free*. People didn't even have to buy anything to get one of these clocks from us; they just had to take a certain action that we wanted them to take. We weren't just giving them out to the masses; **we were sending them out to people who were already extremely well-qualified, and then making them qualify themselves further.** But we even took it beyond that.

These are really big clocks, 10 inches in diameter, which come in a really nice box. When we sent out our sales copy, we showed them a life-sized picture of the clock that we were offering to give them. They'd have to make a small commitment, of course; but otherwise there was no cost, no obligation. I thought it was a great free gift; the atomic clock has that great story to it, so it's exciting. People are crazy about this amazing technology. All this hype and build-up gets them to qualify themselves further, so we can do our best to sell to them — and hey, they know that in advance. **But we're doing things to blow it up, we're making it big, we're making it loud, we're making it aggressive.**

And you've got to be that way! When you're a little controversial, bold and audacious — and maybe even a little bit dangerous — you stand out. **And that's the whole point: you need to design your campaigns to stand head and shoulders above all of the other people in your rather crowded marketplace.** Figure out a way to turn up the volume full blast. You can't be afraid of all of the naysayers and the critics, either. In fact, sometimes, when the critics start yelling the loudest, saying things like, "Oh, you can't do that! You better be careful about that!" that's when you should just laugh quietly and tell yourself, "Hey, now we're getting closer." The more people start telling you that you can't do something, the more you *know* that you're just about where you need to be in order to make a mark in your overcrowded, over-competitive marketplace.

Despite the fact that there are too many competitors in most markets, the truth is that most competitors are just following the follower. **Everybody's doing the same thing, so it's easy to stand out.** Let everyone else blend in, leaving nothing to separate one from another; that makes it easier for you. That's what we were doing with this atomic clock. Oh, we hoped that it would make us money; we weren't giving it away just to be kind, although we think we're kind people. The hope was that it would drive business, which it did. That's what this is all about. **It's about being a showman;** it's about being bold and doing something a little crazy, something that some of our competitors might say is nuts. You know how the game normally works. If you sell something for $1,000 and you have a great free gift, well, the gift was free with $1,000 purchase. So the company is making money, and giving you a free gift; that's the way it works in all kinds of industries, so we're not unique here. But most people would argue that we might be a little crazy to give away a valuable atomic clock just to get someone to raise their hand and go through our qualification process.

But people only buy what they want to buy; you can't force someone to buy something. So if you're targeting people with a product or a service that you know they want, and they're already prone to buy, and you know they're probably going to buy from somebody else if they don't buy from you — then what can you do that separates you from the crowd? How does a person choose whether they're going to do business with you? That's where what we call the Unique Selling Position or USP comes in. **Simply put, it's whatever you do differently to separate yourself from everyone else — and that's where the showmanship comes into play.** That's where being bold and audacious, and going out there with everything to put your best foot forward, becomes critical.

This is what will make you really stand out. Even if the other people out there aren't selling *exactly* what you sell, **there are people selling similar products to your market; so if you line your product up with everybody else's and they're all roughly the same, how are you going to attract people's attention when they come to make that choice?** Well, you could try to be the cheapest in the marketplace, although that's a terrible idea. That's a game everyone will try to play, and some idiot will always undercut you — then all of a sudden you're got no profit, and you might as well not be selling at all. **You're not going to compete on price; get that out of your head.**

Let's say all these similar products are priced exactly the same. What makes someone want to buy yours over everybody else's? **Bluntly put, it's all the intangibles — the extra offers and the showmanship, in whatever form that takes.** You need to be like P.T. Barnum and put on a good show. Be something exciting that people want to get behind and spend time around. Earlier, I talked a little about having seminars and putting on an exciting show for people. Well, what makes one event better than another? **In my opinion, it's how the customer feels when they're there.**

It's not just the benefit from the content that's being shared, although that's important; but the truth is, I could read from a textbook and give you all the information you need, or I could play an audio program that contained the same information. *Or* I could put on a show. We could have fun, we could laugh and joke, and we could tell stories, and we could be entertaining. Now, which event would you rather be at? We all know the answer to that! Everyone will pick entertainment over a dry recitation of the facts, no matter how important those facts are. That's why you have to put on a show for your prospects. **You have to go all out, boldly do everything you can to make people feel good, to make them want to buy from you.** Those intangibles are usually what tip the scale, because if it's just a matter of picking and choosing off the shelf, there's nothing to separate you from anybody else. So do something that raises eyebrows. It's about getting attention. Think about all the free publicity that happens when someone does something weird. Now, I'm not saying you should do something stupid with your business — but look how odd behavior grabs people's attention. Think of YouTube, and all the crazy, viral things that get huge numbers of hits. Remember the balloon boy thing back at the end of 2009? All that weird stuff really gets publicity.

That's what you want for your business. You want to be doing things that people talk about. **You want to do things that create energy and excitement, things that people are drawn to like iron to a magnet. That will be what separates you from all your competition.** Being bold and daring can be an excellent USP — even if your friends say, "You're crazy to do that! Why would you even think of doing that? Look at all the potential for this and that to happen!" Well, you can't think about the bad things that *might* happen; focus on the good things. Nothing ventured, nothing gained, as they say. **It's too easy to be boring in the marketplace** — and everybody else is boring. Why not go to the other extreme? It just might help you sell more products to more people, which is the basic formula for making more money. If you'll do that, you can set yourself up for good profits, because you're offering excitement, and that's where people want to be.

The Secret Weapon That's Stronger Than 1,000 Arguments

A writer by the name of Nathaniel Emmons once stated that any fact is better established by two or three good testimonials than by a thousand arguments. That's the next secret weapon I want to talk about: testimonials. **What you say about yourself isn't *nearly* as important as what other people say about you.**

The same is true, of course, about your product, your service, or the business opportunity you're offering to other people. *What other people say is far more important to your prospect than what you say as a marketer.* Now, there are marketers out there who believe that testimonials are unnecessary; they feel that if you have a good product, then you don't need testimonials. Then there are other people who believe that testimonials are an absolute essential for an offer to be successful.

The truth lies somewhere between; **but I think that more important than whether testimonials are essential or non-essential is this:** *are they believable?* Let me give you an example. Let's say you see a testimonial that says, "I read Bill Gates' book and became a billionaire," and the signature on that testimonial is Warren Buffet. Well, let's get real. We all know Warren Buffet got rich without Bill Gates' help. Yeah, maybe he read Bill's book, and he definitely became a billionaire — but it's a sure bet one that didn't lead to the other. Besides, the prospect reading that testimonial knows that he's no Warren Buffet. He can't relate to that statement at all. But let's say the testimonial says, "My name is Forrest Gump. I'm just an average Joe from Greenbow, Alabama, and I used T.J.'s system to make $68,112.06 in a month." Sounds more realistic, doesn't it? Better yet, it's verifiable. **If the person giving the testimonial is believable, if the reader can feel that like he's like that person, then the testimonial becomes very powerful as a sales stimulator.**

To make the testimonial more believable, you've got to closely tie it to the interests of the audience you're directing your sales message toward. For example, if you're selling to Baby Boomers, you'll need testimonials that address their most important interests — health and money. If you're selling older senior citizens, on the other hand, you'd want testimonials that address their biggest concerns: having good mental function and maintaining the lifestyle they've worked so hard to achieve. **In any case, you want testimonials from people who are like your readers, because people tend to believe people who are like themselves.** There are some cases, of course, where people prefer expert credibility; for example, you could have a doctor give a testimonial for a consumer health product, or you might have a professor from a famous college give a testimonial to a more scholarly market. Or you might do something like this: maybe your testimonial could come from, oh, a former carpet cleaner who started with S300, then went on to become a $100 million Blue Jeans Millionaire. He could direct that experience towards frustrated small business people who want to escape the slavery of their own businesses. People can relate to the testimonial, because they can relate to the person.

Where's the best place to position those testimonials in the sales copy? **As a rule, it should be somewhere near or just following the benefit that you're presenting to the reader.** That substantiates the claims you're making to them; it's proving the benefit, in other words. **The testimonial will carry more authority and be more believable than all the sales copy in the world if it's connected to the benefit you're offering.** And interestingly enough, testing has proven that a longer, quoted testimonial is a lot more effective than the shorter one. In addition, you can really improve the believability and power of that testimonial by including a photograph of the person giving it. If you *really* want to give it power, then include that person's city, state, and phone number. Now, of course you can't just do that randomly; you've got to have their permission to do that. But if you can, it credentializes you; it makes the testimonial believable, more real.

But what can you do if you don't *have* any testimonials? Maybe you've got a brand new product, or you're just now getting into the market. Well, here's what you can do: **use what**

I call *the implied testimonial.* The implied testimonial is just
what that name suggests. For example, you could list well-
known companies that are using your product, or you could list
your Board of Directors on your letterhead, or you could list
groups of people who would benefit using that product. You
could even send a copy of your product to the President of the
United States. It's a real simple thing; they'll send you back a
letter on the White House letterhead, thanking you for that
product and making a brief comment about it. That looks pretty
powerful in your sales copy.

Otherwise, how do you get your clients, those people
you've already sold the product to, to give you those
testimonials? Here's a big secret that most marketers are never
going to share with you: **simple ask your clients for them.**
Remember, you're not just looking for money from a client;
what you really want is a raving fan, someone who can give you
a believable testimonial. **That believable testimonial's going to
multiply your money tenfold or more very quickly and very
easily.** So here's what you need to do right now: NUMBER
ONE, contact all your customers, old and new. NUMBER TWO,
ask them for a testimonial; you can coach them to be very
specific about how they benefited from purchasing your product.
NUMBER THREE, when **you get those testimonials back,
analyze the benefits people have gotten from your product.**
That can help you to create even more powerful sales copy by
pinpointing those benefits in any future promotion.

Now, let me tell you what a good testimonial is not. It's *not*
some guy sending you a statement that says, "Um, your product
worked for me." Boooring. It's not some guy saying, "Hey, I'm
going to become a millionaire this year using your
moneymaking program!" There's nothing wrong with optimism,
but that's just pie in the sky. It's not somebody saying, "Well,
that weight loss product helped my friend lose weight, so it'll

help me." That's not a good testimonial because it's secondhand. **A *good* testimonial is one that reinforces a specific benefit of your product.**

In Michael Penland's now-famous Internet and Joint Mutual Marketing Super Conference, he gives the attendees an evaluation form that asks questions like this: "Please rank in the order of importance why you attended my life-changing Internet Marketing Super Conference." There's a little box they can check that says: *I learned to gain financial and time freedom.* The next one is: *I gained insider secrets for improving sales and skyrocketing my profits.* And so on. Later, they're asked specific questions. For example, a question might I say, "In Question Number One, you ranked the main reasons you attended my Super Conference. Now, please explain how I delivered on these benefits to you personally." Michael leaves a blank space at the end where they can tell him in their own words the greatest benefit of attending that event.

That's the best way to get testimonials from people. **Just ask. Give them a form to fill out asking specific questions, and have them return it to you.** The bottom line here is what you want your testimonial to do. You want the reader to say to himself, "This person is just like me. It worked for them, so it'll work for me. Therefore, it's a good decision to buy right now." That's the true power of the testimonial, because again, any fact is better established by two or three good testimonials than by a thousand arguments. **And the more believable the testimonial, the more money you're going to put into your own pocket.**

One of the ways we've generated hundreds of great testimonials at M.O.R.E., Inc. is by using a variation of Michael Penland's strategy. **We've actually rewarded our customers with a free report if they'll simply take the time to fill out a questionnaire, and give us permission to slightly edit or alter any of the comments they made.** We put together a series of questions that asked things like, "Which of these three things did you enjoy the most?" and then asked, "Please tell us why you checked this." They were all very similar to that, and the things they could check off were specific benefits that our product and service provided to them. Most customers love getting a free gift, so they don't mind expressing their opinions if you give them an easy format to do so.

You know, in going back and studying these responses over the years, the most amazing thing to me is how similar they are: how hundreds and hundreds of responses say a lot of the same things. **You just see the same ideas — and some of our best ad copy has come right out of the words that people have written to us.** This gives you a lot of confidence in your marketplace, the confidence that comes with understanding, because it shows you the commonalities that your customers all have. This lets you get inside their heads and hearts a little bit more, in order to really understand the people you're selling to, and what's most important to them, and why. It's incredible how people who are attracted to the same types of benefits in any market tend to think alike. That's why we call them niche markets. The demographics might be different, the members may be of different races, religions, and ages, they might come from different-size cities — and yet the psychographics are very, very similar.

Testimonials are crucial, and you have to ask for them or you'll never get them. Otherwise, you're likely to hear only from unhappy customers — and every industry, every business, every product has a certain number of people who are upset about it for whatever reason. People are much more apt to complain than to give praise. **So you have to do your best to get your testimonials — and those all-important ideas — from your happy customers.** Here's an example of that. There's a company that sells fans, and they actually named their

company based on a letter they got from one of their clients. You
see, they sell big, commercial-grade fans for big warehouses. I
don't know what the old name of their company was, but once
they got a letter from a customer that raved about their "big ass"
fans. And so they named their company Big Ass Fans, after a
marketing guy actually told them it needed to be the company
name. That goes along with the strategy I talked about earlier —
being bold and audacious and doing things that get attention.
Talk about a company name that's controversial!

So as you can see, you can use comments from your
customers for all kinds of useful benefits. **You can get ideas for
new products, you can find out what your customers are
most interested in, and you can get testimonials that can be
used to help you sell and reach new customers.** Ask for them.
If you have to, tell them what you want their testimonial to look
like by giving them sample testimonials. Consumers in general
don't know how to write good testimonials. As a marketer,
though, you know what you're trying to say and what you're
trying to accomplish. If you'd like your testimonials to talk
about the benefits of a certain aspect of your product, then tell
people you'd like the testimonial to focus on a particular benefit.
Similarly, if you don't want them to mention a certain thing,
then ask them not to. Of course, you can't tell them *exactly* what
to write — and you wouldn't want to, because you wouldn't
want all the testimonials to be same. But you *can* encourage
them to discuss certain things, and avoid others. You can ask
them questions, and out of those questions can come the content
for your testimonial

Since most people don't get testimonials because they don't
ask for them, **you've got to get in the habit of asking for them.**
Offer your customers a free gift if they'll return a comment card;
and of course, **you always want to get permission to use their
testimonial, their name, and their location.** Usually when we

ask for testimonials, we tell people we won't use their phone number or give out their home address, just the name and a city and state — and by name, I mean the full name. Sometimes you see testimonials that only list their initials: J. P., P.T., or T.S. And maybe it doesn't even have a city; maybe it just lists the state, or maybe it doesn't even have that much. Testimonials like those are simply unbelievable. People think you made them up, even if you didn't.

Do your utmost to make the testimonials believable — and that shouldn't be too hard. **Most people are happy to share their thoughts about your product.** Like I said earlier, it's good to get as much information as you can. On some websites, you even see people using video testimonials. You can try that, or you can use audio; sometimes you'll see audio testimonials online, too. If you're doing it in print certainly you can add a photo and a person's title; say who they are and why they should be listened to. And remember: **you want your testimonials to come from the same kinds of people you're trying to reach.** If people can't see themselves as a Warren Buffet, then a Warren Buffet testimonial doesn't matter much; it's not going to be real to that reader. You also want your testimonials to address the issues that you want addressed in your sales copy, the things you're trying to point out to your prospects. **Highlight the main benefits through those testimonials.** Don't just put testimonials in there willy-nilly; use them to tell the story that you're trying to convey to people to get them to send you their money. If you can do that, testimonials can be a huge benefit.

Turning on the Magic Vacuum

Next, we're going to take a look at one of my favorite strategies: how to get down inside that magic marketing vacuum so you can suck unbelievable profits out of your market quickly and easily. **All sales are made in a vacuum.** People buy in a vacuum because of their emotional desires, and so we need to understand that and keep it in mind when we're writing sales copy. The reasons most people buy are emotional, not logical.

Did you ever watch those old Westerns when you were a kid, the ones where John Wayne and Henry Fonda were the heroes? They'd ride off into the sunset — but they would always ride off alone, without that woman that they'd loved or protected. And that comes down to something every good psychiatrist knows: that when people are happy, they don't pay the psychiatrist's rent. It's all about emotional desire, so a psychologist isn't really going to want a person to be happy and fulfilled. He wants to keep them filled with desire, filled with emotion, so they'll keep coming back. We do that in marketing, too: **we help people fulfill their desires, their needs, their wants, but we also bring them to an emotional high in order to keep them coming back.**

Here's a good example that I saw on television some time ago: a commercial for *The Olive Garden* Italian restaurant chain. In this commercial, people are sitting around the table eating together; they're singing, they're joking, they're having really a great time. The message that's being conveyed by that commercial is an emotional one: that when you're at this restaurant you're family, you're happy, you're having fun. It isn't about spaghetti, it isn't about pizza, it isn't anything about the food; **it's about the emotion.** That commercial was pure emotional selling.

The reason we say that all sales are made in a vacuum is because a vacuum is a space in which there's less pressure than on the outside of that space. That's what we do with emotions: we sell off these outside influences, and sometimes it's this logical reasoning that keeps people from buying. **In that vacuum, in that emotional state, we're able to trigger these emotional needs and wants of the individual; and in turn**

they buy our products and services based upon their feelings, not their logic. They're not sitting there trying to reason out why they should or shouldn't do something.

In fact, the University of Rochester School of Medicine published a study based on brain activity imaging that revealed that your prospect's emotions are linked, almost with cement, to the decision process. If you eliminated the emotional guiding factors a person has in his or her mind, it would be impossible for that person to be able to make a decision in daily life. In other words, all the decisions people make are based upon emotions. **People rationalize buying decisions based on facts, but they make those decisions based upon their feelings.** Therefore, their emotions are like a magic vacuum that lessens the resistance to buying. So ask yourself, when you're writing sales copy or creating an offer: what are my prospect's most powerful anxieties and frustrations? **For most people it comes down to self-interest and fear.** The French Emperor Napoleon once pointed out that people are really motivated only by those two emotions.

Back in what some people call 'the good old days,' long before digital cameras, cell phones, faxes or e-mail, there was a guy named George Eastman who ran a little company by the name of Kodak. One day he called all his people into the boardroom and asked a very simple question: "What product are we selling?" Well, Mr. Eastman got a lot of different answers from his people. Some said cameras, some said film; but to each of those answers, his reply was the same: "Nope, that's not what we sell. You're wrong. The camera's just a piece of hardware that anyone can make." And that was true. You see, the founder of Kodak understood that what he was really doing was hitting emotional hot buttons. **What he was selling was memories; he understood the power of emotional marketing, of emotional selling.** Another person who lived way back in the good old days was a boxer by the name of Rocky Marciano. Rocky summed up his professional skill in boxing with these words: "Hit the heart, and the head will follow." It's the same in marketing. **If we hit the heart — that is, their seat of motivation — then we're going to reach them.** They're going to buy our products and continue to do business with us.

And again, two of the greatest emotional hot buttons out there are fear and greed. In the good old days on the farm, a farmer might have a big stick with a carrot on it. His old mule sometimes got lazy and stubborn, so to motivate that mule, the farmer would dangle that carrot in front of him — and then the mule would do what the farmer wanted. Now, did he do it because the *farmer* wanted him to do it? Obviously not. It was because he benefited from what the farmer was doing. He had a fear of not getting that carrot, which he greedily wanted. It's the same with us; **people buy from us because of what's in it for them, not what's in it for us.** The easiest way to help them understand what's in it for them is to appeal to their emotional hot buttons. There's no doubt about it: emotional selling in that vacuum, where there's least resistance to our offer, is the quickest way to make the kind of money most people just dream about.

The last thing we all want is completely happy customers. Sure, people talk about it — but what "happy" really means is "satiated." **What we're looking for are insatiable customers.** We want to keep them coming back again and again. If somebody's happy, they don't always want the benefits that we provide. **So we've got to keep them hungry.** We've got to keep fanning the flames of their desires; we're looking for people who are a little obsessed, a little hungry, a little insatiable, so they're always coming back wanting more. It's like that restaurant I talked about earlier. We really do want people to feel like they're part of something, so they can identify strongly with that. We've got plenty of competition, but we're trying to create an emotional experience that makes people want to continue to be part of what we're selling. It's critical for you to develop that with your customers.

It's all based on those base emotions, fear and greed. It's not a pretty thing, and some people don't want to admit it; they don't even like talking about it. And yet that's how it is. We have to keep telling our sales representatives that all the time, because everybody wants to complicate things. And of course, there are things you can say and do, the more advanced things, that do make it more complicated. **But if you can master those two emotions, fear and greed, you're going to be so far ahead of the competition that you'll never have to worry about them again.**

As an advanced marketing strategy, **fear is what you should really go after.** Everyone's a bit jaded by the greed aspect, partly because it's easy to target that emotion — or at least that was easy for me. The greed thing doesn't take a lot of skill or courage; but it takes a lot of both to do fear. When you're a marketer, you always worry about turning people off or scaring them away; but it doesn't happen that often. You can't be worried about making people feel that what you've done is so great that you scare them, and they don't want to lose out on it. Sometimes it's as simple as just saying — or even implying — that someone will be sorry if they don't grab your product or service right away. A few years back, as I recall, Chris Lakey and I wrote this sales letter that I ended with the sentence, "You'll be glad you did." I started to add "…and you'll be sorry if you don't," but I decided not to. I left that part out because I was too afraid to put it in there. But you know, a lot of marketers *do* put that in there. In the end, we went back in put the "…and you'll be sorry if you don't," and I haven't regretted it. **The fear of losing out can be a big motivator if it's played up right.**

The points I've covered in this chapter are critical ones, and I hope I've provide some information you can really incorporate into your advertising. They're all a part of a valuable arsenal of moneymaking strategies and tips that you can use to make all the money you want, need — and deserve.

Copycat Riches!

As the late, great Peter Drucker once said, **there are only two things in business that make any money: marketing and innovation. Everything else is an expense.** Now, the truth is that it *does* take a little bit of time to fully understand exactly how to use the basics, and sometimes you have to hear things many different times in many different ways from many different sources before they finally click.

Back in 1992, for example, we had a series of what we call Blue Jeans Millionaire seminars. I remember that there was a guy from Los Angeles who came to the seminar — a very intelligent man. He'd been in business for a number of years with a small business. All throughout the day, I must have said at least a dozen times — and I'm not exaggerating here, it probably *was* a dozen times in a dozen slightly different ways — that **the market for a product or service is much more important than the product or service itself.** That's one of my central ideas — and towards the end of the day, he literally jumped out of his chair and shouted, all excited, "Wait! I get it! *The market is more important than anything else!*" That just blew my mind, because that's what I'd had been saying all day long — and he finally heard it!

That's the reason why you might notice me repeating some

of the same things from chapter to chapter. Those things are fundamentals, and they're vitally important to your success. Now, I try to mix it up a bit; but the cynical among you might just think, "You're repeating the same thing over and over; give us something new!" Well, of course — *everybody* wants something new! We live in a society that's absolutely addicted to the new — yet in many cases, it's the old, tried and true stuff that really matters.

Hence the title of this next chapter: *Copycat Riches*. The foundation of *Copycat Riches* goes back to one of my favorite scriptures in the Bible: the statement in the Book of Ecclesiastes that there's nothing new under the sun. That's not entirely true (we do have lots of new things these days), **but in general the more things change, the more they remain the same. If there's one thing that's never changed, it's human nature.** You can always take comfort in that.

All these marketing principles we talk about are directed towards human nature. **Marketing begins and ends with the prospect.** It's all centered right there in the person we're trying to reach, the person we're trying to get to buy from us once and then rebuy from us again and again. **Marketing is basically a combination of math and psychology,** and the psychology behind human nature has *not* changed. In this chapter, I'm going to talk about things other marketers are doing that we can model after. I'm going to talk about things that are tried and true, things that will remain the same in this world that *does* change very fast.

The last century has provided us with tons of innovations. Think of the Internet alone — and yet, even the Internet is just another way to do something that's been around since the beginning of time, and that's communicating. So in essence, the Internet is a new way to do something old. And why not? There's no need to reinvent the wheel. Similarly, **there are all** kinds of methods you can look to, and models you can use, to make money today using things that have been around, in some cases, for centuries. That's certainly true for Direct-Response Marketing in its rawest form; it's a method of communicating that's been around for over a hundred years.

They say that pioneers get scalped; that is, in business, usually the ones who lose are the ones who strike out first in a new direction. Maybe somebody who strikes out first does something new and innovative; maybe that blazes the way for other people later on down the road. **But usually the people who make the most money are the ones following what other people have done, not those who strike out into new waters.** That's one reason we keep repeating these basic strategies and underlying principles. And here's another reason: even if you've heard some of them before, they may just hit you in a new way the dozenth time you hear them — as with the guy in our 1992 seminar. They hit me in a new way all the time, every week. You never know when or why something will hit you in a different way. Maybe it's the life stage you're in. Maybe it's something that's going on in your life this week that wasn't going on last week. Maybe you're just listening in a different way this week than you were before. At any rate, everything lines up and hits you differently.

The important thing is that once these strategies penetrate, you need to take them and actually implement them, because that's where the money comes in. It's not just in the listening; it's not just in the participating. It's not just in the attending of the workshops and reading these books, although all that's great and I appreciate you doing that — but I want you to get out there and actually use these strategies. **So commit to finding at least one strategy in the next chapter that you'll be able to run with, then put that strategy into action and start making money with it.**

It's all about marketing and innovation — and innovation is more than just about inventing something new, it involves finding all the best things that other people are doing and mixing them in a new way. **It's not about being a pioneer; it's about trying to find a new way to combine a whole bunch of old things.** That's what innovation is all about. That's one of the main things that makes a company money instead of costing the company money.

What I'm talking about in this chapter is the ultimate shortcut to get you moving forward. You see, a lot of marketers — in this business opportunity marketplace especially — get frozen. They don't know what to do at all, so they just stand there. It's something we often call "the paralysis of analysis." People say, "I don't want to just copy what somebody else is doing. That's not original; that's no good!" But the reality is that it doesn't matter how original or how creative you are; if you're in business, it matters how well something works or how much money you're making. **It doesn't hurt to model yourself after someone else's success.** Of course, you don't want to copy people verbatim; **it's illegal to plagiarize or actually steal copy.** But you *can* take ideas here and there, and ways of doing things, and roll them into your own business model. You can take somebody else's idea and make it a little bit different, and use that proven strategy to continue to make money in a lot of different ways.

You need to start off by studying the marketing landscape and finding out who the leaders are in your marketplace. Who are these innovators? This works in any marketplace whatsoever, though of course the one I know best is the opportunity marketplace — so that's where most of my examples come from. In any case, you want to go out there and discover who the biggest and most successful company is in your market and find out what they're doing. What types of products are they offering? What's selling? How are they communicating those products to the marketplace? Are they using direct mail? Are they using television ads? Are they using magazines? What are they doing?

Most of these guys have tried a lot of things, and generally what they're doing at the moment is what works the best. **By following the leader and copycatting, if you will, you can become rich — simply because you're following a proven model, a proven system, a blueprint for success.** Using the innovations of others (with the necessary tailoring for your business, of course) is an excellent way to get your business off and running — and to keep it running once you've gotten started.

What you need to realize is that at first, you're going to model these companies or their products and services pretty closely — sometimes as closely as you morally can without breaking the law. **You definitely want to put your own spin on things, of course, but that's easy enough once you find out what someone's doing — which means not just what they're doing right, but also what they're doing wrong, too.** One way to do this is perform a little corporate espionage. You don't have to sneak around to do this; it's a lot easier to do it legally and completely aboveboard. Sign up for their services; purchase their products. Ingest them, consume them, and test them in every conceivable fashion so that you can understand them at a deep level and effectively emulate not just what their selling, but their marketing methods and system. This is the quickest way to get in the game; but once you get started this way, as your knowledge of that industry picks up, you can come up with your own ideas and your own spins, and pretty soon it'll be *you* that other people are looking to as a model for their businesses.

Again, just start taking pieces from here and there and from all over the place and meld them together, and pretty soon you'll come up with something that's all yours (at least on the surface).

Maybe as a result, you're not going to feel like you're particularly original; **but by using a proven model, you're going to be light years ahead of most of the competition.** You're not being the guinea pig here; you're not out trying to forge the way through the wilderness for your fellow marketers. The time to do that is when you're already strong, so you have less of a chance of getting scalped. If you go into your business with the mentality, *Hey, I'm going to follow the leaders, the people who are already making the money*, you're going to save yourself from falling flat on your face by trying to be an innovator before you're ready.

That was the secret to our initial success here are M.O.R.E., Inc., besides the fact that we got a lot of help from Russ von Hoelscher (I've discussed this in other chapters). You've read our story: We started with $300 and brought in over $10 million in less than five years. **We started with a very strong familiarity with our market,** because of all the years I was a customer in that marketplace — when I was buying all the types of things we later got into the business of selling. Without realizing it at the time, I was getting a graduate education in opportunity marketing. I've talked about the importance of being a spy; well, I was the ultimate spy, because I was buying from all these companies. I was on their mailing lists, and I was constantly getting solicited for offers.

All unknowingly, during those years I had absorbed all kinds of knowledge. And I never throw anything away, so when I got ready to create our first little space ad in a magazine, I had all kinds of opportunities I was able to peruse over the course of a weekend. It was from studying existing ads that I learned how to design my own. Basically, sure, I was copying other people. And it's so much easier now! Talk about corporate espionage: nowadays we've got the Internet, and there has never been a greater tool for doing that sort of research. **I think everybody**

**who owns a business should be a spy, regardless of
experience.** You should always look at what all these other
people are doing — because all they're doing is copycatting,
too. You have to realize that.

It all goes back to the limited repertoire that we, as
marketers, have to work with. Look at it this way. There are only
three primary colors: red, yellow, and blue. That's it. Everything
else is basically a mix of all those. And yet from those three
colors, you have an infinite possibility of hues! And look at a
piano: it's got 88 keys white keys. But what people don't realize
is that within those 88 keys, there are just seven notes — A
through G, that's it. Of course, there are sharps and flats; those
are the black keys. But in general there are just seven notes that
can be repeated over and over again in delightful combination.

Another music analogy: You've got all these musicians
who are getting paid millions to do what they do. Almost
without fail, each of them started off by learning to play other
people's songs. Then, in many cases, after years of doing so,
they finally learned how to come up with their own sound. Even
then, they're just using the same few musical notes in different
combinations. I have a couple of friends who play guitar very
well. I'm baffled as I watch them play the guitar, and think about
the fact that, at most, a guitar has 12 strings — but most have
six. And yet they can wring all kinds of sounds out of their
instruments. **It's all in how you play it.**

The same is true in marketing. I've mentioned that Chris
Lakey, my director of marketing, is something of an electronics
junky, who reads a number of blogs that follow technology and
electronic trends — what kinds of cell phones are coming out,
what kinds of computers are on the market. What amazes me is
that when someone comes out with something new — take
Apple's iPhone — within months (and probably within weeks)
there's a competitor that has something very similar. That's

because while there are certain things you can patent and certain processes that you can make uniquely yours, **in general, ideas can't be controlled in the marketplace.**

These people with new products, then, are all just copycats; they're all just doing what everybody else is doing. Whenever someone pops through with a new, creative idea that people like, it's not too long before it's not a new idea anymore — everybody else is copycatting it. That's not a condemnation; it's a fact, and as an entrepreneur, you should be doing it, too. **You should be out there doing a lot of research, spending a lot of time on the Internet, looking at other sites.**

Search engines give us the ability to easily spy on our competition. Just go to your favorite search engine, such as Google, Yahoo, MSN, Bing, or Dogpile. Dogpile, by the way, is a good, unique search engine, because it gives you a compilation of all the top search engines. You can just go to Dogpile.com, enter your search there, and it'll search all the major search engines for you. **In any case, just go to your favorite search engine and type in key words related to the products you sell, and look at what other people are doing.** What kinds of sales letter do they have? What innovative things are they doing to reach their customers? Maybe you'll see some things that they're obviously doing wrong, and you can make sure you avoid those things.

So spying on your competition can be a good, easy, fast way to see what you need to be doing. Just make sure you're looking at the good things, because **some of your competition is probably doing things that you *don't* want to emulate.** One of the things we tell people in direct mail is that when you're studying the subject, keep a swipe file of things other people have done — but make sure to only keep the good stuff, because **just because someone mailed you something once doesn't mean that it worked.** You may get something in the mail that looks really exciting, so you want to emulate it — but you might find out they only mailed it once and lost a bunch of money. Well, in that case, you *don't* want to emulate them.

Look for things that you see over and over again in the marketplace. If you see several of your competitors doing one thing and they're all are using very similar phraseology and methods, that's definitely something you want to take heed of. But don't forget to pay attention to the bad things, just so you can do the opposite.

There's a lot you can learn from watching what other people are doing. In fact, there's a whole new industry that's sprung up over the last three decades called "reverse engineering." It's most often applied to electronics and computers. There are reverse engineering firms all over the world now; you just send them a new product, and in a few months they'll find a way for you to copy it legally. If that's already systemized into the engineering and electronics industries, why can't you use that in our industry? Hey, we always spy on other successful companies, even our allies in the business!

That's the beautiful thing about working with joint venture partners, or striking up relationships with other entrepreneurs, too — because copycatting doesn't have to be done behind closed doors. **You can do it openly with other people who had a good idea,** and say something like, "Hey, do you mind if I borrow that?" It's a great way to get yourself moving forward, inexperienced or not, when you feel stuck.

Going back to that seemingly endless font of information, the Internet, here's one thing to consider: if you get a piece of marketing copy and it has a web-based call to action, **go to the website Alexa.com and check it out.** Alexa tracks web traffic on individual sites. So let's say you want to find out how many people went to that individual website that day or that month;

well, you can type in the URL, and Alexa will show you an actual graph of traffic going to that website. **You'll get real raw numbers right there as to how good and effective that campaign is.**

You can even compare different things. Let's say you've got two or three different pieces of mail, with two or three different websites; well, you can put 'em all in there and it'll draw out the graph and show you exactly how they're doing in combination with each other, too, which is pretty cool. **It's a quick little tool, a good resource you can use to help you identify the winners.** That way, you can copy somebody who knows what they're doing and get going on down the right road immediately.

Now, when it comes to the copycatting, here's something I want to re-emphasize here: I'm not saying to get somebody's sales letter and just sit down and rewrite it exactly. **Your copy should be your own, although you can certainly emulate someone's style.** Or it may be a specific segment of the execution, or a specific way of offering something, that you imitate. There are a lot of things in the marketplace you can model after. Earlier, I mentioned cell phones. A lot of people are competing out there in the market on specific little things; for example, a guarantee, or rollover minutes, or a type of calling plan. Normally, what really makes up the mind of the consumer is one little thing that may not seem like such a big deal, but the whole market share may swing on that one little thing. It may be the one thing that makes them different enough that everybody wants to work with them. You can figure out what that one little thing is, and try to figure out a way you can grasp onto that. How can you capture the essence of that one little thing that makes them stand out? **How can you bring that essence over into your own campaign?**

The more you study a market, the more you understand

how often your competitors will build an entire campaign around one thing that makes the difference, and how you can capitalize by copying them. **Doing that kind of research isn't just profitable, it's fun.** And the kind of "espionage" I'm talking about is perfectly legal: we're not really spies, but it's kind of fun to *think* about yourself as some sort of secret agent — and it makes it more interesting if you're going to make money in the process.

All you're doing, really, is looking for time-tested formulas that are producing wealth for other people, and trying to emulate those as closely as possible so you can roll out your sales campaign and actually be on top right from the get-go. And here's another point about writing successful sales letters or ads: keep doing what I did from the very beginning, even when you've become experienced. **Pull well-written, effective ads and analyze the marketplace every time you develop an ad or sales message, because what worked six months ago isn't necessarily what's current.** That is, it isn't necessarily the mindset of your current customer, what they're thinking *now*. If, say, you find that there are six or seven ads in one magazine targeting your customer base that are executing very similar copy, there's a good indication that you need to try a copycat execution of that, to see if it pulls better numbers than what you originally planned.

You can also test these copycat ideas against your control piece. For example, you might write what you think is effective, and then run that in one magazine; then write what other people show you is effective using the copycat method for another magazine. Then you can see which one pulls better numbers. A lot of the time, you're going to find that your copycat method will pull better numbers than what you think is right. **You're pulling from actual input as opposed to what's been drilled into your head.** You see, a lot of people learn a lot of things that may be applicable at one point in time, but they haven't quite kept up with what's happening. I see this in a lot of creative executions.

For example, years back you could write somebody a 30- or 40- page sales letter, and they would read it and then buy. Maybe that still works for your market segment, but nowadays a lot of people are faced with too much hustle and bustle; everyone's picking up the kids and taking them here and there, going all over the place all the time. **Everybody's busy;** everybody's doing things much more and much faster than they were doing in the past. **That means that they try to speed** *everything* **up in their lives.** My colleagues and I recently tested full-page ads that might be 10 words long — and most people would say *that's crazy*. But I saw somebody else do it over and over, which told me that there must be something to it, or they wouldn't keep doing it." It went against everything I thought about copywriting — but when I tried it I pulled better numbers. You're not really trying something new, after all. **You really need to think about the fact that, if other people are doing it,** *they're* **the guinea pigs.**

That's another good way to identify a winner: if they're willing to do something more than once or twice, it must bring in money. Again, don't pick up a sales letter and put it in your swipe file, assuming that it was a good letter because it was mailed to you. Wait a bit... and if you get that same letter five or six times, *now* put it in your swipe file, because they're willing to spend money repeatedly to send out that same sales message. That being the case, it *must* be effective. It's easier to do this with magazines, because you can look at them month after month and see if the same ad is in there. Same idea.

I've told you before that the way to really succeed in this business (or any business, really) is to **fall in love with all the things that will make you the most money.** Well, this is one of them. Yes, I realize that there's a book out there that basically says, *Do what you love, and the money will follow.* That's not really true — sorry. **What you have to do is fall in love with the things that make you the most money, and do those things consistently — and *then* the money will follow.** Fortunately, this kind of thing is easy to fall in love with, because it can be both fun and challenging. It's also a good idea to see it as an artistic endeavor. We're all cash-flow artists; we create cash flow, and part of the way we do it is through innovation and marketing.

The innovation part, of course, is just doing what I'm talking about here: taking a little bit from many different sources, constantly watching what's out there in the marketplace. Ultimately, you develop a trained eye for things. **You start seeing patterns and common denominators; that's what a trained eye is all about.** And you have to get on the other side of the cash register, too. Stop thinking like a consumer, start thinking like a marketer, and you'll see the things that a marketer sees.

If you're not comfortable with the idea of piecing together your copy from the ideas of others, **consider this; the best ideas are often a combination of many different things.** Chris Lakey and I recently put something together that's a combination of three different things we've seen other people do (with our own unique twist, of course). We've created this tremendous new opportunity, and it's current because these components are very popular right now. If we make millions of dollars, as we believe we will, there will be people on the sidelines just like there always are — and some of those people will be saying, "Man, they got lucky again." And that's a load of crap; we didn't get lucky at all. We're just doing exactly what I'm telling you to do here. **We're finding the best of the best out there, combining them in our own way, and making the**

new opportunity available.

It's about keeping your ear to the marketplace: doing research, spending a lot of time looking at what's out there, determining what other people are mailing, what other people are doing on the Internet, and taking note of those ideas. **It starts with thinking in the abstract** about what's going on out in the marketplace, and what our customers are responding to that other people are mailing them. **Then we move on to thinking about things in a broader sense,** and working those ideas into the products we're already working on and the offers we're already making. It's like making a big pot of soup, where you're not really sure what it's going to end up being, exactly. Now, I'm no chef; I don't know that I've ever made soup, other than pouring a can of pre-made soup into a pot on the stove and heating it up. But I imagine that if I was making some soup and wanted to be a little adventurous, I might start with a soup base — some chicken broth, maybe. Then I'd start throwing things in, mixing them a little bit; and then I'd taste it to see how that worked. Next, I'd grab something else and toss it in, stir it up, and let it simmer for a little while before tasting it again. I'd keep that up until it tasted just perfect, and I'd be done!

That's sort of the way it is when we evaluate opportunities and work on promotions. **We take a little bit of this, a little bit of that; we put it together and mix thoroughly, then stew on it a little bit. We think about it, we analyze it, we sit back, we let it percolate a little bit, and then we go back to the drawing board. We write some more, mix in some other things, and continue to massage it and work out the wrinkles. Pretty soon, you've got an offer.** It's all based on keeping your ears open, keeping your eyes open, listening to what's happening in the marketplace, listening to what your clients are saying, listening to what your competitors are saying, watching what they're doing, ordering their programs, getting on their mailing lists, constantly doing research and our "corporate espionage." You can also do some of that reverse engineering I talked about earlier. **Doing all of those things ends up helping you make the most money in the end.**

And here's another point I want to be sure I don't overlook: **sometimes you're not copycatting other people, you're copycatting *yourself*. Call it recycling, if you like.** It's easy to take elements from other projects you've worked on and incorporate them in your new project. It may be as simple as a line of copy here, a guarantee there, or a headline you can change a little; maybe you just reuse research you've already done. You know, writing copy can be a big pain in your rear. Sometimes it's fun; you get really excited, and words just flow out like they're pouring out of Niagara Falls. Before you know it, you have 20 pages of copy; and as you get better at it, that happens more often.

But at first, writing sales letters can be a very difficult thing, especially if you haven't tried it before. If that's the case, do what I've been talking about: take somebody else's ad and use it as the foundation for your first try. **Once you've done a few, when the words don't seem to want to come, start pulling bits and pieces that you know will work out of other projects to help you create your basic framework.** Mix it all up in a different way, so it tastes completely different. In the end it's a unique offer, but you didn't have to do all the work of inventing it from scratch.

I love this whole idea of copying yourself. A few years back, I was chatting with a good friend visiting us down here in Kansas, and he said, "God, T.J., I don't know how you guys keep coming up with so much new stuff." And I said. "Well, we just keep re-writing the same sales letter over and over again." And everybody laughed — because as with all good comedy, there was an element of truth there. One of the best examples from our own life is a man who's retired now; his name is Luther Brock, and he worked out of Denton, Texas, a suburb of Dallas. For years, he was known as the Letter Doctor. We mailed millions of copies of pieces that Luther wrote for us. They were our control packages for a number of years. And we were just one of many clients that he had.

Luther wrote a lot of copy for a lot of people, and here's the thing: you could shuffle three of Luther's letters into a stack of 30 sales letters, spread 'em all out, and you could easily pick his letters out from the crowd, even if they were for different types of products. Essentially, he re-wrote the same sales letter over and over again. He had a style, he kept using it, and it worked! **It becomes an intuitive process after a while; you see the same common denominators being used over and over again, because there's a language to all good salesmanship.**

Now I'm going to go ahead and reveal one of the marketer's best secrets — and it's very simple, really. Anyone who reads this book can use this trick, especially if you're in the business opportunity marketplace... but frankly, few ever would. **This secret is simply a way of getting the exact material or letter that generated a database of people you're going to communicate with.** One of the ways we acquire lists of people to mail to is by renting the lists of our competition — the people that have bought products from other people in our marketplace. You might think, "Well, that's not new, I've heard that before," but this strategy is a rather new spin on that practice. You see, you can simply call up the list broker and say, "I want to get access to the exact letter which produced this list. Can you contact the list owner and see if they'll share that with me? Tell them that if they don't, I'm not going to rent their list." If you do that with 20-30 different people, you're going to get a lot of different letters; but you're also going to know exactly what list they go with.

Here's a marketing maxim you need to drill into your head: **You can tell everything about a person simply by paying attention to what they spend their money on.** If you have a list of opportunity buyers and you have the letter in front of you that initiated that first purchase, the need for corporate espionage just falls by the wayside. This is an easier way for you to get right to what you need to be paying attention to. **If you can tailor that message to your own product, service, or opportunity, it should work for you, too — especially if you can jazz it up.** Think about it like a mousetrap. If it caught the mouse the first time, why not put the same type of cheese in the trap to see if they'll bite again? **Because people buy what they want, you see; that's a great way to understand their true desires.** Just study what they're looking for. This is the ultimate Copycat Riches secret, I think because you're going to see exactly what the cheese looked like that got the customers to bite in the first place.

If buyers responded to an offer that was sent out by the company whose list you're renting, then they should respond to you as well if you have a similar offer, if you use similar language, if you approach them the same way. And consider this: **if you're renting a large list from someone, you know they've got to be successful, or they wouldn't be renting the lists in the first place.** If they have a list to rent, then they're probably bringing in 5,000 new customers a quarter — because that's usually the smallest list size brokers allow on the marketplace. Someone doing that kind of business is obviously successful.

So if you rented 10 lists and you got 10 sales letters, that's great. Assuming you're renting lists of people who have products and services similar to what you sell, they're each in the same marketplace, you've got 10 different versions of letters that you can copy in some way. You've got a great marketing tool for use both now and later, and it's great corporate espionage, too. And here's another thing: you may not actually have to rent all of those lists you're looking at. Tell the list broker you're thinking about renting a particular list and would like to see the offer that generated it. **You may well end up with a lot more sales letters than lists you actually end up testing.**

By the way, don't forget the Internet! If you know that a company whose list you're considering is on the Internet, **you can usually get their sales letter online, too, right off their website!** Now, with a website there's a lot more testing done, so you can't ever be sure that the offer and the sales letter you see online is the same one they're mailing offline to generate the list you would be renting offline — so you need to keep that in mind as well.

The reason that this strategy of getting the letter that produced the list is so important is because the data cards on all these lists may not be accurate. There's nothing that says they can't lie when they say these 10,000 people bought a product offered for $20. If they're not willing to show you the letter, then how do you know what they're telling you is the truth? All your competitor is doing by renting that list to you is creating a situation whereby they can make more money, based on the stored energy of that list, by offering it to other people in the industry. But they don't necessarily have to tell the truth! **If they're not willing to do put up or shut up, weed them out, because they're probably a junk list.** Focus only on trustworthy people who do what they say they'll do.

It's also a good strategy if you don't have a lot of money and you can't really afford to lose any. Once you have a "war chest," you can afford to lose a couple of battles, because you've got plenty of backup. **But when you're first getting started and money is a concern, you don't have a margin of error.** Look at my case, for example. We sold our carpet-cleaning van for $300. No margin of error there! That's why I pulled my hair out looking over all those ads to come up with a solution that I thought emulated what the marketplace was looking for. The less money you have, the more research you should do — and that's something a lot of people don't understand. You can afford to make mistakes later, when you can actually *afford* to make mistakes. But don't do it early on. **Take all this stuff to heart and take action on it.**

You know, I've never heard anybody else teach that as a strategy, but it *is* the ultimate way to know the value of the list. **Every sales letter you can get your hands on is equal to one less guess; and the fewer guesses you have to make, the more spot on you can be with your marketing.** Just drill it into your head that if you want to sell something to somebody, figure out what they bought the first time around.

You can also copycat other people who are marketing to you. What did you buy last time, and how can you find an offer that was similar to what you just paid for? These are all things you need to be thinking about. **Again, it's not about being original.** If someone has already done what you're doing, then good! Somebody else proved that it either works or didn't. Cash flow artist or not, the whole point of going through this exercise is to produce something that produces. You're not trying to make it pretty; you're not writing the next great American novel. **You're writing a letter that stirs people to action — a letter that moves the emotions.** If a letter comes across your desk and moves your emotions, chances are it's going to move other people's emotions as well.

Finding other successful letters that generated your mailing lists is especially effective with smaller markets; this is where it's really important to get tough and tell the brokers, "Look, I'm not going to rent the list until I see the piece." It's less necessary in the bigger markets; you can generally go to the SRDS book — the Standard Rate and Data Service — and get what you need. **In**

very competitive markets, the list brokers themselves commonly make all of that information available, because there's so much competition for the individual mailing lists.

Think of yourself as a salesperson. **That's what we're all supposed to be doing here: closing sales.** It's not the standing ovation we want; we want people to rush the stage, trample over each other with their money in hand, fighting each other so that they can be the first to give us their money. We're salespeople here. Oh, some people don't like to be called salespeople — but that's a problem you're going to have to get over real fast. Sure, there will always be a few bad salespeople that give the whole group a bad name, and everybody loves to call themselves a marketer... but honestly? **We're salespeople. That's what we do: We sell.** So put on your salesman hat and start thinking like a salesman. If you have no sales experience, then I suggest you get it.

If nothing else, go out there and work flea markets for a couple of years; sell stuff to people when they're walking by all day. Or do what you have to do: Knock on doors, or get a job somewhere where you learn the principles of what it takes to get people to part with their money. That's all we're doing. **And here's another thing:** *know yourself.* **The better you know yourself, the better you'll know other people.** When you're all excited about something, don't be blinded by all those crazy emotions. Try to figure out what's exciting you so much. When you're out there spending your money unconsciously, stop and wake up and try to realize, "Why am I buying this? Why? Why am I so excited? Why am I getting ready to give this company $3,000 of my hard earned money?"

I think you should get the idea that you're something you aren't out of your mind. We're salespeople. **Marketing is just a way of selling on a massive scale to a larger group of people,** and this copycat strategy can definitely help you make a lot of money if you put it into action.

One more thing, before I end this chapter. I've always believed that a USP, a unique sales position, is crucial if you want to achieve maximal success. But let me qualify that a bit. People like to say you need to stand out in the marketplace, so you have to strive to do something absolutely different from everybody else. And that's not *entirely* true. **You don't have to be different from everybody else out there, you just have to be different *in the mind of your consumer*.** The people reading your ad have to think, "This is different from everything else out there." It doesn't matter if it truly is or not, because after all, people buy in a vacuum. The reality is that there may be 500 things just like what you have to offer. But they're still going to buy from you because your letter, or your ad, or your message, got them excited. As long as they're excited, they'll certainly buy from you. **So while a USP is important, you don't have to be revolutionary; it's all about trying to build relationships with people.** And there's no harm in copying the ways other successful people have done that; in fact, you're foolish if you don't.

People want to do business with other people, so yes, you do have to take those things that are already unique about you and put them into your marketing. Otherwise, just let people know who you are; that's the way to differentiate yourself, by just by being you and by trying to serve people in the highest possible way. **As soon as people start thinking all you're about is trying to get their money, they're going to run away as fast as they can. Don't let that happen!**

The Greatest Secret That Nobody Tells You About — and Nobody Ever Uses!

If you ask 100 different experts what marketing is, they'll give you a 100 slightly different answers. If they're highly educated "experts," they might go on and on forever and you may only understand a small fraction of what they say. But I think all people who have anything to do with the subject of marketing will agree on this one simple explanation that *we* have: **marketing is everything that you do in your business to both attract and retain the best customers within your marketplace.**

I like to compare marketing to chess, in that you can learn the basic rules very easily — but it takes years to really master. That's because it's subtle and full of nuances, and it takes a while to learn the strategies, tips, and tricks that make you thrive. For the first chapter of my latest epic here, I thought I'd pull out one of those Direct-Response Marketing (DRM) secrets that most people don't talk about much, and that most marketers never actually use; hence the title at the top of the page.

Let me start this way. Have you ever noticed how very addicting online games are? Exhaustive studies have been conducted by researchers to learn the causes of the formation of this online game addiction that a lot of people have; in this case, they used college students. There was an empirical approach involved; in other words, it was something that was measurable and repeatable. The results indicated that the behavior repetition was the main contribution to online game addiction.

Well, that same addiction factor, when properly harnessed, can significantly improve your sales and profits and improve customer retention by 300% or more. This is highly important, so pay close attention here! Human beings in general repeat the same behaviors over and over again. If you can get them to do something one time, then you can get them to do it the next time. In most of us, that's what we refer to as a habit.

A noted American psychologist by the name of William James, who lived between 1842 and 1910, wrote an essay about human behavior for a popular science monthly back in 1887. In that essay, he said that habit is the "enormous flywheel of society"— that habitual behavior patterns and repetition are "part of the inescapable folds of mental drapery that are set like plaster." A flywheel is a huge, heavy wheel that regulates how fast and how uniformly a machine works. I thought the way he concluded that essay was especially interesting: "It is well for the world that in most of us, by the age of thirty, the character has been set like plaster and will never soften again." In our case, the flywheel is those behaviors that are repeated again and again. The machine, of course, is the human machine, the person repeating those behaviors. **Given enough knowledge about a person, we can determine and forecast what actions they're going to take as a result of their particular habits.**

Furthermore, we can trigger this repetition of behavior in people by painting mental and emotional pictures with the words we use in our sales copy. Remember, when people go to see a movie, they go to *see* a movie. They don't go to listen to a movie, do they? So it isn't just the words that you write; more importantly, **it's the emotional and the mental picture that you create in that reader's mind that causes him or her to repeat a desired behavior.**

Again, people love to repeat the same behaviors. If you can get them to do something once, it becomes easier to get them to do it again and again. Television stations, and especially their infomercial clients, learned long ago that repetition automatically increases the likelihood that the content being broadcast is going to be absorbed in the minds of the people watching. **Repetition is kind of like a magnifying glass: it magnifies certain mental and emotional effects that trigger the action we want the viewer to take.** For example, if you see an image or an event repeated onscreen, the impact is dramatically increased each time. A good example of that was the Rodney King beating by the Los Angeles police. Remember how that was broadcast again and again, time after time? Soon it became permanently etched in the minds of the viewers; it became an emotional reality in their minds.

Now, this reminds of me of something I learned about from my friend and colleague Michael Penland. When he was a kid on his grandfather's farm in the backwoods of north Georgia, Michael was always fascinated by this hand pump his grandfather had at the farmhouse. That pump always had to be primed in order to get it to repeat the desired action; in this case, it was moving the water through the pipes so that it could be used. It's the same in marketing. People need to be primed each time you want them to take a specific desired action. **This is known as *repetition priming.*** That refers to the theory that an initial presentation presented in a certain way will cause an individual to respond when it's presented again at a later time.

In other words, the repetition keeps them doing the process; and repeating that priming process — that is, getting our sales message to the prospects — is going to influence that person to respond to our offers and to what we're doing. Now, there are marketers out there who obviously believe that your marketing message needs to be changed often in order to prevent it from growing old in the reader's mind. **But the truth is, repetition is the marketer's best friend.** Just because *we* may get bored with our sales copy doesn't mean it won't work, or that it isn't working. **The truth is, when boredom sets in for you as a marketer, the chances are that your sales message is just beginning to trigger the action that you want from the reader.** It's not going to happen on the first exposure; it happens after repeated exposures, because again, people love to do things over and over. That's why the most successful marketers send sequential mailings to their prospects and clients: Those followup mailings help trigger that emotional response in the reader, with the result that he takes the action that we want him to take.

Ninety percent of all buying decisions are made in the unconscious mind at a deep emotional level that we really can't lay a finger on. **The way we access that as marketers is through repetition. The idea is to produce in the prospect an "aha" moment.** In other words, we want him to come to that moment in time when he or she realizes that they have finally found exactly what they're looking for to solve their problem, or to empower their passion, or to add to their pleasure. The Internet is a great example of how humans love to repeat the same behaviors over and over... and we don't even have to consciously think about it. People have their favorite start page, their resource pages; I know that every time my computer boots up, it's going to start on Google. Now why is that? Because people navigate the Internet first by habit and then by instinct, and so they repeat, over and over, certain habits. That behavior is formed through repetition.

Why has Google been able to dominate the search engine

market and related markets, without ever doing any real advertising? All their competitors spend huge sums of money on advertising, but they're not able to gain that market dominance. The reason is that people don't think about Google; they just do it. It's a repetition, a habit they have.

And here's an amazing fact: motivational experts have for years told people to look into a mirror as they imagine, or as they picture, what their future's going to be like, as they see themselves achieving their goals. Now, why do they do that? Simply because when people look into that mirror, their behavior is altered, at least for a short time. **Because when you see yourself, it makes you think about your behavior before acting.** As marketers, what we want to do is mirror the person to whom we're marketing, even if it's just for a short time. We want that person to think about their repetitive behavior. **Our goal of course, is to get them to stop doing what they've always done, and then to buy our products and solve the problems they're facing in life.**

Here's something that Michael Penland has recently been testing, and I know it's kind of on the edge, but I think it's a good idea. What he does is include a small, inexpensive reflective area in the sales copy of his Direct-Response Marketing sales letter so that the person reading that sales letter can actually see a reflection of himself as he's reading about the benefits of Michael's products. In other words, he tells the reader to imagine himself as successful and financially free, as the proud owner of Michael's product. Now, imagine the impact of that sales letter if you were to personalize it by putting that reader's name in bold face type, just below that reflective mirror area.

The bottom line is that higher customer retention and greater long-term profitability are possible when you leverage the fact that human beings love to repeat the same behaviors over and over. **If you know this, if you can get them to do**

something one time, you can get them to do it the *next* time. Repetition is the marketer's best friend.

Now, people have always accused me of being repetitious, and people have made fun of my sales letters. One guy, for example, came to one of my seminars and said to my mentor Russ von Hoelscher, "My God, T.J. needs to learn how to not be so redundant. His sales letters are just the same stuff over and over again." And Russ paused for reflection and then said, "Well, how much did you pay to be here?" And the guy said, "Five thousand dollars." Russ replied, "That's it. That's why he does it."

People complain — and yet they buy. That's one of the reasons we love two-step marketing, because if you get people to make that first commitment to you, it's so much easier to get them to make the second commitment to you. For the last 21 years, almost year-for-year, we've been mailing an average of about three million lead-generation and customer-acquisition pieces a year to people who have already bought the same kinds of things that we sell. Now, think about that. Their past behavior has indicated to us that they may buy, since they've bought from other companies that sell the same types of things that we sell; in fact, they're the *most likely* people who will buy. **We never try to sell something to somebody who doesn't already have a past established pattern of behavior.** People are creatures of comfort and habit. You can set your watch by how they live their lives, day after day, and they do tend to repeat the same behaviors.

As marketers, we can use that to our advantage. I know that when things don't go the way I'm used to them going, I get agitated, upset. It puts me off my game; I don't feel comfortable. For example, I tend to browse the Internet in the same way every time. I have the same websites I go to consistently, and I usually go to them pretty much in the same order every time.

There are occasions where I end up seeing a link that I click on and I go somewhere else, but generally I do things in the same order. And if I get out of that repetition for some reason — maybe one of the websites isn't working that particular day, or something takes me away from it and I don't do it in the right order — it feels uncomfortable.

I think that's the way a lot of people are. They have their routines, the way they do things. We're all creatures of habit; and I think that if you can tap into that from a selling standpoint, it gives you a tremendous edge. You certainly want to work within that. I think if you try to get people to go outside of what they're used to, or get them to change their habits, it's something of a deterrent. You've gotten them in an uncomfortable position, where you're trying to go against their natural tendencies. **When it comes to selling, people have to see the same thing over and over again; they have to be comfortable with you, and they have to be exposed to your offer several times.** That's why we do follow-ups to people: to get them familiar and comfortable with our sales message before they're ready to buy.

The recognition of this typical, habitual form of behavior is something that any business can harness to survive and even thrive during a recession, a depression, or any other money-sucking business-jeopardizing economy. I know everyone wants to learn how to do that — because if you turn on your television, you hear more and more each day about how bad the economy is, and how the recession's affecting business. Well, most of my colleagues and I personally decided a long time ago not to let that income-reduction machine, the TV, control our attitudes or determine whether or not we're successful. There are plenty of things I can do personally for my own business so that it not only survives, but it actually thrives during any economy.

First of all, you've got to learn how to survive, because

survival is the key. If you look at a book on survival, it'll tell you that the number one trait of successful wilderness survival is flexibility, and it's the same in business. **The flexible person learns to bend; he learns to adapt, while those who aren't flexible just break.** Their businesses crumble, and in the process, they lose a lot of themselves. **Being flexible is all about changing, it's about growing, it's about adapting, and it's really about moving forward.** But instead of doing this, many business owners tend to go around in a circle, arriving right back at the point they started at, and so they lose their livelihood.

Years ago, in some of the colder northern snow states in the United States, there were farmers who would run a rope from the front door of their home to the barn where their livestock stayed. They did that so they could find their way to the barn to feed the livestock, and then find their way back to the house during blizzards. Otherwise they could get lost in a blizzard, and they could actually lose their life. There are persons, hikers, who have gotten lost in the mountains, and they have found that they actually walk around in a circle just trying to survive. And that's because, with everyone, without exception — this is true of all of us — we have one leg that's just a little bit shorter than the other leg. And so we naturally move in the direction of a circle when we don't know the exact way to walk in order to survive.

So to keep on course, the wise thing to do when you're lost is climb a tree or a high rock, and find a point that you can focus on to walk towards — and then from time to time, check to be sure you're still on the right course. It's the same in marketing, especially during a recession. **You got to be connected;** it's kind of like that rope from the house to the barn. Where you're at and where you want to get to are two totally different things. Just like that hiker lost in the mountains, you have to stay on course so that you don't just go around in circles.

Here's how to do it: these are the exact steps to take in

order to survive and thrive during a recession. **You have to follow this formula step-by-step,** and if you do, you're going to enjoy success, greater profits and, of course, bigger sales for your business.

The FIRST STEP is: don't panic. Avoid making crazy, rash decisions. When a person is lost in a snowstorm or in the mountains, a lot of times they'll panic; they'll make some crazy decision, and it proves detrimental to their survival. In the nearly 40 years that I and my closest associates have been doing marketing, we've seen recessions, near-depressions, and inflations come and go. **So always understand that this too will pass. It's just part of life.**

The founder of the science of economics, Adam Smith, never spoke or wrote about recessions. What he *did* write about was what he called economic fluctuations. He talked about the cheap year, when the crops were great; he talked about the dear year, when the crops were short. **So STEP NUMBER TWO is to keep standing, to keep fighting, because it's really during these difficult economic times that fortunes are made quickly and easily in marketing.** During the great depression of 1929 to 1932, prices fell — and Americans got poorer. They couldn't buy cars, homes, or take a vacation, and gasoline was limited to three gallons a week. They rationed meat, eggs, and butter. And then in 1989, at the beginning of the worst period of economic decline since the Great Depression, most of the experts predicted that businesses were going to crumble completely, that there was going to be no more wealth. Yet many experts today are predicting that during the next 5-10 years, we're going to see household wealth double again, in the U.S. alone. We're going to see up to 10 million new millionaire households.

Think back to the 1970s. It was during that decade that Bill Gates started Microsoft, Frederick Smith launched Fed-Ex, and Time, Inc. introduced *People* magazine. During that recessionary period, it was a great time to start a business... **and now is a great time to start a business.** From 2005-2007, there was a 12% increase in business start-ups. **So keep standing, keep fighting.**

   STEP THREE is to take special care of your existing clients. Give them what they want. Remember, they're facing tough economic times, too. So let them know that you personally appreciate their business and that you care about them. **STEP NUMBER FOUR, again, is to be flexible.** If you're only marketing to the business opportunity seekers, for example, then widen out and market to more affluent small business owners. If you're marketing just to small business owners, then widen out and market to business opportunity seekers or to other markets. Just be flexible.

   STEP NUMBER FIVE is to give more than others are giving, because obviously they're going to be giving less during these tough economic times. STEP NUMBER SIX is: don't lower your prices! Let me say that again: don't lower your prices. That seldom increases business enough to justify the action. If anything, what you need to do is give more value, raise your prices, and sell to a market that has money to spend. **STEP NUMBER SEVEN is to follow up with leads more often, and to follow up with your old leads again — *every single one of them.*** If you've got phone broadcasting, use that. If you can make a personal phone call to them, call them and let them know you appreciate their business.

   STEP NUMBER EIGHT is the last one I want to share; this **is what I call the Redneck Millionaire's Rule.** It goes something like this: **Don't be spending too much of your time on stuff that don't make you any money.** Don't be spending too much time watchin' TV, as it's just telling you how bad things are; it's not going to make you money. Worrying about the present economic situation won't make you money. Waiting and

THE GREATEST SECRET THAT NOBODY TELLS YOU ABOUT — AND NOBODY EVER USES

doing nothing won't make you money. **But performing these steps that I've outlined here *will* help you to prosper even during this recessionary period, or in any economic time.**

I know for a fact that, while most people suffered greatly during the Great Depression, there were plenty of people that made huge sums of money. The Depression built their fortunes. **But keep this in mind: *you must be self-employed* to really cash in.** Give up this idea that you're going to somehow make it as an employee of someone else's company. You've got to be self-employed to really profit. You've got to take charge of your own financial future. **And flexibility is so important.**

Hey, listen, I'm an optimist. I know that times are tough. But we've gone through several such times already, and you never know exactly what to believe. It happens that I believe in the future and in the Baby Boomer generation, that generation of Americans who were born from 1946-1964. The future is bright. **You've got to take things into your own hands, and let your whole focus be on doing everything possible to serve as many people as you can in the highest way.** The economy is on people's minds right now, and they're worried about what they're going to do to make ends meet. Some people are losing their jobs, others are worried about losing their jobs, and a lot of people are doing exactly what I said earlier: They're watching the news and they're fretting. They're worrying about what's happening, instead of being out there trying to make sure that what's happening to everybody else doesn't happen to them.

Now is *not* the time to panic. Now is the time to prepare and be smart in your thinking. You hear some economists saying, "Get out of the stock market now! Put the money in your mattress and run! Hide! Bury it in the backyard, whatever; get it out of the banks!" And you hear other people telling you, "No, now's a great time to be buying. When the economy's down, when the market's lower, that's a great time to buy up all kinds of bargain stocks. And if you hold onto those for five or 10 years, you could make a huge fortune."

So the pundits are talking their heads off, and they're talking out of both sides of their mouths. They'll tell you whatever you want to hear. You'll have people telling you one thing while someone else is telling you something the exact opposite; so who do you trust? Well, why don't you make it so that you don't have to worry at all about what they think? Let the talking heads talk about the economy until they're blue in the face. Let them say it's up, let them say it's down, let them say it's good, let them say it's bad, whatever. **You can make money regardless of whether the economy is up or down.** You can focus on making money using these strategies I'm sharing with you now.

Now, let me re-emphasize a few points I made earlier. **First, if the economy's down, who is the best person to sell to? People who aren't affected by that — the affluent.** Sell to the super-rich, people who already have money and who aren't affected when the economy's going down. **And again, expand your marketplace.** If you're just selling to a niche marketplace, think about how you can expand out to an even bigger marketplace, to bring in a bigger herd of people that you can sell your products and services to. **And never, never lower your prices.** People have a tendency to do that; it's the first cut-and-run move. They think, "Business isn't good, so I've got to sell my products for less." That's usually not going to help you. It may get you a few more orders, and maybe some people who wouldn't have bought before might decide to buy; but it's not going to be an effective long-term strategy. **So it's better to find more people who want to buy what you have.** Add value, do things to make your products and services even better than before, make them even worth more than what you originally planned on them being worth, and expand them and sell them for even more — and you *can* be successful.

Strategies like these aren't dependent on what the economy's doing. It doesn't matter whether it's good or bad, up or down. It doesn't matter whether the people are telling you to pull your money out of the stock market or telling you to flood your money back into the marketplace. Whatever those people are talking about, you can just sit back and relax, knowing that you're using these strategies to make huge amounts of cash in any economy.

Next I'm going to talk about smart marketing secrets, which transform new marketers into millionaire marketers. Most people have heard the expression "Work smarter and not harder." Well, that's a neat little cliché, but very few people ever explain how to do smart marketing, so I want to talk about that here. **And I'm going to use SMART as an acronym,** with each letter representing something. The "S" means Specific: direct it to a highly targeted niche market. "M" is Measurable, and "A" is Action-oriented — that is, taking an offensive stance rather than a defensive one. Do something proactive. The **"R"** is for Results-oriented, and direct response advertising is just that, unlike institutional advertising. And the **"T"** is for Trackable. Be sure that you track everything you're doing.

SMART marketing covers a number of key areas:

1. Giving people what they want.

2. Developing products or services that appeal to a specific market.

3. Making sure those items have the largest profit margin possible.

4. Developing marketing systems that identify the right

prospect, and communicate the right message to them.

5. Reaching and selling to those people as fast as possible for the largest profit.

6. Reselling to them as often as possible.

7. Creating sales messages that build strong bonds with your customers.

8. Positioning yourself so that you seem unique.

9. Creating offensive marketing strategies that allow you to control the selling process.

10. Making specific offers to your customers on an ongoing basis.

I'm not going to go into detail on all of these, but I do want to talk about a few, the first of which is giving people what they want. Some of the worst examples of not following this key area of SMART marketing are Internet websites that use flash and splash screens. **Market study after market study has unequivocally demonstrated that people using the Internet are doing it to get the information they want when they want it.** They're not doing it to watch some fancy flash presentation. So, with your marketing you've got to give people what they want. And hey, they all listen to the radio marketing station WII-FM — you know, What's In It For Me? **So you have to give people a reason to remember you, a reason to make your product or business a part of their life.** The way you do this is by giving them exactly what they want.

So what do people want? Well, before you answer that question, you've got to understand why people actually buy. **People buy your products to feel good. They buy them with**

emotion. They'll try to justify it with logic, so that means you've got to sell the benefits and not the features of your product. **Remember, they only care about what's in it for them.** So no matter you're selling, you should always ask yourself, what's the emotional hot button in this offer? And you've got to understand that people as a whole are very egocentric. Everything they do is centered around the self, around them. People look at the world, at your offer, in terms of how that relates to them personally. Again, what's in it for me?

Now, **people want to obviously avoid risk, so the desire to avoid losing something has a lot more power in marketing than the power of them getting something.** And understand this, too: **People don't trust you, at least not right away.** They don't know you, and most have never even heard of you, much less seen you. So you've got to lower the risk by providing in your sales message answers to questions like, "Does this really work? Do other people trust this guy? Can I get my money back if it doesn't work?" You see, people are always looking for something. **They live lives of quiet desperation and dissatisfaction.** What they want is love, wealth, better health/security and comfort. **They want to take back control of their lives, because 99% of people** *don't* **have control of their own lives.** That's why you must give people what they want.

The second marketing key area that I want to talk about here is developing products or services that appeal to a specific market. How do you determine this? Well, one way is to use the Internet. Go to Google, enter the search term "market trends" with a plus sign, and then type in the specific market you're marketing. For example, "market trends" + "health and wellness." What you'd find, according to A.C. Nielson's studies. is that one of the world's fastest growing categories is food and drink.

With the information that you find about any specific

market, you can create an information product — for example, an insider report that you could sell to people who are interested in that subject. And again, please don't underprice your products! I know that there are a lot of these low-priced e-books on the market — but there are also many, many electronic books that sell for huge amounts of money. For example, a good friend of mine sells his e-book for $997. In the health and wellness industry that I just talked about there is a health and wellness trends report that sells for $13,000. Let me say it again: $13,000. It's a simple PDF document, an e-book — but 100 sales of a product like that will net you a cool $1.3 million. And prices like this are possible because the products are developed for a specific target market. In that example there, there are 12 chapters — and what that marketing company does is sell the individual chapters for $2,500 to $3,000 each, in case a buyer doesn't want the entire e-book.

So what you're looking for when developing products or services is a specific niche market. **By marketing to that specific niche, you're going to stand out from the crowd** — and that's going to give you an opportunity to create products that address their problems, their passions, and their pleasures. In other words, you want to fish in a pond — not an ocean, and you want a pond that's filled with fish hungry for what you're offering, so you can satisfy their hunger.

How do you find out what they're hungry for? **Simply read the magazines they're reading, paying special attention to the letter column.** If you read those, you're going to spot gaps in the market that you can fill by developing a specific product or a service. **You can also study Amazon.com.** Look at the 11 or 12 departments there, and learn what people are buying. And don't forget to click on that link that says **"emerging technologies,"** because you can locate hot new trends that people are passionate about. **You can also go to a large public**

library and go through a copy of the SRDS Direct Marketing List Source Directory. You'll find over 60,000 lists of buyers from 230 different business and consumer markets listed there — and with the online version, you can get 30 new list opportunities each day. Your chances for success when you do that are multiplied a thousand-fold, because you're not trying to find a market for a product; **instead, you're creating a product for a market.**

And here's another secret that I want to leave you with, and it's one that's overlooked by most new marketers: *sell to the market that you're already a part of.* If you know business opportunities, then create products for that market; you understand that market, because you're a part of it. **What you want to do is get on the other side of that cash register, and begin creating products for that market and selling them** *exactly* **what they want.** This is the SMART marketing secret that millionaire marketers follow to earn their fortunes in Direct-Response Marketing.

You know, whatever we sell, we're all in the relationships business. That's the reason why people keep coming back to us. **You have to really understand the market in order to have a relationship;** you can't have a relationship with somebody that you don't really know anything about. If I had to put my greatest secret on one little 3 x 5 index card, that's what it would be. That's what made my whole career, my whole fortune: the fact that for years I myself was an opportunity junkie. I was addicted to buying every plan and program, and the dumber they were, the more I wanted them. Those stupid ones were my favorites: the kind where supposedly you just put it under your pillow at night, and you'd wake up the next morning and have a million dollars right there. So when it came time to getting into the marketplace, I already knew exactly who the people were in that marketplace. It was easy to build relationships with them, which was what #7 up there is all about. **You have to know these people you're wanting to sell to — and they _are_ people. They're not numbers, they're people. It's all about relationships.**

And that bears on #10 as well. **You have to keep going back to them; you can't just expect them to come to you.** That's one of the greatest problems marketers suffer from: So many think that just because they do have a relationship with people, those people are going to come back and want to do business with them again. Nothing could be further from the truth. We have a 21-year-old company here, and if we were to stop mailing, it would be only a matter of weeks or months before there would be no more phone calls and mail coming in. That makes it easy if we ever want to shut down, but we're not going that route!

Okay, now, this is the moment you've been waiting for, and I've kind of really been pounding along, going through these things I've been sharing. But on this one **I want to kind of slow my pace a bit and really share with you, seriously, from my heart, what I _know_ is marketing's greatest secret that no one tells you and most people never use.** Learn it, use it, and prosper abundantly. **And here it is: Learning is a process, not an event.** Let me repeat that: Learning is a process, not an event. And let me illustrate it this way: Two years ago during the summer Olympics, I watched Olympic swimmer Michael Phelps win eight gold metals. How did he do it? How did he beat 1972 Gold Medal Winner Mark Spitz's record? The answer is the secret I'm sharing with you now: Learning is a process, not an event.

Michael Phelps didn't simply pack a bag, fly to China, jump in the pool and win; no, he trains for six hours a day, six days a week, without fail. Even if a holiday falls on one of those training days, he does a full day of training. It's that total dedication to learning, to training, that's made him a champion. **Similarly, all the skills you want as a marketer can be learned — and they *must* be learned.** And yes, education can be a very slow, very painful process. You can increase your knowledge through books, through thinking, through dreaming; but there's no substitute for hands-on experience. You've got to get out there; you've got to do it.

Michael Phelps could've read about swimming, he could've watched other people swim, he could've dreamed about being an Olympic champion — but his dreams would never have come true, and he probably would never have learned to swim. It's the same when it comes to learning about marketing, especially Direct-Response Marketing. **You have to get into the water. Each day, you've got to go through the process of learning, through the exercises, the testing, playing the game.** And no great Olympic champion ever becomes a champion by himself; he's got a trainer, he's got a coach, he's got several people who work with him. And fortunately you have that also, through this series of books. **The very information that you're now reading can be like a springboard to a greater achievement for you as a marketer.** Maybe you've already got a great business idea, or maybe you're just now formulating that idea in your mind; that's important. But you've got to take action. **You *must* take action.**

Trying a new business idea is kind of like climbing up on a huge diving board. You fearfully climb to the top, and then inch your way to the end of that board. You try not to get dizzy... and then you jump. Of course it's scary, but the more you do it, the less scary it becomes. And finally it starts being *fun*. You learn to enjoy the rush, you learn to use the adrenalin, and the fear becomes enjoyable. Learning to dive, learning to swim, **learning how to do marketing successfully so you become a marketing champion is a process, not an event.** Aristotle once said, "What we have to learn to do we learn by doing."

Learning relies on you acquiring different types of knowledge, supported by information. And that leads to the development of new skills and of an understanding, so that you can experience the things that you desire — prosperity, abundance, wealth. **Repeating these thoughts and these actions is essential to your learning.** It's believed that after several repetitions of a different daily activity and thoughts, change occurs in the synapses of the brain. I call this the transformation trench. That is, I believe there's a neural pattern or trench formed that becomes deeply ingrained in your mind, so that at some point when you try to do something you begin to do it automatically, instinctively. **You take the necessary actions, and the result is success to you as a marketer. But again, that takes time.** There's a Chinese proverb which states, "Learning is like rowing upstream; not to advance is to drop back." But the end result here is that you're going to be successful and financially free — and that's what you desire, isn't it? Are you going to fall along the way, are you going to fail? Well, of course... **but learn to fail forward, and don't drop back.**

Let me tell you about a failure. He failed several times in business, he suffered a nervous breakdown, he suffered from depression throughout his life, he failed in politics eight times... but he never quit, and he never stopped learning. In fact he learned through the process of failure, and he eventually became the 16th President of the United States. His name was Abraham Lincoln. Abraham Lincoln wrote about learning. **He said, "I don't think much of a man who is not wiser today than he was yesterday."**

Recently Princeton University, which teaches the process of learning, put together a formula they called the 70/20/10 Formula. **The idea is that 70% of learning takes place when a person applies the acquired skill in a real-life situation, 20%**

comes from feedback or **observing, or working with a role model, and 10% comes from formal training.** Interesting, isn't it? Obviously, the most important part of the learning process is applying what you're learning. That takes time and patience; it's like a journey, and there will be detours, there will be roadblocks, you're going to have accidents, and there will be distractions along the way. It's a process, not an event. **Ultimately, learning is a change in behavior as a result of your experience — and you can never have the experience until you actually apply what you've learned.** The instructor, the teacher, the trainer, they can't do it for you. You can only learn from personal experience through application of what you're learning about marketing, and your learning has to be an active process.

People are not sponges; we don't simply absorb knowledge like a sponge does water. Just reading about it, just listening to it, or just watching information about marketing isn't learning. Just knowing the systems of marketing isn't learning. **Learning is the active process of applying and using that knowledge and information personally.** So let me ask you this: what stage of learning are you presently at? **STAGE ONE is when you're trying to absorb information.** Usually there's a lot of frustration and failure involved in that stage. **STAGE TWO is what's called the integration stage;** that's the internal process where you take what you're learning, what you're trying to absorb, and you try to integrate it with what you already know. This is sometimes confusing, and it can become stressful. And then there's that final stage, **STAGE THREE, which is expression — you actually begin applying your knowledge.** You experience failure, you experience success, but the more you learn and apply, the greater your successes and the fewer your failures.

Now you've just learned marketing's greatest secret, which

no one ever tells you and most people never use. I encourage you to use it, and to prosper abundantly. **Never stop learning:** apply what you learn, because learning is a process, it's not an event.

My sister is a physical trainer — she helps people build their bodies and get in shape. I was introduced to her boss a while back, and he's in such great shape. He's got all these pictures of him on the wall, where he's gone to these weightlifter kinds of contests. It's just him in this little Speedo, and you can see that all of his muscles are ripped, and he's got this championship weightlifter type of body. I was in his office once commenting on what great shape he's in, and then he opened up his drawer and pulled out these pictures of this real fat guy — this fat, dumpy looking guy. I wondered what in the world that was all about, and then he says, "That was me 10 years ago." I had to look, and look, and look, and I could only see just a little bit of resemblance — but I saw enough to know that it really *was* him 10 years ago. And I said, "Look, what's the secret? Give me the secret, man, I want that body that you have right there. I want that!" He goes, "All right, you want the secret? I'll tell you what the secret is. **It's diet and exercise."**

And I said, "No, no I don't want to hear that, I want to know what the *secret* is!" Well folks, the secret is that there *is* no secret. Everyone is promising shortcuts, and they do exist; sure, there are things that you can learn to get to Point A to Point Z faster. **But what people want is the magic pill offering a softer, easier way. And they want somebody else to take care of everything.** That's not going to happen.

The great Earl Nightingale once produced a program called *The Strangest Secret*. It came out 50 years ago on an LP record, and you can still buy it to this day in other formats. **Basically** *The Strangest Secret* **is that everybody wants the results — but they don't want to put in the action that it takes to get the results, whatever those results are.** Earlier, I was using the analogy of my sister's boss, the guy who's got this perfectly ripped body. Everybody wants the payoff, they want the bonus, they want the results... but as Zig Ziegler once said you've got to put the wood into that wood stove first. You can't just sit there going, "Where's my heat, where's my heat?" You have to put the wood in and light the fire, and then you'll get some heat.

So I would encourage you to be willing to pay the price if you want the results. There's some work involved, some time involved; but the payoff is definitely worth it. **In this business, as with any business, the way that you get really, really good is by going through some adversity.** It's another secret that nobody uses, because most people just give up way too soon. They put in a little bit, they don't get the results that they want, and they're gone. They just give up.

The people who make it big time are the people who go through all kinds of pain, all kinds of problems, all kinds of adversity, all kinds of obstacles and challenges. That's the only way that we really learn anything, by the way: **we learn it the hard way, especially those of us who are stubborn as hell. Sadly, it really does take daily work and discipline.** There are some things that are a helluva lot of fun, but there's also a lot of what they call grub work. But the payoffs can run in the millions. The payoff is that you can have a business no matter where you live, and the money just comes rolling in, just like rain falling down from the sky. **The payoff is that you can be totally in charge of your own income and create money at will, as much money as you want, whenever you want to make it.** Let that be your rainbow here, the end result, but learn how to fall in love with the work, too. It's exciting. Direct-Response Marketing is a thrilling business.

Take writing sales copy. It seems that everyone wants to learn how. **Well, the way you learn how to write copy is to write copy.** That's the whole secret right there. I mean, anybody can write a sales letter; but it's writing a sales letter that's going to make you a million dollars that's the tough thing.

You know, it's kind of funny. We humans do so much to avoid pain, to avoid uncomfortable circumstances, to avoid things that make us uncomfortable or that we don't necessarily like... **when it's usually those very things that make us grow the most and that we learn the most from.** If we had our way, I suspect we'd all live a cushy life with no struggle, with nothing negative or uncomfortable involved. We'd all just float by, and we'd all have everything we needed. Yet if you ask somebody who's gone through some hardships and who's struggled, even a successful business person who has had some failures, maybe some bankruptcy in the past, they'll tell you how much they learned from all that experience they got going through the ditches.

What that tells me is that while you should try to avoid pain, you should realize that even in the pain, there are lessons to be learned. Even in the struggle, even in the failure, there are things you can learn that will help you grow, and you'll come out of it a better person. Several years ago, Chris Lakey read an article where they followed up several lottery winners, people who had won many, many millions of dollars in the big multi-state Powerball and big state jackpots, just from picking the right numbers. They went back and looked at their lives and said, "Man, I wonder how they're living today."

And it was amazing how many of them were flat broke. Most just blew the money and completely lived high on the hog for a while, didn't invest anything, bought fancy cars and went on huge vacations — and were back to nothing again. Some of them tried to get into businesses, but they really didn't understand how to be business people and they lost all their money that way. Some of them got taken advantage of by family and friends. In any case, a significant portion had no money left just a few years later. Easy come, easy go, right? **Well, people who fight for their money, people who struggle for success, people who work hard at it, who are dedicated to it, tend to keep it.** It's just like the guy who used to weigh a ton and was really unhealthy, and now he's super-fit: When you work for it, you have an incentive intrinsically built into your mind, and you put so much heart into it that you have a different mindset about that success. You don't take it lightly, and you do everything you can to keep it. Similarly, Chris Lakey's grandfather had a heart attack once, and he was much healthier afterward, because he became determined to exercise after he had those heart problems. I can't remember how many miles he walks every day now, but he's a lot healthier because of the struggle he went through.

So don't be afraid of struggling. Don't be afraid of going through some bad times, because you can learn from the experience, as long as you're out there doing it and working hard. **The key is action, because inaction just breeds *more* inaction.** If you're doing something, if you're moving forward, you'll continue down that road towards success. **You can learn from your mistakes and failures.** You can learn things along the way that will help you. That way, you'll have a much better appreciation of it when you actually achieve the success you've been looking for — and you'll become smarter in the process.

I believe that problems are good, as long as you handle them right. Problems spur you into action — and a lot of times, that's the *only* thing that spurs you into action. And again, action is what life is all about... at least, taking the right kinds of actions in a repetitive way. For years I dreamed of making millions of dollars — and then, when the money just started coming in, I got so damned depressed I couldn't even believe it! Why was I depressed? Because the reality wasn't living up to the fantasy. What I've learned since then is the money really doesn't make you happy. I realize that people who have money always say that, and it used to drive me crazy when I heard it.

Now I'm saying it myself, because I've learned the truth: **the pleasure in this business is the process of *learning how* to get the money.** Once you fall in love with the things that you do to get it, once you make it a game, that's what will keep you healthy and happy — and wealthy.

How to Make a Seven-Figure Income

I happen to believe, quite fervently, that if you put
enough work into your business and keep educating
yourself, you can eventually make more money than you can
spend. I'm living proof: as I've mentioned before, my company
has made well over $100,000,000 in just 21 years. And I happen
to know quite a few people who have parlayed hard work and
self-education into big money. **In this chapter, an example
you'll see me use repeatedly is Jeff Gardner, a Dallas
businessman who makes a seven-figure income every year.** In
just his first two months as a member of our Direct-Response
Network (DRN), he made more than $100,000 — and that's on
top of the money he's made with all the rest of his endeavors. So
in the next 30 pages or so, let's look at some of the secrets he's
used to do all this — including the main secret he used to
generate more than $100,000 with the DRN in just two months.

When Jeff was only 15 years old, he was already in what
was then called the mail order business; we call it Direct
Response Marketing (DRM) nowadays. He was already running
ads and getting money in the mail. He would come home from
school, and the first thing that he would say was, "Mom, did I
get any mail today?" And she'd say "Yes, son," and hand him a
stack of envelopes full of cash, checks, and money orders. That
was over 20 years ago — and he's been making a living the

same way since. Jeff Gardner is a great example and a great teacher, because he's passionate about the business. He grew up with it; he understands *everything* when it comes to making money through Direct-Response Marketing. He's a good friend of mine, and I hope these secrets of his I'll be revealing in this chapter will make him a good friend of yours, too.

Let's jump right in, shall we? I've already alluded to the fact that one secret has been more responsible for his fortune, including the $100,000 he generated with DRN in his two months, than anything else. That secret is simple: **Jeff has focused exclusively on the business opportunity market. That's a market that includes of millions of people, all around the world, who want to know how to make more money — and with the Internet, they're easier than ever to get to.**

You know, if you ask people what they want more of in life, they don't say, *I want to work more.* **In most cases, what people want above all else is more money.** That's really the key to success in the biz opp market. With my company, and with Jeff's as well, it's all about going out there and serving this market, delivering high-quality products, services, and opportunities. In doing that, I've been able to generate tens of millions dollars over the years — and Jeff isn't far behind. He's been doing it as long as I have, in his case, well over half his life. It's a market we absolutely love, and it's been phenomenal to us; it's helped us create lifestyles we could only have dreamed of not too many years ago. **It's something we're trying to help other people get into, too... because once you jump into this business with both feet and understand the moneymaking power of the business opportunity market, you can make money very quickly.**

That really was the key to Jeff's success with DRN: he went to the right market and used a few techniques he already knew to very quickly generate a lot of money. Now, I expected that everybody who reads this book has, almost without exception, been a customer of many of the companies selling business opportunities. And what we tell people, over in over — in audio productions, seminars, workshops, in print — is that **the number one rule in marketing is to know who your customers are and what they want more than anything else.** Armed with that information, you can then develop a wider set of products and services that are customized for those specific wants and needs. **You have to get on the other side of the cash register.**

If you're already involved in the business opportunity market from a consumer viewpoint, then you're already equipped to get rich in this field. **Because realize this: The business opportunity market is made up of tens of millions of people who are *just like you*.** This is an important point, because too many times I see people who want to make a lot of money from home, but they get stuck in that consumer mindset. They're constantly buying "get rich quick" programs, moneymaking programs, and business opportunities; and in fact, a lot of these programs and opportunities are of very high quality. They can actually work, and you see people often getting out there and making a little bit of money, and in some cases, a *lot* of money.

But what I try to tell people is this: **If you really want to open that vault and make a killing, you have to stop thinking like a *buyer* of moneymaking opportunities and start thinking like a *seller* of moneymaking opportunities instead.** I always love that look in their eyes when they finally get it. It's kind of an "aha" moment. And in some cases, it takes giving people an actual example of how other folks are doing that. The example that Jeff usually gives people is a gentleman on T.V. who sells a real estate course. He's been selling that same real estate course for 20 years now — and it's doing very well. Any night around 2 or 3 AM, if you turn on your T.V. and look for paid programming, you're going to see his infomercial.

Now, what's the message he's giving you on that infomercial? Simply this: you can get filthy, stinking rich with real estate. You want to buy wholesale real estate, you want to flip properties, etc. According to this guy, real estate is simply the best way to get rich. Now, if you're just a buyer of moneymaking opportunities, you're likely to listen to what he's telling you, let it sink into your brain, and say, "You know, I think maybe he's right," and you may well buy the program. And maybe you'll actually use it... or maybe, as is often the case, it's going to collect dust on a shelf. In either case, by then you're going to believe that the number one way to get rich, based on what he's telling you, is real estate.

But if you step behind the cash register, you can ask yourself this question: How is *he* making most of his money? Is it in real estate? Well, yes, he's probably making *some* money in real estate. But if he was making more money in real estate than he was selling his *information* about making money in real estate, you'd never see him on T.V. He'd be out there spending 100% of his time getting filthy, stinking rich in real estate. Yet he's making a huge profit selling his real estate moneymaking course, which is why he'll still be on T.V. flogging his course for not one year, not five years, not 10 years, but 20 years on. What's making him rich isn't real estate; it's that moneymaking course that he's selling to thousands of people. **So again, it's all about not being a buyer of moneymaking opportunities, but a seller of them.** Once you get that into your head, you're ready to act on that knowledge and make some real money.

Getting to this point, though, is easier said than done. So many people get stuck in the mindset of buying and being a consumer that they never see the opportunity that awaits them on the other side of the cash register. This means you, Dear Reader. **You've got to stop looking at things like you've been looking at them, and start seeing them with new eyes.** When you get a package in the mail and it has an offer in it, **there are two ways to look at it.** The first is how most people look at it: *This person is trying to sell me something. I'm a consumer. I read over the offer, I look at what they have to offer me, and I decide whether I want to buy it.*

The second way to look at it is this: *I am an entrepreneur. How can this product or service help me advance what I'm trying to do as an entrepreneur? What can I do with this product?* Maybe that means that you buy it and use it as research; maybe that means you buy it and use it to make money, or maybe that means you just pick it apart and evaluate it, and learn things that you can use in your business. Sometimes it's the advertising copy itself that's the real value, because it can act as a model for your own.

In any case, it's critical to re-think how you analyze the offers that come across your desk or through your e-mail. **Forget the consumer's side of things; and begin to think about things from a purely business standpoint.** That's where a lot of people break down; they can't separate the two. For example, they get something in the mail or they see an offer, and all they can think about is analyzing it from a product/service standpoint of, "What is this product going to do for me as a consumer?" Until you get out of that mindset and start thinking about it like a businessperson, you really can't become a successful entrepreneur.

It's hard to realize exactly how you do it until you've done it, and once you've done it, you never go back. **But you've got to make that flip** — and each person has to go through it in their own way, and come to that realization independently in their own mind. **Until you do, you really can't move forward.**

In fact, as far as I'm concerned, you really can't get to the next level without making that switch.

Of course, once you start getting money in the mail, that changes you! That's another one of those "aha" moments I was talking about earlier. Here's an example: Like me, Jeff Gardner was in this market for a long time before he really succeeded. Like me, he not only has bookcases filled from floor to ceiling with all the moneymaking and opportunity books, manuals, courses, tape sets, video sets, CDs and DVDs he's bought, there's also a storage closet with boxes and boxes of them to handle the overflow. You see, there was a time when Jeff thought *that* was the key to making money. He was buying all these up and storing them on bookcases, and sticking them in boxes and under the bed, and putting them on the coffee table, and he was like, "I'm not getting rich. I don't understand what's going on. They tell me if I buy these things, I'm going to get filthy rich!"

Finally, Jeff realized, **"Hey, wait a minute: the people really making the money are *the people promoting these*."** One of the very first things he did after that was get involved in a turnkey opportunity. It came with a ready-to-go product and ready-to-go sales materials. He took that information, put that product out there, and lo and behold, money started showing up in the mailbox.

When you start getting those checks in the mail, you want more. When you start seeing that bank account go up, you definitely want more. It's really an adrenaline rush. **And the best thing about it is that not only are you making piles of money, you're helping other people at the same time — so it's a great win-win situation.** Once you're hooked, you're pretty much hooked for life, I think. But it's a positive addiction... and the only side effect is that if you really get into it heavily, you may suffer from lack of sleep, because you want to get up every morning really early and get cracking. Personally, I get up at 5

AM or so. Jeff gets up about 5:30. It's great to be up that early...
but it's hard to get there if you don't want to go to bed, because
you're so excited about your life and what you're doing.

You see, this business is one of those that really grabs you,
because it's such a fun thing to do. You end up wanting to spend
most of your time doing it, and I think that's one of the exciting
things about getting involved in the business opportunity
market. **Frankly, this is one of the few things I've found
where if somebody gets hooked on it, it can be a very positive
thing** — so that instead of dreading going to work and dreading
getting up in the morning, you're eager to do both. And you
don't want to go to bed. because you know that it's just a few
more hours until you've got to get up.

So it's an addiction, but it's a positive one — and frankly, I
can't think of a better way to live my life than to do something
that I'm passionate about, that I want to do and that makes me a
lot of money at the same time. And yes, this is the kind of thing
where, some nights, you wake up at 3 AM because the ideas
won't stop flowing. You have to wake in the middle of the night,
sometimes, to act on those ideas and write 'em down.

The coolest thing about being an entrepreneur is serving
customers who look to you to show them new and creative
ways to make money. That's what serving the opportunity
market is all about. **There really is an opportunity to profit
around every corner.** You can spend all of your waking
moments doing so, if you let yourself — though **I recommend
giving yourself some free time to unwind.** Go watch a movie,
play golf, etc. You'll probably end up thinking of business
anyway, but at least you end up with some downtime, so your
brain can think other thoughts.

**Another great thing about being in the opportunity
market is that every day is a new day to profit.** There are

always new products and services on the horizon, based on new technologies, and if you're savvy about it, there's always a new way to sell them. That last bit is important, by the way. Too many people get stuck thinking, "Okay, I bought this product and it comes with this sales letter or this website, and I have to do it *this* way because this is the way the book says I need to do it. And I'm going to do these things, 1-2-3, and then I'm just going to sit back and wait for the money to come."

Well, not necessarily. Sometimes that's an okay strategy, but being an entrepreneur in the opportunity market is so much more than that. **There are *so* many ways to cross-pollinate, where you can take a little idea here and a little idea there and merge them and come up with a whole new product or service, or a new way of marketing that product or service.** That's how we got started at M.O.R.E., Inc., in fact, with our *Dialing for Dollars* program; we merged two effective moneymaking programs, tossed in our own ideas, smoothed out the joints, and made millions off it. There are always plenty of new ideas to throw in, new products that could be free gifts, new this, new that; there are so many different things out there that you'll see clearly, once you get on the other side of the cash register. You'll become aware of those opportunities for profit, or for improving on a service or product — rather than just getting stuck in the mindset that you have to do things "by the book."

If you keep doing things the same way, you never learn everything — and there's so much to learn. I'm amazed at the fact that I've been involved in this now since 1988, and I'm *still* constantly learning on a regular basis. In this field you're always growing, you're always finding new things. You're never at a level where you think you know everything. The longer I'm in it, the more I realize that there's more to learn and more room to grow. And believe me, that's one of the great things about the business opportunity market.

There are people in this market right who that are just thrilled to pieces to be making a full-time income, where they don't have to work for a boss. Just selling $20, $30, $40 booklets — they're happy with that. You've got people in the middle somewhere who are selling slightly more high-dollar things — $200-500 deals, say, and maybe they do a seminar every so often. Then you've got bigger companies that are generating hundreds of millions of dollars yearly. They're doing multiple seminars all year, every year, and they're sending out big programs and plenty of direct mail. They're doing radio and infomercials and similar advertising. So there are different points and places to come into the field, and there's always room to grow. You can always decide whether you want to stand pat in one place, or learn and earn more. You decide that you either want staff or you don't, or you want to do seminars or not, or maybe that you want a newsletter, or a teleseminars deal, or a membership site. **Whatever it is, you have the ability to grow and do exciting new things.**

There aren't many of those types of opportunities in the workaday world, where you've got a job and a boss, and few chances to grow beyond some basic limits. So yeah, it's a really exciting place to be. If you want to make millions of dollars, you've got the potential to do it — but if you just want to make $100,000 a year, you can do that instead. **The amount of money you make is *not* contingent upon the number of hours you work, by the way.** So many people are out there trading their life for a paycheck — that is, they're trading the number of hours they work for pay. But people who make money in the opportunity market have the kind of freedom and flexibility that allows them to get beyond that. There's no clocking in and out and being forced to stay for a certain number of hours, no matter what, with a lousy two weeks a year for vacation. Do you really want to sell off a good portion of your life that way?

I'm not saying you shouldn't try to make money. We've all got bills to pay, things we want to buy, and lifestyles we want to enjoy. But there's a different way to get those things and to live that life. **When you work as an entrepreneur in this type of a market, you can actually make more money by working fewer hours.** Now, I know that may seem crazy, but one very successful business opportunity marketer has a saying that applies here: "The less I do, the more I make." One of the things he's talking about here is leverage. **When you're in the business opportunity market, there are different systems you can put into place where you can actually leverage other people's time and resources.** For example, you can outsource tasks. That is, you could hire people to do specialized or repetitious tasks that they can do more cheaply and effectively, while you focus exclusively on the tasks that make you the most money. Or, you can sell very high-dollar items. So instead of having to work for $10 or $20 an hour, you can sell a course for $500, $1,000, $5,000, or even $10,000, or do seminars at similar price points. **With very few sales, you can very quickly make the same amount of money in a couple of days that you would usually make in a month.**

That's the power you have with the business opportunity market. **You can actually create a life and a lifestyle where you're in complete control.** You have a better quality of life, and at the same time you have more free time to enjoy the things you want in your life. I think that's one of the biggest benefits of this business. When you're stuck in a job — even if it's a high-paying job — you may not have the time to enjoy the brand new car that you just bought, or that nice new home, or to go on the trips you'd like. But when you work for yourself in the business opportunity market, and you're making a lot of money and have all that extra time, well now you're able to enjoy your vehicles, and you're able to enjoy your home, and you're able to go on all the trips your heart desires.

You see, **this is really about creating a lifestyle; think of it that way.** Yes, we're talking about a business, and I know that turns some people off; they think, "No, I don't want to be in business." But you're really in a *lifestyle* business, the way I look at it; because instead of feeling like you're stuck behind a desk, **you're really designing the life and lifestyle you want — and enjoying it.** I honestly think that's what we're on Earth to do.

Even highly paid doctors, lawyers, and business professionals who make fifty or a hundred dollars per hour are still limited by the number of hours they can work. It seems like they should be the ones living high and enjoying the freedom of having a high-paying job — and yet they still pinch their pennies, sometimes worse than people who make a lot less than they do, and they still don't have all the time they want. **Even the best-paying conventional jobs don't pay anywhere near what a self-employed entrepreneur can make.** A lot of people in those professional industries are slaves to their jobs, not just monetarily but in terms of time. They have no ability to just decide to take a day and go to the beach, or take a week and go to Europe on vacation. Even people who seem to have everything still labor under a lot of restrictions.

Not so for entrepreneurs like us. Sure, we work hard — but **we're getting paid on the number of products we actually develop or sell for other people.** We don't usually sell other people's products here at M.O.R.E., Inc. (we have so many of our own!), but I know Jeff Gardner has done a lot of that over the years. He's made literally millions of dollars by selling other people's products in addition to his own... and that's one of the great things about this business. There's always a way to make money.

Jeff has a quote that he considers a foundation of his success, one he goes back to again and again: *You can make money, or you can make excuses, but you can't make both.* He first heard it from the great Dan Kennedy. Very often, those of us who help other people reach for their dreams hear those people complain, "But I don't know how to do this. I don't know how to create a product. I don't know how to write a sales letter." Those are excuses, and they're not particularly valid ones. I tell these people, "Look, you don't have to know how to invent a product or write a sales letter, or how to do any of that stuff at first. It's a good idea to learn, but there are companies out there that will sell or license you the rights to their ready-to-go products. They'll even provide the copy to sell the products with. All you have to do is advertise."

In some cases, the companies have already sold the heck out of their product, and they realize there's still some life in it, so they'll license it to others. **You can buy the rights, market them to your customers and clients, and build up your business that way.** Sometimes, a company has a product they're doing very well with, so you can contact them and say, "Let's do a joint venture. Let me use the sales materials and I'll mail it to my list, or I'll go out there and market it fresh in the magazines or through direct mail, and we'll split it 50/50, 60/40, 80/20, whatever. "

That gives you the ability, again, to leverage, so you don't have to crank out your own 300-400 page product. Let me give you a quick example. There's a product on the Internet, an e-book that Jeff bought a number of years ago; it's an awesome moneymaking book, 300 pages long. It was written by this fellow who was just brainstorming all sorts of different ways to make quick money. He provided literally dozens of ways do so. When Jeff saw this on the Internet, he was very interested in buying it for research purposes; and the fellow sold it for maybe $20-$30; it was quite inexpensive for a 300-page e-book. So Jeff downloaded it, and stayed on the guy's list. Well, not too long ago he e-mailed his list and said, "Look, I need to make some quick money to pay off my tax bill, I'm going to sell people the ownership rights to this 300-page e-book." Jeff was reading this sales letter thinking, "Okay, he's got this big tax bill. It's going to cost me hundreds, maybe even thousands of dollars for the ownership rights to this book." He was figuring it was going to be a huge expense.

But he was wrong. To get the full rights to the book, to change it, add to it, do whatever you want with it, put your name on it, change the title, whatever, Jeff thought it would be expensive — $2,500, $5,000, $10,000, especially since you got the website, the sales letter, everything. So Jeff went to the website... and it was $67. Jeff couldn't get his credit card out fast enough! Here was a product ready to go, a 300-page proven seller with testimonials and a sales letter, for $67. Now Jeff can do anything with it. He can print it out himself, he can break it into articles, he can put it on CD-ROM, he can print a physical copy and put it in bookstores, or create a distributorship — however he wants to sell it. **It's a ready-to-go product for $67. With deals like that available, there's no excuse for somebody *not* to get into this market and make a huge amount of money.**

Those ready-to-go products are out there. And let me tell you a little secret: After you start selling those ready-to-go products and get comfortable in this market, you're going to realize that creating these products isn't so difficult. This is how our example entrepreneur, Jeff Gardner, really got started in the business. After he started selling other people's products, he wanted to create his own to see if they'd sell. He put his first product out there, and sure enough — he made $100,000 with it. He thought, *This is great!* He put another one out there and made a quarter of a million dollars with it — and ever since that time he's tried to create a lot more of his own products. **Now he sells other people's products *and* his own.**

It just goes to show that if you just want to dip your toe in the water and get started, and gain some confidence in the process, one of the best things you can do is sell other people's turnkey products.

A while back, Chris Lakey and I started working with a guy out of Indiana. He came up to me in Chicago and said, "I've got this business I'm involved in where I make $4,000 on the average job. It takes me less than a day to do it, there's no competition, and millions of homeowners need this because I save them thousands of dollars. I keep 65% profit on every job I do. So all I have to do is one job a week, and I make over $100,000 a year." Chris and I got excited about the idea. I'm not going to go into the details here, but we're working with him now, and we plan on making millions of dollars selling this to other people looking for a simple, fast, easy, way to make over $100,000 a year and only work one day a week. You know, those types of opportunities are *everywhere*, and there are literally tens of millions of people in the United States alone looking for the perfect way to work just a few hours a week at something that's enjoyable and make huge sums of money. **All you have to do is connect the opportunities with the people who are looking at them, maybe after polishing them just a little to make them stand out.** That's basically what our DRN is all about.

Finding businesses you can start for a low amount of money, certainly less than your typical franchise, without a lot of regulation and overhead — that's the ultimate entrepreneurial dream. But it's not just a dream, because those things are out there. You don't have to become a franchise robot to take advantage of these opportunities. Speaking of which, look at the typical franchise: at minimum, you spend up to $200,000 or more, and you've got this company above you telling you *exactly* what you can and can't do as far as the franchise goes. You buy into their franchise, and they've got all the cards — and yet you spend all this money to be in business.

Well, we teach people how to get into Direct-Response Marketing and work for themselves. Whatever business you're in, you can use direct response strategies to build it up. **But what it's really all about is about working a little, making a lot, and enjoying the freedom that comes with that.** A lot of that comes with experience — but you can always learn as you go. And one of your most important tasks is to start building a mailing list, right away.

As I mentioned earlier, Jeff Gardner was able to do over $100,000 within his first few months in the DRN, back in 2007; he's made a lot more since. **Part of the reason he was able to do that was because he had confidence that comes with experience, which I think is very, very important.** But another reason he was able to do that is because he had a mailing list of customers who loved him, trusted him, respected him, and knew he was a good person looking out for their best interests. And yes, I realize that that's probably what keeps most people from getting started with this business.

I've got to be completely honest here: I have a huge customer list, and Jeff has a large customer list, and we were both born with those customer lists. We've had them forever, since we came out of the womb... NOT!!! But most people *think* that way. They look at companies with these large customer mailing lists and think, "Oh, I can't do that. I don't have a customer mailing list." **Well, here's a newsflash: Every single person in the business opportunity market, from the person doing it part time to the people with their own jets, all started without a single name on a customer mailing list.**

This is all just marketing, folks. **It's easy to rent mailing lists, and almost as easy to build your own.** There's a huge market of ravenous, hungry buyers for moneymaking and business opportunities. **These are all good people who want financial independence, and they're easily reachable.** They want to buy high quality products, services, and opportunities. The way Jeff Gardner was able to make $100,000 in less than two months in the DRN was because he already had a list of people who had done business with him before, a list that he had built up over time. He was able to go back to them with this opportunity; he said, "This has my highest recommendation. I think it's great to get into for these reason, so why don't you join?" A lot of people did join, and that's how Jeff did so much business in a short amount of time.

A lot of people use the excuse, "I don't have a customer list." Well, *don't* use that as an excuse. Start with one person and then two people, and then keep doubling and doubling and doubling. **Jeff started out in this business with free advertising and a lot of joint ventures.** After a year or two, he only had 282-286 people on his mailing list, total. That's not thousands or tens of thousands, but roughly 282 people. And he was able to generate a six-figure income year after year! Why? A couple of different reasons. First off, **business opportunity seekers are ravenous buyers.** Let's look at another market: the weight-loss market. If someone wants to lose weight, are they going to buy one program, one product, one deal, one workout? No, they'll buy everything they can get their hands on. They're watching the infomercials, they're buying the Ab Rocker, they're going to Jenny Craig, buying the books, buying the food, doing everything they can.

It's the same way in the business opportunity market. **Business opportunity seekers are looking for a solution to their problem, so they're buying everything they can get their hands on,** going to seminars, buying courses, books, memberships, all these things. That's one of the great things about the business opportunity market. You can have a very small list, but still get people to buy over and over again because they want more information. **That's really one of the keys: Just get started and understand that these people are buyers.** They're going to buy from you repeatedly, and as you build up that trust with them, they're going to be long-term buyers. Plus, you can continue adding to that list over time. Don't think you have to add 5,000 people to your list immediately; start with a few and grow it from there. Try to keep doing front-end marketing and lead generating to add people to your list, and over time you're going to build a list you can really profit from.

Don't let those excuses hold you back! Realize that this is a vibrant, dynamic market where you can make a lot of money and have a lot more time in your life. You know, I think it's incredible exciting that for years, Jeff Gardner made millions of dollars with *282 customers*. I can't think of a more inspirational story for those people who say, "Well yeah, sure, you've made millions of dollars — but you've got this huge mailing list."

But really, it's not all just about the size of the list. **One of the most important factors in building a list like this — in any business, really — is relationships.** There are some companies that literally have hundreds of thousands of customers on their lists, and they get a very small percentage of a response to any offer simply because they haven't built up those relationships. They're going for the masses; they want the biggest list possible, because they're looking at the overall numbers. Well, that's not a particularly good strategy for most companies.

I always look at the relationship. That's why I try to go above and beyond every time we deliver a product or a service, to build that relationship and deliver high quality. **If I have a good relationship with my client base, if I'm giving them high quality stuff, if I'm giving them great customer service, then I don't** *need* **hundreds of thousands of customers.** I can do very well with a few thousand or tens of thousands, and as you've seen, some of my colleagues are happy to do six or seven figures in sales a year on a very limited number of people.

As for Jeff, there were times when he would send a $1,000 offer to his list of 282 people, and would get a third of those people to buy that product. Now, on any mailing list, getting 33% of your list to convert on a thousand-dollar offer is almost unheard of, but Jeff was able to do that because he has a great relationship with a small group of people. **Now, as your list builds over time, it can be more difficult to keep that kind of personal relationship going. But in just delivering great products and doing certain things like holding seminars and teleseminars, and trying to keep in touch with your client base, you *can* keep that relationship going.** Do that and you'll have great conversion rates, make great sales, and make your customers happy at the same time. I can't think of a better way to live your life than making lots of money and helping other people at the same time, can you?

List building is something that every direct marketer is passionate about, because **without a mailing list, you really can't accomplish much in this business.** Sure, you can run ads and sell products; but unless you build a list, you're never going to have a lifelong revenue stream. **Whether you're selling by mail or on the Internet, *you've got to build a mailing list.*** And it's really not that hard: there's just a formula you have to follow. Most people don't do it right, so they never get around to building a decent list; but if you follow the formulas and you do the right things, you can build a nice, solid list that continues to grow. **And it doesn't take a very big list to get started and to generate a nice revenue for you on an ongoing basis,** as I think Jeff Gardner's 282-person list pretty much proves. The bigger it gets, of course the more revenue you can make from that list.

The good news is, it's possible to build a mailing list for

very little money — or even no money whatsoever. There are so many different ways to build a list — and of course it's that "little or no money" part that throws the big wrench in the works, because there are lots of ways to do it if you have a lot of money to throw at the problem. You can easily buy or rent a mailing list... if you have plenty of moolah. But if you're new to the game and your budget is tight, you need to build that list for the least amount of money possible. **How do you do that? Easy: give something away for free.**

In fact, give something *great* away for free. The best example I've got of that is movie trailers. Watch the "Coming Soon" features at the theatre, or those "Coming Attractions" on DVDs, and you'll see what I mean. If it's a $30 million movie, they've got $20 million in that two-minute clip that they put together of the very, very best of the movie. They give that away, and of course it's all the most exciting stuff: cars blowing up, bombs going off, ships sinking — the most expensive scenes they shot, the biggest action, the greatest thrills are right there, packed into that two minutes, and they just give it away to you free. Why? Because it creates lines at the box office. This isn't the same as building a list, quite, but it *is* very similar. They're doing direct marketing in a way; they're just not collecting names at the other end.

The point is, they're giving something of high-value away for free, and you should do the same. On the Web you *definitely* have to do this, because that's the only way I know of to get the largest number of people to willingly hand you their names and e-mail addresses, along with permission to e-mail to them. **This is crucial, because the best program in the world (like our own DRN, of course!) isn't going to sell unless you build a list.** Even though the DRN has tons of automatic list-building features built in, lots of what I call "stick attractiveness," you still want to build a list that you then send that offer to,

223

because you also want to build a relationship with that list.

Let me re-emphasize this, because it's so important: **Customer relationships are the lifeblood of any business —** and most marketers just completely miss this. With rare exceptions, everybody out there who teaches about list building just talks about building the list and then selling them something. **They forget there's a step in the middle: build the list, build a relationship, and** *then* **you can sell something to your new friends.** That's what's missing in 99% of the list-building courses, systems and programs that I and other marketers I know have bought, tested, and tried over the years. They just miss that middle step. Building a list and immediately going after the people on it is like meeting someone at the grocery store that you hit it off with, and they say, "Hey, why don't you come over for cards tonight?" Can you imagine what it would be like to arrive at the door, and the first thing they do is whip out some Tupperware and try to sell it to you? That kind of thing happens all the time. The only reason you put up with that is you're trapped. You're in a social situation where you either have to look like a jerk and either say, "Oh, just forget it," and leave, or politely put up with the whole evening and try to get away without buying anything. Online they don't know you, they don't trust you, they don't have a reason to buy from you — so when you come running after them going *buy this, buy this,* the first thing they'll do is click away. No obligation, no social situation, no pain; they just leave.

So you make them come to you. If you just say, "Here's something of incredible value. Just give me your name and e-mail address and I'll provide it to you," they do. **And then they hear from you two or three times with some useful information,** a tip, just an introduction, some ideas on how to make money; whatever works. **This is how you build a relationship where they start to trust you.** Now you can start offering them things. You can say, "By the way, here's a free thing you can go get," or "Here's something that's only $14.95," or "Here's a cool thing I found for $39.95," and they'll start buying. Once they've bought, then you move up the ladder and start selling more.

Incidentally, **experienced Internet marketers like the my friend Alan R. Bechtold now recommend that you collect more than just a first name and an e-mail for your list.** That's because e-mail delivery has a lot of problems, more now than ever before. **And I'm talking about the legit stuff — actually trying to get e-mail to people who give you their real addresses.** You see, people get so many emails that they've started to just delete every single e-mail they see unless it's from somebody that they know for sure. The number one problem here is that it's hard for people to recognize what's legitimate, from people that they requested information from, and what's not. Because of course, all the spammers want you to *think* that you requested their information.

Another prevailing problem (for marketers, at least) is that **a lot of Internet service providers think that they know better than you do how to protect yourself from spam** — and sometimes they do. But nowadays, messages that you want to get through are often being filtered and put into junk folders by the ISPs. So you could have all the good intentions in the world, and your customer wants to receive stuff from you — but for some reason it's just not coming through, because AOL or Verizon has set some arbitrary rules about what is and what isn't spam. **Your message may be crafted just the right way, and *still* won't get through because you've got some ISP filtering it out.**

That's why if you stick to just collecting an e-mail and a name, you've got a list that could end up worthless in a week. I've seen some of these ISPs band together, in fact, and

225

crank up what they call their "spam safeguards" to such a degree that 90% of all marketers sending e-mail couldn't even get through to legitimate subscribers. This went on until they backed off because they got so many complaints. The truth is, these ISPs have the power to literally say tomorrow, "Okay, it's $0.20 per e-mail you want to send." Are you prepared for that? Can your business handle it? If you've got a mailing address too, you now have a way to send out a postcard; or if you've got a phone number, you've got a way to send out a telephone call and say, "Hey, we're trying to reach you. Please go to this website." **A good postcard campaign may cost a few bucks, but your response rates can go through the roof if you handle it right and send them to a website.** Postcards are dirt cheap, compared to most mail.

Any way you do it, you've got to get a list in order to be a successful marketer. **You can go buy lists, but it's better to build your own.** Now, you still have to drive some people to that list, but there are ways to do that. If fact, the method that Alan R. Bechtold has used to average about a million dollars in sales a year over the last 25+ years is absurdly simple to do online. **Here it is, in just three simple steps: Publish an e-book. Launch an eZine (an electronic newsletter). Give 'em both away for free.**

Now, when we reveal that secret to people, they usually wrinkle their brow and ask, "How do you make money doing *that*?" Well, that's the subject of an entire course Alan has put together. But that's not the issue here: The issue is that whole list-building system. **It's based on giving away free information, at least on the front end.** What's the number one most popular item being sought after on the search engines today? Freebies. Free information, free newsletters, free books. **These are natural list builders, and you can very cheaply build a list by putting together the right free offer.**

Alan has come up with a system, based on his larger course, that combines all this. Because I highly recommend it, I'm going to go into some detail about it in this chapter. Among other things, he launched a little thing called *Mind Gold News* about six or seven years ago. This is an automatic electronic newsletter that gives people the ability to send someone to a page where they can sign up to subscribe to a free newsletter. That free newsletter is then filled with 1-4 articles each week and automatically sent to all of your subscribers for you by the system. **You get the list of people who subscribe and you can go into a back office area and plug in ads that appear at the top, middle, and bottom of each issue of your newsletter.** It's an incredible service; I've never seen anybody quite duplicate it yet. **All the articles are about business and home business;** one week they might focus on marketing, a second week writing good headlines, another week how to work with eBay, and all kinds of other incredible information that you can send to people for free, no obligation on their part.

Alan also created something called *The PowerPointer's Page* close to seven years ago — and it's still going, every week. **This is a website that changes constantly.** You can put your name up there and add a link to another website. As I discussed in the last chapter, Google loves websites that change constantly; and what this site does is feature five really cool, interesting, or unique websites every week, kind of like Cool Site of the Day. And again, it's automatically updated. **You get people to sign up to that page, and people tend to make that page their home page** because then when they bring up their browser there's five little sites to go visit, and it changes a lot for them. **At the top is the link to your business.**

Alan has had a lot of luck with people selling these services, because they're very powerful. But about five years ago, he combined them into a recruiter-level program that helped people to give away a free web business that sells the *PowerPointer's Page* or *Mind Gold News*. This free web business asks people to provide their name, their e-mail address, their mailing address, their phone number, a cell phone, and a fax number if they have them. The reason he asks for that information is to contact the business owner if there's a problem or a question, *and* to determine what contact information the owner wants to appear on their free web business. **Of course, all this information is also going into Alan's list in his back office, so he can automatically add people to that list.** If someone takes that, they're sent a whole series of offers to upgrade their free web business. They can get a ton more time, hosting, assistance, and material. They get all this information, help, and assistance for just $195 — and the recruiter gets $100 of that, so there's a chance to earn commissions.

In order to build those lists for recruiter-level members at the lowest price possible, Alan came up with the idea for an advertising co-op. That's where 8-10 people could pool their money to pay for print ads for the entire group. **As leads came, they would share them.** This worked very well for a while, until the law of diminishing returns set in, and Alan canceled it. **He replaced it with a Gold-level newsletter program called *Ticket2Wealth*.** It's a great way to tap Alan's mind, to get the benefit of all of his teaching, knowledge, and the 25+ years of experience he's had marketing online, publishing online. He does it in a 12-16 page newsletter that's printed and mailed to the door of every *Ticket2Wealth* Gold Member, and **then he holds a live telephone call once a month where he does Q & A at the end and presents in-depth on one subject,** such as copywriting for the web, writing meaningful headlines, or subject lines for e-mail, creating an e-mail sequence offer, coming up with a great free offer, combining things — all sorts of very in-depth stuff that's made simple by the way he presents it. Then he opens it up for Q & A at the end and answers people's questions. **He burns that to a CD after the call and mails that to every member, once a month.**

But people always want more, so Alan created a Platinum membership level combining that powerful recruiting program for the *Mind Gold* news as well as the *PowerPointer's Page* recruiter-level program for a single price that was low enough that he and his customers could afford it, and still pull out a chunk of money every month to put it directly into advertising, much as his early co-ops we were doing. At the Platinum level, they could pool a lot more money and thus have a much bigger budget than pooling just 8-10 people together. **Everybody would get leads — that would more than cover what they were paying every month for the membership.** Some of his recruiters have participated in ad pools and ad co-ops and done other marketing to promote their businesses, Alan tells me, and in many cases those commissions just at the $195 level have added up pretty quickly. Plus, they've got a nice list they can reach through Alan's system just by sending him an e-mail twice a month — whereupon Alan's system sends an e-mail to their list automatically. While this may cost a bit, it's still much cheaper, in the long run, than the typical e-mail marketing method of setting up your own servers, buying software, and actually spending the time to set up, write, and send those e-mail messages.

Now, you may be wondering, "Why would Alan do this?" Well, he's not in it just for the good feelings, although you can bet that's a factor! First off, while his programs are an excellent value, you'll still pay $1,795 each to get involved in both the *PowerPointer's Page* and *Mind Gold* recruiting programs. And here's the second reason: Though he's paying recruiters that $100 commission for the people who buy the $195 package, he's getting the other $95 from everyone. **So naturally he wants everyone to do well — because it's in his own self-interest.**

He's not doing this because he's an altruist. I think that's the sincerest form of help — assistance whereby the persona helping you also profits. That's a very powerful motive. I would strongly suspect *anyone* who says they're trying to help you just because they're a Good Samaritan.

In Alan's case, it's another instance of a rising tide lifting all boats, as they say. Alan has built a system that raises the tide for him as well as all of those who get involved; the higher it rises, the better off he is. All you have to do is swing your boat in the harbor and hook up to the dock — and he's made that very easy to do, too.

One of the things that Alan does with his program is to pare down the mailing lists as people become unresponsive. **There's no point in sending mail to people who just aren't ever going to buy from you.** Let's be realistic here: if you've got 200 names on a list and they haven't bought from you in six months or a year, they're getting cold. They dry up for many reasons. People die, they move, or they get out of the market for one reason or another. Maybe they simply change their e-mail address, so the e-mail bounces. That's no good. In Alan's system, he prunes them occasionally for his users — but he also continually adds new names to the list, which is crucial. **Whatever system you're using to build your list, you should *always* be bringing new leads and customers in with your front-end marketing, so that you can replace those who become inactive for some reason or another.** Otherwise, the pond will dry up. It may take a while, but it *will* dry up.

I can't over-emphasize the value of building and maintaining a good list, however you go about it. Believe me, **it can be done for very little money and a modicum of effort,** as Jeff Gardner has proved. You can build it even faster online using a simple but hyper-effective system like Alan Bechtold's. **I guarantee you, you'll never make any decent money if you**

don't obtain a decent list — whether you rent one or, as I'm urging you to do here, build your own. **Once you have it, maintain it scrupulously; deepen and develop your relationships with your list-members sufficiently, and you'll never hurt for money.** There's an amazing amount of financial kinetic energy, if you will, stored in a well-maintained list. All you have to do is take care of your members, and you can tap into that energy whenever you need cash.

At the risk of repeating myself, it all boils down to relationships. At our seminars, we teach people the restaurant analogy. Imagine your favorite restaurant — and of course everybody's got one. Mine is a Mexican food restaurant that my wife Eileen and I started going to more than 20 years ago. When we first started going, the little kids of the family used to serve us our chips and hot sauce, and they used to refill our iced teas and our soda pops — and now those kids run the restaurant while Dad and Mom are spending a lot of time in Mexico having fun.

Everybody's got their favorite restaurant, and the key to getting rich in the restaurant business is the simple fact that you have to have regular customers who keep coming back again and again, who invite all their friends and tell all their neighbors and relatives about the restaurant. They build a regular crowd this way. **We teach people that that's the secret to getting rich in the business opportunity market, too — and most people don't seem to understand that. Somehow, they just don't make the connection.**

Maybe this is because a plate full of enchiladas is more tangible, in many ways, than a moneymaking program. I suppose it can be hard to make that transition in your mind. But what you should focus on here is the fact that **this is really is about connecting with other people.** Let's use my favorite restaurant as an example. You get such phenomenal service that you want to go back; and not only do you want to go back, but you want to spread the word — and word-of-mouth marketing can be amazingly valuable.

Now, in the business opportunity market, there are a lot of scam artists and schemers — a lot of people who are trying to prey on people's dreams of financial independence. **In this type of market, your relationship with your customers is very important, because your reputation is always on the line.** If you've got a bad reputation, believe me, word travels very quickly. People are always more happy to beat somebody down, and complain, argue, and whine than they are to tell people about a good experience. Always keep that at the back of your mind, as I do. **I always know that whenever I deliver something I have to *over* deliver,** because when somebody gets that opportunity I want them to have such a *WOW* experience that they not only want to write to us and say *I love this, this is great*, but they want to tell other people about it.

That's how you build a great reputation and get a high conversion rate like Jeff's. *That's* how you build a strong business. That's the flipside to the scam artists you see on *20/20* and *60 Minutes*. There are companies in this market delivering so much value that their clients and customers absolutely love them. These are the companies that are really helping people — and that's where *you* want to be. So don't dare think it's all about selling people get-rich-quick stuff that doesn't work. **This is about building a long-term business by delivering value.** Do that, and you're going to have people buy from you again and again, just as I return to my favorite restaurant again and again. You're going to have great word-of-mouth advertising, too; people are going to sing your praises if you'll just work to keep them happy this way.

And let me say again: People will be quicker to damn you than to praise you. I can recall going to new restaurants and getting excellent food and service and being very happy — but then I didn't tell anybody. Oh, I would have if they'd asked, but they didn't. But you can bet that if I'd had a bad experience (especially service-wise), I'd have told the restaurant manager and five or six other people. **Bad experiences travel a lot faster than positive ones, which is why you have to over-deliver to your customers, doing things above and beyond their normal expectations.** Create a positive experience, a fun experience, a profitable experience for your clients, and make them want to talk about you in a positive way. Do that, and you'll never have to worry about the negatives.

You can't make everyone happy, but you can ensure that the happy people are many times more numerous than those who aren't. You've got to hope that those you've made happy will talk about it, and tell all their friends. Now, in this marketplace, telling all their friends probably doesn't mean talking to their family about it, because their family probably doesn't buy the same kinds of products and services they're buying. But it does mean that any time they're on a discussion board on the Internet, they can back you up. You can use them as a testimonial, too. **Because there are so many con artists and criminals out there, when you deliver real, honest-to-goodness value, you'll shine like a diamond in the dirt.** People will want to grab onto you and continue to do business with you, because compared with the other people in the same market, you're simply a gem. Receiving value well beyond their expectations will quite simply blow their minds.

So commit yourself to delivering the highest quality and value to your customers, in the best possible way! That's the key to making a six or seven figure income every single year.

RULE TEN:

Three Foundational Skills

You know, I wish somebody had told me 30 years ago that making money was a *skill*. Because that's exactly what it is: **it's something that you can learn.** It's not a talent or instinct that's inborn in certain special people; **no, anyone of normal intelligence and common sense has the potential to learn to make money.** It's something that you can develop and hone. **And it's fueled by desire:** The more you want it, the more you're going to be willing to work for it. In the beginning, when you don't have a lot of skill, that desire will keep you in the game. It'll keep you moving forward. It'll keep you getting up every time you get knocked down, and it'll help you get past all the initial adversities and setbacks you're going to face along the way as you develop your skills.

Once you do develop them, from that point forward you have a tremendous power to do incredible things. Others who watch you do these things will say, "Man, that person is blessed! They've got some special abilities." Well, you *do* have a special ability—but it's a skill. It's something that you *learned*. **You developed it along the way; you weren't born with it.** There's a myth that people who accomplish great things in life are somehow blessed. Sometimes they do have some natural ability; but for the most part, they developed themselves every step of the way. They worked very hard to get where they are, so don't

235

buy into that idea that some people are born with it and some people aren't.

If you really want something, if you're willing to do whatever it takes to get it, the question is not, "Will you make it?" but "How much will you make and how fast will you make it?" and "What will you have to go through on the way?" This is especially true when you're talking money. **You have to be willing to endure some hard times and work like a maniac. That's what makes it all worthwhile when you ultimately get what you want.** So I want you to think about that: all the adversity, all the setbacks, all the pain and problems and disappointment that you have to go through on the road to riches. When you finally do get those riches, that's when you appreciate it the most.

So be willing to pay the price. **Be willing to go through the adversity. As long as your desire is intense, as long as you want it so bad you're willing to do whatever it takes, then when you get there, you're going to love yourself that much more.** You're going to feel that much more proud of yourself when it finally *does* come together. Then, when all of the people around you say that you got lucky, you can just give them a wink and a smile. You're never going to change their attitudes, but you'll know in your heart that luck had very little to do with it. Whatever luck you had you created for yourself.

In this chapter, I'm going to discuss three foundational skills you absolutely must put into play, with great desire, in order to succeed in our business. **These are all Direct Response Marketing (DRM) skills, and they're not just a good idea— they're a necessity.**

At some point or another, most people think deeply about what they're going to do to earn a living. Many people have useful skills, and they turn those skills into businesses of one kind or another. Consider your local service businesses. For example, someone who is a good mechanic, who has the *skill* of fixing cars might decide to open a shop on Main Street. Or let's say someone is a trained plumber, whose skills involve knowing how to fix a broken toilet. These are businesses where someone has developed a *skill*, and is offering that skill to the public. Some of those businesses are successful; some aren't. Some are here today and gone tomorrow, while other ones last many years.

So there are all these skills out there in the marketplace— **but one thing you rarely see discussed is the *skill* of marketing, the skill of being able to bring in new customers and do more repeat business with your existing customers.** That's a skill most business owners and managers lack, frankly. In this chapter, I'll challenge the way you think about skills in general, because we tend to think only about the skills related to whatever we do or sell in our businesses, or the services we provide. **We don't think about marketing as being a skill, and about the skills required to be a good Direct Response Marketer.**

In any case, in any business, you've got to bring in the customers somehow; therefore, **marketing skills should be among the most important assets of any business owner,** because if you can't bring in customers, then the specific skill set relating to your business just isn't going to provide for you. It all comes down to the marketing. In this case, I'm teaching Direct-Response Marketing; so the skills I'll discuss here in Chapter 2 will be the three basic skills directly related to making the most money as a Direct Response Marketer.

According to the dictionary, the noun "skill" means "proficiency, facility, or dexterity that is acquired or developed through training or experience." There's a secondary definition as "an art, trade, or technique; particularly one requiring use of the hands or body." In this case, they're talking about skills related to labor. I think the first definition is especially apropos here. **When applied to Direct-Response Marketing, then, a skill is simply proficiency, facility, or dexterity that is acquired or developed though training or experience in Direct-Response Marketing.**

Note that this says nothing about having to go to school to learn the skill. It doesn't say that a skill is acquired or developed through getting a four-year degree at a university—though it can be. It doesn't say you have to read a book to pick up a skill. **A skill is developed through training**—which, admittedly, could be through books. But it could also be gained by attending seminars, participating in coaching, or via direct experience practicing the skill. Someone who knows nothing about Direct-Response Marketing can throw themselves into it and, through experience, become skilled. So it's not about a university degree; **you can acquire or develop a skill in many ways.**

And the learning of the skill isn't sufficient, either. One of my favorite quotes is, "You can't learn how to ride a bike at a seminar." **The point is that you've got to get out there and get some experience.** Many times it means getting knocked down repeatedly, whereupon you get back up. You have to endure adversity and setbacks in acquiring or developing any skill; your first few tries aren't going to be as good as your later attempts.

Let me use an example from my own background. Early on, our mentor, Russ von Hoelscher, took my wife Eileen and I by the hand and showed us how to turn our initial success into a real, long-term success. I would often call him up, excited as a little kid in a candy store. I'd say, "Russ, I've got this great idea…" and proceed to go on for about 10 minutes of non-stop talking. And then he would pause for dramatic purposes, and all of a sudden he'd say, "Won't work." I would get so angry! Time after time I'd give him my best ideas for making money, only to have him tell me it wouldn't work. I would always say, "What do you *mean* it won't work?"

And then he'd proceed to tell me exactly why it wouldn't work; and I would be thinking, "Who are you to say whether it will work or won't work?" When I would protest he'd remind me that he had over 20 years experience, and I was just getting started. The punch line is this: nowadays, now that *I* have more than 20 years experience myself, people come up to me at our seminars and say, "Hey, T. J., I have this great idea!" And then I'll listen to it, and before they even talk for 30 seconds or a minute, I'll know that it won't work, and I'll know why it won't work. Could I be wrong? Of course. **The only real way you can know if something is going to work or not is by testing it. Otherwise, you learn through experience whether something is going to work or not.**

With time and experience, you can get a pretty quick read on whether an idea has potential or not. Maybe it's already failed for you, so you know it can't work. Now, that's not to say that there aren't going to be challenges with any idea, or that a certain business ultimately will or won't succeed, because sometimes there are forces at work greater than any of us could ever control on our own. Sometimes you have a great business idea, and when it just doesn't work you're left dumbfounded. And then there are other times where you think an idea is so stupid that it could never work—and it brings in millions of dollars! **So it's not a universal truth, but there *are* simple formulas you can use to decide whether or not an idea has merit.** Similarly, by drawing on your experience, you can quickly look at a product or service and you can tell whether it has potential or not. Which is why, as part of our business, we look at hundreds of business opportunities on an annual basis. It's easy to tell which ones have potential—and they're rare.

We do workshops and seminars for our clients on a regular

basis, so we're standing in front of them regularly—unlike some consultants, who deal with clients on the phone and rarely have any face-to-face contact. **And you know, it's really hard to look someone in the face when they're really excited about an idea... and then to have to tell them it won't work,** like Russ did to me all the time back at the beginning. I try to break it to them gently, of course.

The point is, once you've got the skill in place, it doesn't take very long to recognize good or bad ideas. That's something that comes with time. It's something like the way a veteran musician recognizes good music or bad music; he's got an acquired ear for it. He can tell right away whether something has potential, whether it's got that right combination of things that could make it work.

Now, admittedly, some people do have special abilities in things like music, or they're predisposed to being better at some things than others. For example, no matter how much I want to be a good singer, I'm not likely to become great no matter how hard I try. I know this because I *did* try. I was in a rock band with four or five other people that came and went one summer. We learned 30-some songs and only played a couple of gigs, but it was a great experience. I wanted to be one of the background singers. I played drums, but I also wanted to sing in the band. And no matter how hard I tried to convince the rest of my bandmates that I could be a good background singer, they never let me sing background... ever. No matter how much I practiced, no matter how much I performed for them, they never would let me ever do it in front of anybody but them. So yes, there are some natural abilities here that, no matter how much you try to develop them, won't turn into much. That's why I confine my singing to the shower. **But learning to make money in Direct-Response Marketing? Just about anyone can develop that skill.**

Before I reveal the three foundational skills of Direct-

Response Marketing, I want to say one more thing. **There are four different levels that we all go through as we develop any skill or any ability.** I think it's important to know them. **The first is what we call "unconscious incompetence."** It simply means that you don't even know that you don't even know. **You're totally blind; you don't even understand anything about it.** There are a lot of businesspeople out there who are just following the follower. They're doing everything the way that their competitors are doing it. Many don't even do any advertising. They're completely ignorant about Direct-Response Marketing, and they don't even know what they don't even know.

The second stage is called "conscious incompetence." You still don't really know how to do it on your own, but you do know that you're beginning to learn some things. You're waking up to a whole new world, and you're starting to become aware of all the things you don't know. That's a little overwhelming, so **most people never get past that stage.** They get frustrated. They get confused. They quit.

Those who continue to push on and break past those barriers of frustration and confusion get to the third level: "conscious competence," where they can now do it (whatever "it" is). You're fairly good at doing it... sometimes. You have moments where you're great at doing it. You're still working hard. You're still going through periods of real frustration. It's still difficult to do it at times, but at least you're getting the job done. And at least you're not stuck in that second level that most people never get beyond.

Usually, unfortunately, you stay in that third level for a long time. I had to stay in that third level of Direct-Response Marketing for years—I don't even want to tell you how long, because I might discourage you! But I was definitely in that third level for a while... *and I still am sometimes*, despite the fact that I've been doing this for 20 years now. But mostly I'm in the fourth level, and this is the goal. **The fourth stage of learning anything new and becoming skilled at it is what we call "unconscious competence." That's where you do it without even thinking.** That's where it becomes natural. It becomes a part of you.

I think that once again, music is a good example here. When somebody first starts out playing the guitar or the piano, they've got to learn their chords. I took piano lessons for eight years just so I could learn some basic structure of how the chords all work together in the scales, and that type of thing. There are certain things you have to learn when it comes to music; you can't just sit down and just start rockin' out. (Well, some people can, but they're freaks of nature.) Most of us have to make a lot of mistakes along the way. **You learn it slowly, until finally, after playing long enough, you become fluent with it.** The people who are the most committed are the ones who make it. Bruce Springsteen, who is one of my favorite musicians, only took several years. But for those three years that it took him, he locked himself into a bedroom (basically) and he had absolutely zero social life. He just stayed in his bedroom for three years practicing, until finally he got good enough to perform in front of other people. So, yes, if you practice long enough, eventually you can get out there and do it without even thinking. **That's where all the creativity and joy happens— the passion, the fulfillment, the creativity, the fun! That's where it's all worth it. That's your payday.**

Sports are similar. Think of a football game. There's a defender down in his stance. Maybe he's a lineman and the ball is getting ready to be hiked; his job is to sniff out the ball and make the tackle or whatever. Well, in football (especially at the professional level) the athletes are so good that everything has to be reactionary. It has to happen instinctively—that is, as a quick, unthinking reaction to the action taking place opposite you. So if you're a defensive lineman and the quarterback snaps the ball, you don't have time to stop and think, "Okay, now, let's see... in this scenario I want to try to go right and stop him from passing." By the time you think, you're too late! The game happens so fast that if you don't just react to what you're seeing instantly, based on instinct and what you've learned, the play is already over—and the running back who got the handoff is already beyond you and down the field.

In business it's much the same way, though it may not happen quite so fast. **You want to be in a position where you just do what you know needs to be done without analyzing the playbook first.** You want to have it so ingrained in your thought processes that it's a part of the way you think, so that when you know that you need to advertise, you don't have to read a book about advertising. You just know the strategies; they're in your head. You've developed that skill. If you need to write a sales letter, you've got the skill of writing sales copy down, and you know how to do it.

Now, you may want to hone that skill, or you may want to do some more research; you may even want to look at some models. You may want to take a glance at your swipe file, in other words, and see if you can find some strategies that you can adapt to your needs. That's just being a smart marketer. The basics are already there. They're a part of your ingrained thought process. **You don't have to study up to figure out the right play. You don't have to figure out what your next move is, because you just know instinctively. It's a part of how you think.** When you can get to that level, that's when you know you've got that skill down pat.

Chris Lakey tells a story about how he took Spanish in high school—all four years of high school—and he remembers something his Spanish teacher used to say: "If you dream in Spanish, that's how you know you've mastered the Spanish language." If you had to try to figure out what the right word was, then you hadn't mastered it yet. But if you know the Spanish language well enough that you dream in it and you're thinking subconsciously in the language, then you're fluent; you've got that skill down. For Chris, it was Spanish; it could be any other language you're trying to learn.

In Direct-Response Marketing, if you don't have to stop and try to think about what the rule is— if you just know the rule, and it's in the top of your mind because you've acquired that skill—that's how you know that you're finally at the place where you possess the required skills. Anything less than that, and you're somewhere else along that learning curve. That's not a bad thing, as long as you're moving and making progress. **But the idea is to master that skill so well that it's just a part of who you are and how you think.** That's when you can just hear an idea and know if it's good or not, just from the way it sounds.

Again, you're not right all the time—and testing is the only way to know for sure. Some of the ideas we didn't think were going to work all that well, or that we weren't too sure of, turned out to be our biggest hits ever. So it's not an absolute, but for the most part experience *is* everything, as long as you continue to learn and you're not just living the same year of experience over and over again.

Okay, let's move on and get those three skills out into the open. I'll give them all to you first, and then go over them one at a time. **SKILL #1 is the ability to generate massive quantities of the very best prospects for whatever it is you're selling.** It's all the things you do to get the best prospects in your market to come to *you* rather than your competitors. There's a skill to that, and I'm going to talk about the basics behind it.

SKILL #2 is your ability to convert those prospects into

customers, and earn a profit very quickly through a series of sequential follow-up steps. So in the first skill you're getting the best prospects to come to you, and then you're converting the highest percentage of those people into immediate buyers so that you can make a quick profit. You're doing that through systematic follow-up marketing.

SKILL #3 is the ability to extract the largest possible profit from each customer for the longest possible period of time. This has to do with your relationship with these people — building a bond with them, a friendship where people *want* to come back and keep doing business with you.

Let's talk about **Skill #1** first: getting the very best prospects to come to you. **This requires an intimate knowledge of who those people are to begin with.** Where can you reach those people? What mailing lists will reach them? What magazines or other media can you advertise in to reach them? When you determine that, what do you say to them? What kinds of offers will appeal to them the most?

In addition to an intimate knowledge of who those people are, **this also requires an intimate knowledge of the marketplace that you want to reach.** The good news is, thanks to the wonderful world of the Internet, it's never been easier to gain that knowledge. At M.O.R.E., Inc., we use the Internet to enter markets that are totally new to us. I can't imagine *not* having this tremendous resource tool available, because it makes everything we're doing so much easier. **We can get most of the information we need by studying the companies that are already selling to the marketplace we want to sell to.** What kinds of messages are they using? Who are they targeting?

Of course, the more you look at all this new information, the more confusing it can get; you have to learn how to live with that at some level. You have to make it your friend. Confusion is part of the process. Frustration is part of the process. **Just deal with it, accept it, and learn how to live through it—because you also learn a lot, too.** At first, you just see a lot of different people doing a lot of different things; but soon you start to see certain patterns, certain common denominators. **You begin to understand things you weren't able to understand before—** just as a musician can listen to a song and can tell you which key it's in, and identify the chord progressions. Just like somebody who's very familiar with a specific genre of music can tell you which influences that band follows. Eventually, you too will develop a sixth sense—an intuitive knowledge of your field. **It all comes from experience, but is a part of willingly subjecting yourself to and throwing yourself into the subject.**

This is where it all starts with Direct-Response Marketing—the ability to generate massive quantities of the very best prospects for whatever you're selling. There's a lot wrapped up in this statement, because this isn't just the ability to get big numbers of prospects to raise their hand and request information from you; **they've got to be the *right kinds* of prospects.** That's why I emphasize "the very best prospects," not just any prospect. Anybody can go to the phone book and compile a list of people, but that list will be useless. To really profit, you have to develop the skill of generating massive quantities of the very best prospects for whatever it is that you're selling. **You start by knowing who your customers are and by learning exactly what they want to get.**

You might say, "Well, I don't have any customers yet; I'm just getting started." Well, if you don't already have customers, just imagine that you do, and think about your product and who's most likely to buy it. Put yourself in your business five or ten years from now, when you have scores or hundreds of customers. Who buys from you over and over again? What are they responding to? **What makes them want to buy, not just**

the first time but over and over again? That knowledge will fuel your ability to develop this skill.

Having the ability to generate massive amounts of customers is entirely dependent on knowing who your prospects are, and knowing why they respond to you in the first place. **You've got to create offers they want to buy.** If you have an offer that you think does a good job of selling your product or generating and building a mailing list, **but it's not written to attract the right kinds of people, then either you'll attract the wrong kinds of people, or you won't attract anybody at all.** Either is a bad scenario.

Chris Lakey recently mentioned to me that he was having a conversation with one of his sons about the simple economics of television and radio advertising. They were listening to the radio, and the boy was asking how radio ads worked, and why people chose to advertise on the radio. He was baffled by the fact that the same advertisement could cost two different prices, depending on where it was run. Chris was telling him how expensive it was to run an ad during the Super Bowl. That was an amazing thought to his son: that a 30-second commercial could cost millions! That's because you can advertise during the Super Bowl and know you're reaching a huge marketplace. Pretty much *everybody* watches the Super Bowl. On the other hand, maybe those aren't the right kinds of people. **It doesn't do you any good to build a mailing list of people who aren't likely to do business with you.**

Instead, you could spend tons less and advertise in a magazine that reaches *just* the readers that you know are the most likely kinds of people to be on your customer list. See, it's a piece of cake to compile lists if you're just looking for large numbers. But finding large numbers of the very best prospects... that's a little more difficult. **So at the beginning, don't focus so much on the large part; focus on just building a list of the**

best prospects you can find. I could give you example upon example of people who've made huge amounts of money with small numbers of people on their mailing list, including the colleague I talked about in the last chapter, Jeff Gardner.

So it doesn't always take large numbers, but you do, ultimately, want to build a big list. All it takes to get started is that first customer; then you get your second one. And from your second one, get your third and so forth. Eventually you'll build a good-size mailing list. The quantity will come as you continue to develop your marketing skills, and as you continue to do more and more business and bring in more prospects. **From that best prospect list will come the second skill, which is the ability to convert those prospects into customers.**

I once lost over $100,000 very quickly because my best friend bought a pest-control business, and I had money invested in it, too—so I proceeded to go out there and spend a lot of money on advertising and marketing, thinking that I understood the marketplace. My first business was a carpet cleaning business, and since with carpet cleaning I knew that we were selling to housewives, I thought I understood the pest-control business, too… and so I proceeded to waste money because I *didn't* understand the business. That was 10 or 12 years ago. Now I know a lot more about the pest-control business than I did them, so let that serve as an example to you.

I think that in the beginning, especially, you should go with the markets that you understand the most—the ones where you're already a very good customer. Think about that: In what marketplace are you already buying a bunch of stuff right now? Get into that same marketplace, and start selling to the people who have a lot in common with you. **In your ability to understand yourself, and what it is that causes you to buy, you'll gain a tremendous head start into understanding the mindset of the typical buyer.** That was our secret with Direct-

Response Marketing. For years, I sent away for every single money-making plan and program I could get my hands on, so I was already a customer of that marketplace. When it came time to get involved in the marketplace ourselves, I already had a good, intimate knowledge of the average customer, because I was one.

The second foundational skill of Direct-Response Marketing is the ability to turn your prospects into customers right away, for the most profit possible. You do that through crafting a good offer. How well you do that comes with your knowledge of the marketplace, of course, **but what you really need to do is give people what they want the most.** So many people think that just because they get all excited about something, other people are going to get excited about it, too; and that's true, in some cases. But for the most part it isn't. **So find the competitors who are doing the very best in your marketplace, the companies that are making the most money possible, and then do what they're doing.** Sell similar things. Get your feet wet, get some experience, and develop the necessary skills. Make some money, and put it in the bank. Then, in time, you can try new things.

To explain this concept to people at seminars, I draw a little triangle and say: "This triangle represents everything you could sell to your customer. It's all within this triangle." What you want to do is focus on the very top of that triangle, the smaller percentage of the better ideas that you know they want the most. This is important for both of these first two skills. You're trying to attract the very best prospects; so you want to have something they really desire to get them to raise their hands and initially come to you, either on a free or low-cost offer. You're not asking new people to do a lot, but you do want to get them to spend some money. **The more attractive the offer is, the higher the percentage of people you convert to first-time sales.**

You've got to follow up with them. You've got to be relentless. You can't just send people an invitation to buy something from you once, and then if they don't buy, assume that they never will. No! Continue to go after those people again and again, until it becomes unprofitable to do so. **You *can't* give up on them too soon.** That should be the battle cry of Direct Response Marketers everywhere. Even seasoned marketers often get this one wrong. I know this because our colleagues often gasp when we tell them how much we follow up with our prospects. And I don't know; in some cases, it seems like we do too much following up; but in others, I think maybe we should do more. So this skill is important, because it's not enough just to build a big prospect list. **You've got to take it beyond the prospect and into the customer relationship, where someone actually does business with you.** Your business doesn't exist just to give away free stuff and build a customer list. **The ability to convert those prospects into paying customers is critical.** That's part of why you're in business: to serve your customers and earn a profit.

So what do you do to convert those prospects? Well, hopefully you've done Step #1 right and have built a solid prospect base. Now, obviously, not all of those prospects will become customers. In fact, most won't. Don't be offended when most people don't buy from you. It's just the nature of the beast. In fact, in some Direct Response models (depending on your profit margins and what you're selling) you can have 9 out of 10 people not buying, which would be a pretty good 10% conversion rate. Sometimes you can have 99 out of 100 say no. We've had models where 997 out of 1,000 say no—and we still make a profit. **You can make huge profits with most people saying no.**

So most prospects don't become customers. **But the way you convert the biggest percentage of them to customers is**

through a series of sequential follow-ups and by not giving up. If you're using direct mail (which is what we recommend) then continue to mail them. Or maybe you're using phone calls, and have a sales staff helping you close sales and convert leads. Whatever you're doing, you must do it in a systematic, sequential manner. **You send them the material the first time, then continue to send them the material again and again.** Maybe you send them new offers, new invitations—all built around the same offer that they responded to the first time. You're trying to convince as many of them as possible that they should be doing business with you. They should be sending their money to you for whatever they inquired about in the first place.

The main principle I want to make sure you understand here is that it's all based on a series of sequential follow-ups. It's not enough to invite your prospects to buy from you just once and then forget about them. **You need a system for continuing to follow up with them.** Many times, people have asked me, "Well, how do I know when to stop following up? " The easy answer is, "Whenever it's no longer profitable." Generally speaking, the more you follow up with people, the less responsive the list becomes, because you're continuing to filter out the buyers. So if you started out with 100 prospects and you've had 10 of them buy, well, those 10 are no longer in your prospect list for that product. They've already bought. But there may still be money available in the 90 who haven't responded. **So the next time you do a mailing to that 90, maybe you get two or three more orders; or maybe you don't get any.**

At whatever point it becomes unprofitable to mail to them, that's when you know it's time to wrap it up. Generally speaking, most people give up way too soon. Although it's not universal, in our model of marketing we can safely run 6-12 weeks of follow-ups, where we're mailing a couple of times a week to our prospects. And we'll continue to make that profit down the line, as we remind them that they still haven't done business with us. Your model might be different; you might not have the profit margin to sustain that intense a follow-up campaign, but you've got to do the numbers and look at your model to determine that. **Just know that the principle here is sound.**

So **Skill #2 could be summed up as, "Don't give up on your prospects too soon."** If you can acquire the skill of patience, you'll be rewarded with increased profits *and* an increased customer base, which sets up the third skill of doing business with them on an ongoing basis. In other words, **if you're giving people what they want, and your products or services deliver on your promises and really do help people, be relentless.** With that as your premise, you should do everything possible to sell your products. Do whatever it takes to make the sale. Don't pussyfoot around. Just get out there and be totally relentless. Don't quit until you have to.

The third foundation skill of Direct-Response Marketing is the skill of building a relationship with your customers for the longest possible period of time. I'll give you a couple of keys on how to accomplish this. **First of all, people want to do business with other people they like and trust and have already done business with successfully before.** All things being equal, given the choice people will always choose to do business with somebody they've already given their money to, someone who has treated them well and whom they feel a bond with and whom they trust and feel connected to.

The second key is this: You have to remember that people are, for the most part, insatiable. Insatiability is like a bottomless pit that can't be filled. This factor is more pronounced with certain markets, of course, but for the most part people just want to continue to buy. Oftentimes a purchase becomes more fuel for the fire, in that it makes them want more. **In other words, the more they buy, the more they *want* to buy.** You may have seen it in yourself. Usually, you don't stop with just one purchase. If you're interested in a certain subject, if you're moving in a certain direction with your life, you usually just continue to buy more and more of the associated products.

To maintain this level of insatiability in your own customers, you've got to take good care of them. I like to use the restaurant analogy to describe this concept, because it's so appropriate. No matter what business you're in, you've got to think of it as a diner in a small town. You want, and need, the same customers to come back and eat again and again. That metaphor is appropriate to all businesses, because all businesses make their biggest profits by doing repeat business with existing customers.

I mentioned earlier in this chapter that we're preparing to move into some exciting new areas. But as part of our overall business plan, we're also thinking about our current customers—people who already like us, trust us, and want to do more business with us. Although we're striking out in new directions, we're asking ourselves, **"What can we do so that the people we already have relationships with can come along with us? What kinds of things can we put together for them?"** Any business that doesn't do that is foolish. You're losing money that could and should be yours if you're not thinking about your existing customers. *Always* **focus on that.**

This third foundational skill is where your long-term profitability really comes into play. Here's an unfortunate fact about Direct-Response Marketing that some people are afraid to tell you, because they don't want to mention pitfalls or the possible negatives: **Direct-Response Marketing is expensive. In some businesses it's more expensive than others.** Now, there are less-expensive ways to do direct response, but they're not as effective. **So the way you make long-term profits through Direct-Response Marketing in your business is with Skill #3: the ability to extract the largest possible profit from each customer over the longest possible period of time.**

Those people who try to build a business around one-time sales... well, either they're selling to a marketplace they don't believe in, looking for a quick buck, or they just don't understand good Direct-Response Marketing—**because *it's not enough* just to acquire a lead and then turn that lead into a one-time sale. The ultimate purpose of all of this is to develop a relationship with your prospects and customers.** That's one of the reasons you'll hear Direct-Response Marketing also referred to as Relationship Marketing. It's all about building a relationship with people and doing business with them repeatedly... like the restaurant example, or a coffee shop, or something like that where you've got a relationship going with people you deal with constantly.

Even if it's only a business relationship, there's nothing wrong with that. You know how it is: If you've got your favorite Starbucks or your favorite local donut hangout or a little dive downtown that you go to all the time, you walk in and the owner says, "Hey..." and you say, "Hey, Joe, how's it going?" They talk about the weather with you and you shoot the bull for a while. But you always spend money with them. That's a business relationship built on the long-term. Theirs is a relationship business. **They know you; you know them. They provide a valuable service to you and you don't mind spending money with them on a regular basis. That should happen with every Direct-Response Marketing business.** Now, you may not see your customers face-to-face all the time; in fact, maybe you never meet them in person. But you're still building a relationship that turns into something more. **It turns**

into the ability for *you* to do business with them on an
ongoing basis and to bring profits to your business through
that relationship. They get something out of it, as well,
because you're providing value to them. They're willing to
spend money with you because of that. You want to provide
value to them on an ongoing basis, so they know you, like you,
and trust you, and want to continue to do more and more
business with you. In some cases, the resulting relationship
might be a relatively short-term one that lasts a few weeks or
months. In other cases, it can last for years. **It's those
customers who provide you with ongoing profits, which is
the lifeblood of your business.**

**All three of these skills are important. They all work
together as part of a 1-2-3 punch bringing in new prospects,
turning those prospects into customers, and then ultimately
turning them into life-long customers.** One you acquire these
skills, and get them rolling all together, they can provide you
with a lifetime stream of profits for your business, no matter
what business you're in. **Your ability to develop these three
skills will be your meal ticket for life.** No matter how much
money you want to make, it's there for you—if you put these
three basic skills of good Direct-Response Marketing into play.

It's what good selling is all about. It's business building at
its best.

The Simple Copywriter's Secret That Has Made Millions

In this chapter, I'm going to introduce a simple copywriting secret that I know from experience can make you millions of dollars. **And it really *is* a secret, because most people just don't know about it — and even those who do aren't using it nearly enough.** Will it make you millions? Well, that's up to you. It all depends on how committed you are, how dedicated you are, how passionate you are, and how willing you are to do whatever it takes to master this idea and continue to use it consistently.

Let's start with the basics: **Copywriting is the ability to put words on a piece of paper, or a website, or even on an audio or DVD program to effectively sell a product or service.** The format doesn't matter; it's the words that convince people that what you have to offer is worth far more than the amount of money you're asking them to give you in exchange. **How well you use those words determines how well you make a case for whatever product or service you're promoting.** You need to communicate the fact that you're offering so much value that by the time people are finished reading your sales letter or listening to your audio program or going through your website, they just can't take it anymore.

They're excited and eager to give you the money. **If you've got the right offer in front of the right people, with a little timing and a whole lot of luck, you'll rake in the money.** Luck favors the bold; and the decision, the commitment, and the willingness to do whatever it takes to make a fortune creates its own form of luck.

Then floodgates can open and millions of dollars can come pouring in. If that sounds too good to be true, well... it *is* too good to be true for most people. I don't want to kid around here. Most people will never make millions of dollars. **And yet, if you're willing to do whatever it takes, if you're willing to master these principles, then the sky truly is the limit**. However much money you want to make, it's all out there in the bank accounts and credit card authorizations and the cash and the available lines of credit of the millions people who are looking for whatever it is you want to sell them. **Using the secrets and strategies I'm sharing in this book, you can unlock the vault.** You can get those people to give you their money in exchange for what you're offering.

Success isn't going to find everybody. **It's a reality of life that most people are going to keep doing what they're doing rather than reach out and grab success, or even reach out and grab the first rung on the ladder.** There are all kinds of opportunities available. In America, we have certain freedoms, and one of those is the freedom to succeed—or the freedom to fail. **You can be just about anything you want to be.** From a young age, you can choose to excel in music. Constant practice gets you down that road towards success. If you want to be an athlete you can decide at a young age to be involved in all kinds of sports. Your parents can steer you in the right direction, and when you get a little older you can determine what to do yourself; you can decide you're going to be in the gym three hours a day, or however long it takes. You can excel in that direction, and you can set yourself up to be in the best position to make it to the NFL if that's your goal, or play in the NBA, or be a professional golfer. You can also choose to be a professional couch potato! **That's one of the great things about America. If you want it, you can have it... no matter what it is.**

People all across this great nation are making decisions, right now, that will have a lasting impact on them. No matter whether you're young or old or in between, **the actions you're taking determine whether you're on the road to success,** or whether you're on some other road. **That other road could lead to complacency or just inaction.** But *you* determine that, in large part—no matter where you came from, no matter your socioeconomic background, no matter where you live, no matter what kind of family you grew up in. **It's all up to you and your determination. The things you're doing today will put you on the road to where you want to go; or you'll take some other path by default.**

Because you see, we're all going somewhere. If you don't choose a way, it doesn't necessarily matter whether you "want" to go a certain direction or not. You could say, "Well I'm not trying to be a couch potato," but your actions may determine that that's what you are. Or, you could say, "I'm not trying to be a millionaire." Well, it looks like you are to me, because it seems like you're trying really hard to be successful! **We *all* determine which path we're on—and unfortunately, most people choose the lazy way because success doesn't come easily.** It requires a lot of hard work, a lot of dedication to the craft of entrepreneurship, to writing sales copy, to learning how to be an entrepreneur. **It takes determination. It's a long road that can take a lifetime to achieve. Success is rarely an overnight thing, so it's not just a matter of arriving.** It's not just a matter of being successful and then deciding that you're there and you can take it easy at that point. **It's constant pedal to the metal.** It's constant full throttle, doing everything you can to be as successful as you want to be. **You can determine how much money you want to make, how successful you want to be, how many hours you want to put in.**

It's sort of like turning the knob up and down on a radio; or better yet, turning up the gas on a stove. If you want to make more money, you can turn it up, generate more heat and light. If you want to sit back and enjoy an easier life, and maybe just live off your earlier investments, you can turn the knob down and keep the money coming in... but not quite as much. **To a large degree, it's all based on what you're willing to do to make the money you want to make, and only you can determine that.** We're here to provide the tools, to help you with the resources, to provide information that you need to succeed... but we can only take you so far.

So here I am, ready to provide you with some great information, some great resources on writing sales copy, and how to become a master at the art of putting words in print or online that make people want to respond enthusiastically to your offers. **I'm here to help you as much as I can, as much as you're willing to be helped — but you have to decide to reach out and grab it!** The opportunity is here. The time is now. What you'll do with it is up to you, but let's get going!

What I'm sharing right now is simply entitled The Simple Copywriter's Secret That Has Made Millions. This is a method that I borrowed from my colleague and friend Chris Hollinger, who switched from school teaching to entrepreneurship a few years back. **He would use this set of exercises to practice his ability to write compelling copy.** I wanted to start from scratch like this for people who are saying, "I'm just not a good writer. I've never done this kind of thing." I want you to start building some practices and strategies, and start getting better and better until you reach the point to where you can write sales letters and ads that get people's attention—ads that generate money!

This simple copywriter's secret starts with writing headlines; then you write the copy that goes below the headline. That sounds simple, but it's a bit more complex than you might realize. One of the things I want to stress is that **writing as many headlines as you can is great practice. The headline is the most important ingredient of any advertisement.** It's the ad for your ad, if you will. It gets the reader's attention and pulls them into the copy. The headline gives you ideas and themes for your body copy; and **the headlines that don't make the grade can be used as sub-heads and body copy for your ads and sales letters.** They may not be good enough to make the main headlines, but they're still powerful enough to build your sales material.

Now, when it comes to the opportunity market, a lot of times we use fear and greed as motivators. When I first started, I would sit down and I would read as many different long-form sales letters selling as many different programs, opportunities, products, and services as possible. Many marketing experts have started out that way (including Chris Hollinger). Sometimes I would copy them; sometimes I'd would study them thoroughly, and tweak their headlines. **It really *does* start by simply writing those headlines.** You'll get a good feel for how to build fear, greed and motivation into your headlines, and you'll also get better at writing them.

If you have an idea for a product, service, or opportunity, sit down and write as many headlines as you can that illustrate your main selling points or benefits to your prospects. **Then go back and choose the best ones—the most powerful, the most hard hitting, even the most provocative. Those headlines will get people's attention. Keep them simple, keep them compelling, and make big promises.** Don't be afraid to go over the top. I can guarantee that you can very rarely be too audacious. So start writing headlines today. It takes dedication and practice to become a good copywriter. **It won't happen overnight, and it's not going to happen as if you've just turned on a switch. But that *can* happen, with time.** You're going to get better at it, you're going to get more confident at it, and it'll lead to more compelling headlines that get people's attention.

As I was preparing this chapter, I was looking at my swipe file—my collection of great copy written by other people. **Everyone should have a good swipe file full of proven headlines and copy.** I came across one that I wanted to share with you to show how, in this market, a great headline can get someone's attention. This one's from my friend and mentor Russ von Hoelscher. It's a good headline to start practicing with, to see how many different ways you can change it, because it's applicable to many different opportunities. Here's the headline: "Do you need a money miracle right now?"

Now, think about that in terms of the opportunity market and this economy we're experiencing. There's a language to writing copy, and there are plenty of people who have gone before you. **All the answers you're looking for are already out there, so you don't need to come up with anything original in the beginning.** You just need to work on all the old themes and adapt them to your needs. The best way you learn anything is to learn by doing, **so simply take excellent headlines that other people have written and rewrite them over and over.** That's the same way a musician learns how to play an instrument. They don't start out by writing their own songs; they start by playing other peoples songs first. They learn the chords and chord progressions; some learn how to read music, some don't. Either way, they start by playing other peoples songs' over and over, until finally they start learning how to create variations on a theme and come up with their own songs.

After doing it for over 20 years, I've probably got four or five different methods that I use to write copy, **but this method of modeling after what other people have done is one I often use, especially at the beginning of a project.** Chris Lakey and I have one of the greatest and biggest swipe file collections in Direct-Response Marketing. There may be somebody alive in this world who has a bigger swipe file than us, but if there is, we don't know of that person! Our collection is massive—I'm talking tens of thousands of pages of copy that other people have written and used effectively, and I'm not exaggerating. **We're not plagiarizing by any means, just looking at what other people have done and adapting those ideas for our market.** They act as a sort of creative spark for our own mighty fire.

This is a process where you don't even think about what you do; you just write as much as you can. The whole thinking and editing process comes later, as you're trying to decide what's best and what goes where. Don't bother with that in the beginning; just write like crazy and look for ways to re-theme existing ideas. **Then, of course, when you achieve success of your own, you can find ways to re-theme your own stuff.** When you you've been in the business for a while and you've got dozens of sales letters and ads already written, you can easily find a way to rewrite it, adding new stuff as you go along.

Here's how simple it can be. Recently, Chris and I were working on an old promotion that we'd run three or four years previously, and the headline was: "How to mail ONE MAGIC PAGE and be set for life... GUARANTEED!" It was a great headline, followed by a great sub-head: "And we can even mail the ONE MAGIC PAGE for you!" This was great promotion, and we did quite well with it. So for the new promotion, all we did was change the headline and subhead to: "How to give away a toll-free number and be set for life... GUARANTEED! And we can even give it away for you!"

This is not rocket science! It doesn't take any special brain power. **It's simply variations on a theme. You take one successful element, and change it into something else.** It's fun, it's creative, it's fulfilling, it's rewarding, and it really can make you millions of dollars. You just have to do it!

I look at headlines a lot. They're in ads I receive in the mail, they're on billboards and in email, and they're on the Internet when I'm looking at websites. News websites are a great way to study headlines. One cool thing about the Internet is that sometimes you'll see headlines change throughout the day for the same article. You can tell they're trying to figure out which headline is going to get the best readership. **I look for headlines that are not only good, but mutable; that is, ones where you can change out the copy and make it work for just about any promotion you're working on.** The headline I mentioned earlier by Russ von Hoelscher, "Do you need a money miracle right now?" is just such a headline. You can substitute some key words and change the meaning altogether. "Do you need a *health makeover* right now?" or "Do you need a *thousand dollars* right now?" or how about, "Do you need a *home loan* right now?" There are all kinds of things you could substitute here, depending on the industry you're selling to.

So you could take a headline, tweak it just a bit, change some key words, and make it fit to a specific model you're working on. If you're in the home mortgage business, someone in your market might be looking for an affordable interest rate. So, "Do you need a *3.9% interest rate* right now?" might work. Last I checked, interest rates were higher than that; so that would be an extremely appealing interest rate to someone looking at refinancing. You make the headline change, based on what your offer is. **You don't even have to limit your swipe file to ads that cater to the marketplace you sell to.**

Here's another famous headline: "They all laughed when I sat down at the piano, but when I started to play…" All you have to do is keep the "They all laughed…" part and change the rest to fit your needs. For example, "They all laughed when I said I was going to be a millionaire by the age of 35… But when the cash started rolling in…" You see how that works? **You can take a headline that doesn't even apply to your field, that wasn't originally written for your marketplace at all, and change it slightly to fit your needs.** It's still a good headline no matter what.

So be very aware of headlines, because they offer a great way to start your quest to learn how to write good sales copy. Keeping a swipe file or a similar record is so important, because you can literally plug and play the headlines. If you have a list of, say, a hundred of what you would consider really good headlines that you've collected, they can serve you well for a long time, just from making those minor changes to the key phrases. Again, consider Russ's example of, "Do you need a money miracle right now?" It boils down to, "Do you need a _____ _____ right now?" **Write this down, and think about the things in your market that your prospects want the very most. Insert different words in the blanks to try to come up with a good headline that will work in your marketplace.** Once you've got a good headline, or something you *think* is a good headline, **the next phase is to test that headline and find out if it's as good as you think it is.** Find out if your prospects respond to it, if it resonates with them.

Like I said, I'm always looking at headlines. There are headlines everywhere. **Headlines can also appear as lead stories on your local news.** They've got headlines for what they're going to talk about when they get back from their commercial break. Those are teaser copy, brief things to get you to pay attention, and there are useful nuggets of information there. You can use them to craft your own headlines, if you'll just write them down as you hear them or see them. It's easy to copy and paste right out of a website, too. Just don't steal the headlines outright, word-for-word; that's plagiarism. **Take the basic ideas, the central themes; then incorporate them in your copy, rewriting them enough to make them your own.** That can be a great foundation for sales copywriting in general.

Now, let's take a look at the copy itself. **One of the things you really want to work into your copy is a story.** That story must be emotional, simple, positive, and compelling. And I don't want you to think that this example is out of context here, because it's one of my favorite things to read and to draw inspiration from, but, quite frankly, a lot of great copywriting has a lot in common with the Bible—especially the New Testament. Speaking of emotional, simple, positive, and compelling stories: Jesus died for your sins. That's a pretty compelling promise there! **In our copywriting, we make those big promises, like salvation now—not later. It must offer hope. It must appeal to greed and fear, as I said before. It must promise people the opportunity to rise above others.**

Developing your copywriting skills is a process, not an event. It takes a lot of time, work, thinking and re-thinking, and practice. **You need to *constantly* practice writing those headlines, writing the copy, and making it simple, positive, and compelling.** It won't happen overnight. The best ideas develop after brainstorming sessions and hard work, because you absolutely have to flush out those great-selling ideas. I love the old saying, **"Genius is 99% perspiration and 1% inspiration."** You do have to put in work to be a good copywriter, but it's so worth it! Another thing that I like to point out is that **you have to sell from your heart. Build emotion into your copy, and the reader will feel it.** Being convincing and being able to convey your emotion and your enthusiasm into your sales copy makes a big difference. That comes with practice, too.

Another thing I'm always thinking about as I'm writing is this: **What are the three biggest things my prospect wants, and how can I give it to them? When you answer that question, tweak it, work it, refine it, polish it, and then shout it out as loudly as you can.** Let the people in your market hear it in the clearest and most compelling way. Your biggest task, and the most difficult sometimes, is getting all that copy to come together in a way that forces them to act the way you want them to. So start thinking about the practice that it takes to develop those messages—because, again, it's not going to happen overnight. You're going to have to build up those behaviors and attitudes by buckling down and getting to work on your headlines. Don't just throw your hands in the air and say, "Okay, I've done enough." **The more you do it, the better you're going to get!**

Persuasion is the ability to get people to do what you want them to do, or get them to move in the way that you want them to move, without them really being aware that you're doing that. The real masters of persuasion influence people without them having any real recollection or awareness that they're being influenced. That's the art and skill of all persuasion: making people feel something was their idea, not yours. Chris Hollinger tells me that when he was in college, he attended a lot of churches, checking out all the different forms of Christianity out there. He sat in on some sermons that were just electrifying... that had him all pumped up, and he loved it! And then he sat in on some sermons that just didn't resonate with him. And there's something similar there between a really good persuasive piece, and one that's not so good.

I would encourage anybody in the field to watch some of the more prominent televangelists. You can hate them, that's okay, but watch them! They didn't get that air time by accident. They are very, very good at what they do. They know how to move people emotionally. And even if you have a different faith than theirs, and you don't believe the things that they believe, you'll still find yourself being somewhat persuaded sometimes! **That's the power of** *making people feel it!* It's part of the emotion behind all persuasion. **What you say is not nearly as important as how you say it; that's the principle here.** You can take the very best sales message, the greatest sales presentation out there, but if it's delivered in a way that's stale and flat and boring, you won't make any sales. On the other hand, you can have a halfway decent sales presentation, amateurish in every way, but **if you can present it with enthusiasm and make people just feel it, if you can inspire people by the way that you deliver it, you can make a ton of money!**

Now, let's look again at this concept of focusing on those three main things that your best customers want the most. **You should** *always* **be thinking about what the people within your market really, really want.** If you're in the business of serving a certain market and somebody comes up to you and says, "What are the three main things your customers are looking for?" you ought to be able to reply immediately. If you don't have a quick answer for that, you're sabotaging your own efforts. It means you haven't been thinking about it enough. **You** *always* **have to think about it from the customer's point of view. That's part of the art of communication; that's part of the art of persuasion.**

And nothing works here as well as stories! People remember stories; they go way below the radar, which is exactly how it should be. You see, people have lots of sales resistance these days. The more sales messages people are exposed to, the thicker the layer of resistance they develop. People are better now than ever before at blocking out sales messages, so it takes more to get them excited. **They're skeptical;** it's like they're standing there with their arms crossed, not believing a word you say. **But when you start telling stories, they perk up. They'll listen to stories because they like to hear stories.** We're conditioned to that. When I was little, my mom used to rock me to sleep, telling me bedtime stories. I don't really remember so much of it, but I know that she did. We grow up with stories. That's what movies are; and we love to watch movies. Almost every movie has this theme to it: Here's a situation, and then something happens, and then at the end things have changed. **So there's a "before" and an "after" kind of thing.** Almost every movie has that theme: before and after... and something important transpired in the process between. There can be other formulas for storytelling, too, but "before and after" stories are the best, and they're the simplest and easiest to tell.

There's a story that has made us millions of dollars in the last 21 years. It just keeps working... and I'm sick of telling it. It's the story of how I used to struggle financially, how I used to send away for all these get-rich-quick programs... while my friends and family told me I was a complete moron to believe I could actually get rich. But I refused to listen and, because I stuck with it, I finally found some good programs, put them into effect, and millions of dollars came pouring in within the first five years.

Now, I just told that story in the most boring way. But in a sales environment I tell that story on Volume 10, cranked up full blast. That story has literally made us millions of dollars, because our customers all want to *be* in that story. **It's a way for me to connect with them; it's a commonality that we share.** They're always sending for these get-rich-quick programs, you see. They're the ones whose friends and family are telling them that they're crazy. They love that story! They never get tired of hearing it.

I think that there's a reason that storytelling works in salesmanship. It works no matter whether you're selling face-to-face or if you're on the phone talking to people. It works if you're writing an Internet sales letter and if you're selling in print. **No matter what format your selling is taking, storytelling can and should be a big part of your sales process.** Think about it: Storytelling is such a big part of our culture and our history. All societies have stories that have been told all throughout history. We tell stories of our ancestors who did things, and stories of current family members. When we put our kids to bed at night, we read them bedtime stories. Musicians tell stories through their music.

We talked a little already about pastors and preachers and storytelling from the pulpit, as well as storytelling in the Bible. Storytelling has been around a long, long time, and it's part of who we are. We like to hear stories. We like to tell stories. If a couple of old guys are sitting in the coffee shop, they're shooting the bull, telling stories. It's just a part of our fabric; we like to hear stories and we like to tell them. **And so when you're building relationships, which is required to make a sale, you tell stories. They go a long way toward making the sale.** And, of course, the stories can be anecdotes or little jokes. They can be parables or fables, teaching stories that aren't true but are used to illustrate a point. But some stories are real. **Some stories are "here's my history." These are the real stories—the true stories—that make up who you are.** Things like me talking about my history, and how I discovered how to make money.

I think the reason they're so successful is because the idea of telling a story is ingrained in us. It's a part of our DNA, almost. We like to hear other people talk about something they experienced or learned. It doesn't matter what the story is; we all want to hear a good one. **And stories build connections to people; a good story builds a bridge, a bond.** You start telling someone a story, and all of a sudden they're paying attention to you. **They're listening to who you are. They're finding out more about what's important to you.** They feel the emotion that comes with telling of the story, especially the personal ones—the stories that are real for you, because they're part of your real experience in life. People identify with that.

Now, this next tip is intended to help make your copy pop and to sizzle and get people's attention. **Great copywriters spend a lot of time focusing on small details, because including a lot of details in an ad or Direct Mail package can dramatically increase your sales and profits.** Separately, these details aren't that important; but added together, they can make a dramatic impact on your bottom line. I'm sure that you've seen some real dud mailing pieces—ones that didn't get your attention at all. And where did they end up? In the trash can. But you want to make your Direct Mail sizzle, and you do that by paying attention to your details. **Give it drama! Find ways to make it super exciting! Jazz it up!** Shake the prospects out of whatever stupor they're in so they'll rip open your package and look at it! It all comes down to paying attention to those details.

Look at the mailings you receive. I'm on all kinds of mailing lists, so I get all kinds of mail from all over the world for all kinds of products, services, and opportunities. I look at them all, and put some of them in my swipe file. I study the headlines; I look at the entire mail packages and ask myself, "How compelling is it? Does this piece make me want to rip it open? If so, what makes me want to rip it open? Is it the headline? Is the color? Is it the way the paper feels? What's the message I'm getting?" **When you're building a mail piece, *every aspect* of that mailing needs to be evaluated through what I call the "salesmanship prism." You need to look at every little detail.**

Take, for example, the typical lead-generation letter. Is it in an envelope? If so, does it have a great headline? Does it have great copy? Does it have great colors? Does it offer a compelling reason for someone to open that letter? Because it doesn't matter how much time you've put into that marketing piece, if the prospects don't open that envelope, you're dead in the water. (Actually, you're in the trash can.) **So look at the mail you're getting.** Quite likely you've received some mail from M.O.R.E., Inc. at some point. Look at those letters. Look at the envelopes. There's color, there are headlines, there are many compelling reasons why you need to rip it open right now! **Use that as a lesson. Evaluate what makes it so compelling. Admittedly, that takes an experienced eye, one that you have to develop if you want your mail to be opened.**

Some of the sales letters you see in your mail were written by people who've been in the business a long time and have a lot of experience. You might read those letters and be intimidated; you might say to yourself, "Oh man, there is no way I could ever write like that!" **But here's the thing: Those people didn't learn it all overnight. They worked on every detail, and they modeled their work on techniques used by other people,** just as I've talked about in this chapter. **Then they tweaked the copy until it was perfect.** They may have edited it a thousand times; you can't tell just from looking. Don't think that they just threw something together and put it out there.

Oh, and by the way, when you read a long-form sales letter, do *not* think that the person who wrote it just sat down, wrote the headline, then wrote the "Dear Friend," went straight on through the copy, and five or six hours later wrote the "Sincerely Yours," P.S., P.P.S., and all that. No way! **It never happened, not in a million years! Those long sales letters (and even a lot of short letters) are written in what we call "patchwork quilts"—a little bit of copy at a time.** That's how we've written a lot of our letters. Personally, I take little patches of this and that and blend it all together. I use the copy and paste function on my computer a lot. **I often rewrite existing copy, and I repeat myself a lot.** I'm trying to go for a sale, not win awards. I'm not trying to win anybody's respect, either, *except* that of the people who give us money. I'm trying to win their business, which is one of the reasons I use a lot of repetition. I drive those main sales points home again and again. **Ultimately, a lot of small changes equals one big result.** So just think about that, and realize that these letters are edited carefully, they're rewritten carefully, and they're also written by people who've done this so long that they really know what they're doing.

Another thing: **In order to understand other people, it helps to understand yourself.** In fact, the better you understand yourself, the better you can understand other people. That's Psychology 101. **Good marketing is just psychology and math, that's all.** You try to get a feel for what excites you. What really turns you on? What makes you respond? What makes you grab your wallet and go for the credit card and call the toll-free number, or fill out the order form and rush it back?

Once you've answered those questions, try to get beyond the emotion of it, because emotion and logic are two separate things. You could spend the rest of your life trying to understand your emotions; but the more you do, the more you know about things that turn you on, the more you can see that those are the things that turn *other* people on, too. **Just pay attention; get on the other side of the cash register.** Start looking at the sales material not from an eye of a consumer, but from the eye of somebody actually in the business, or someone who has an interest in being in the business, and try and determine what makes it successful. **The more of it you look at, the more you're going to develop the trained eye that you**

need in order to push your prospect's emotional buttons and get them to buy.

It's simple enough. If you read a thousand sales letters, you're going to be pretty smart about what makes a good sales letter or a bad one. If you read ten thousand, you're going to be even smarter! **You're going to start figuring out the formulas... and there *are* formulas.** You'll see it. Just as there are formulas for movie-making and songwriting, there are formulas for writing copy, too. **It's all pretty simple once you see the formulas, though it's not always easy.** But it's the kind of work that gives you the greatest sense of fulfillment. It's really not even work in a traditional sense; it's creative work. It's fun! It's challenging! It's interesting! And if you can just get it right, all the money that you want is out there, waiting for you.

We've got a big goal for our company right now. As of this writing, we know exactly how much money we're trying to bring in every month— and it's a huge number. Let's just say it's about twice as big as we've been bringing in every other month. But we set the goal, and we know how we're going to hit it. We're going to get a promotion going that's super-successful, something that really gets people jazzed, really gets them exited, gets them pumped up—and that's the whole key to doubling our sales. That's the key to making all the money that you want to make, too! **All the money that you want is out there for you, *if* you just put the right offer in front of the right people in the right way.**

Of course, there are other strategies that must be applied. We taught a copywriting workshop a few years ago, and both Chris Lakey and Chris Hollinger were instructors. I did a 10-step list of my top, favorite things about being a copywriter and what to learn, and only *one* of those things involved writing copy! The other nine involved specific strategies. **So you have to take good copy and put the right strategies in play behind**

274

it. When you can do that, look out, baby — because any amount of money you want can happen for you! It's happened for others; it's happening for others as you're reading this right now. **It can *definitely* happen for you!**

And let me re-emphasize here that sales copy is rarely written in one piece, all at once. But as I've mentioned before, that's usually not how it happens — not for me, and not for other copywriters I know. I'm sure there are some people who do that, but it's rare. **Most sales letters are written a little bit here, a little bit there, pieced together from fragments. Rarely is a single headline written.** A bunch of headlines are written, and then one is finally settled on. **Different parts of the letter are written at other times.** You might sit down and write some paragraphs that become the main offer, and then other parts that become filler for the middle, where you're talking about the main benefits the prospect will receive if they respond. Maybe you take some of the failed headlines and turn them into bullets, or subheads, or weave them into the text. You write all these different pieces, and eventually it comes together and looks like a sales letter.

The prospects don't see it that way. They certainly don't read them that way; nor do they analyze them from that angle. All they know is that here's an offer, and they're deciding whether or not they want to respond. They don't think about it as a marketer would. **But as a copywriter, you *have* to analyze your sales letter differently than a consumer would.** You might then put them together on sort of an assembly line, like putting together an airplane. We've got airplane manufacturers in Wichita, and occasionally you'll see trains or semi-trucks transporting these big airplane parts. You know it's an airplane part because it's obvious; big wings or the big main hollow tube will be driving down the highway. But it certainly can't fly like that! It's just a piece, a part, and yet you know that eventually, that piece is going to be welded together with all those other parts to form an airplane.

It's that way with a sales letter; with any ad, really. **You put together all the parts and you work on them a while, tinkering.** Over here you put together the order form and there you put together the headline, and somewhere else you write some bullets. You work on refining all these different things, and it all starts coming together; and in the end you've got yourself an offer, a sales letter that you can mail.

Constantly being in a state of learning, I think, is important. Think about all the other things I've talked about in this chapter: writing headlines, the art of storytelling, and things like that. These are things that don't always come easily or fast. **You'll never be an overnight success, although you can have overnight successes.** After some experience, you can craft an offer and mail it out, and all of a sudden it's wildly successful.

One great practice that you can get into right now — other than starting to compile a swipe file — is to just sit down and write. It's a good way to start. You don't have to worry about writing a whole sales letter right now; **just start writing headlines.** And maybe instead of just keeping a swipe file, create a computer file and re-type all the headlines you see. The act of typing them will make you actively think about the words you're seeing. Then try writing your own, unique headlines. **Think about ways to mix and match some of the best headlines you've seen.** Even if you don't have an offer yet, make one up in your head. Tell yourself, "Here are some of the things my prospects want... so I'm going to start playing with some headlines for that marketplace."

Next, work on the copy. Incorporate some storytelling — write *your* story, if you like. Maybe you've never told your story before, and you don't even think about it like that, but it can be advantageous to you. Tell the story of who you are, and maybe even tell the story of who you will be. You hear people talking about affirmations and things like that all the time. Well... some of that's junk, and I don't necessarily think it's helpful. But it can be useful if you're thinking about where you want to be. So if you like, go ahead and write your story as if you've already achieved the things you want to achieve. Just don't use it in print until it's true, because you don't want to make things up. But do write your story, because it helps you think about where you've been and where you come from. If you come from a military background, write about your fight of your life when you were in Iraq, or Vietnam, or whatever your story is. Just share that story.

When you read an autobiography or a biography, or when you watch a movie about someone's life, you know that it was probably wasn't as exciting as it sounds. But they use the right words to tell the right story, to paint the right picture in the reader's or viewer's mind so that it *sounds* exciting, even if it was only marginally exciting. Practice that in your own story. **Use terms that brighten your story and make it sound as exciting as possible.** To you it might be boring... but other people may be very interested, and it can help them identify with you. Maybe you've got a story about struggling with a disease when you were a kid, and you grew up and triumphed over that illness. Share that experience in writing. That story will become a part of who you are as you begin to write sales copy, and will become valuable as you learn to put those words and experiences in print and add them to your sales copy.

Practice doing those kinds of things, and that will become the foundation for your copywriting success. This really is a skill, something anyone can acquire. You don't have to be born with any special abilities: **you just have to be disciplined, and you have to want it bad enough and be**

willing to do whatever it takes. I became the copywriter I am today because I used to watch Russ von Hoelscher do it. He'd come over, and we'd go over the copy together. I was so impressed that I said, "Man, I've got to get good at this!"

Russ inspired me. **We all need somebody to inspire us.** So let this chapter be your inspiration, until you can find a good mentor of your own to work with.

The Six-Step Million-Dollar Sales Letter Formula

In the previous Rule, I pointed out that copyrighting is based on formulas, just like almost any other skill or art. I've talked about a few in this book already. In this chapter, I'll introduce you to another: the Six-Step Million-Dollar Sales Letter Formula! **These are the six steps that you can use to write a sales letter that can make you millions of dollars.** Now, can I promise you that you *will* make millions of dollars? Absolutely not! Anybody who makes you a promise like that is lying to you.

But what I *will* promise you is that this same exact six-step formula has made us millions of dollars here at M.O.R.E., Inc. **We use this formula (or a variation thereof) on a regular basis.** We learned it from studying other sales letters by master copywriters—from doing just what I told you to do in the last chapter. **We broke down the sales letters that were making other people multimillionaires, derived this simple formula, and used the heck out of it.** It's a formula that you can use, too. **As you'll see, it can work for almost any product or service.** I'll admit that the formula works better for some products and services than it works for others; but if you'll carefully consider these six steps, **you'll realize that copywriting really is very simple and formulaic.** It's just a set of processes that you go through.

All this will help you get on the other side of the cash register. **The more you do that, the more you'll see commonalities in how these steps are used.** That will take the mystery out of it, and will empower you to write your own sales copy. Hopefully, it will give you great confidence, so you can develop your own sales material that can, in fact, make you millions of dollars. The money's out there, in the pockets, purses, and lines of credit of tens of millions of Americans, let alone the people from other countries whom you can easily do business with nowadays. **There are *billions* of people looking for all kinds of products and services.** You can use formulas just like the one I'll tell you here to offer people such useful things that they'll gladly give you their money!

I love talking about marketing, and copywriting specifically, because it's such a vital part of the Direct Response business. Some people might try to tell you, "Ah, you don't need to know how to write sales copy." **But I think that if you're serious about being a Direct Response Marketer, you *must* learn how to write good copy.** It's one thing to have someone else write a sales letter for you once, or to use an outsourced copywriter occasionally; **But if you don't know how to write your own sales copy, you have a severe disadvantage compared with someone else who does.**

So learning how to be a good copywriter is vital if you're serious about being in the Direct Response business... or really, in my estimation, being in any business. I think that every business out there—no matter what it is, no matter whether it's online or offline, no matter whether it's someone working out of a spare bedroom in their house or they've got a retail storefront selling on Main Street, U.S.A.—can benefit from Direct-Response Marketing. **Every business can benefit by having its owner or its Marketing Director learn how to write good** sales copy.

We have 6 steps in our formula; other people may be using the same basics in writing their sales copy, but maybe they've got it down to a 5-step formula, or possibly their formula is 10 steps. You could probably expand or shrink this concept to fit whatever model you want. But the basics are here. **These six steps can help you write killer sales letters that can bring cash into your mailbox, into your e-mail box, over the phone, or however you take orders.**

Early on, Russ von Hoelscher—the man who helped us make millions of dollars initially—told us that **all it takes is one good sales letter to make a million dollars.** We've had quite a few do that for us! And then, of course, **we tend to rewrite the same sales letters over and over again, so we've had many sales letters that have generated more than a million over the years.** That's not to brag; certainly other people have made our success look pale by comparison. It's just to show that this really does work!

The FIRST STEP is this: You've got to tell people something revolutionary. It's got to be something wild, something that gets their attention. You have to make them a strong promise. Get them pumped up, and they'll get interested. Make them a strong promise, or tell them about something outrageous you're about to reveal, and then go on to something else for a moment. **Here's a working headline, an example of this first step:** "I'm going to show you how to make $4,854 a day while sitting in your underwear! And I promise, you'll never have to put in more than 30 minutes a day. But first…" **Then you go on to something else. But now they're hooked!** This keeps them reading. It snaps them into attention. There's nothing new in this first step. In fact, in the late 1700s a man named Dr. Johnson said, **"The big promise is the soul of an advertisement."** That was known 300 years ago. In Step #1,

281

you're making people a big promise. It's bold! It's outrageous! It gets them excited and wakes them up!

Listen: More than ever before, people *need* something like that. **To wake people up it's got to be huge in order, because people these days feel like that they've heard and seen everything.** They feel jaded. The things that used to excite them don't anymore. They're skeptical. They doubt everything. They're immune to hype; they don't trust anything.

So your message has to cut through the clutter. **It has to be unique enough that it doesn't even *sound* like hype.** For instance, consider an opportunity that lets people save 30-70% off their grocery purchases on over 10,000 different items — with free delivery. It's all done over the Internet. They can scroll through over 10,000 discounted grocery items and pick what they want, pay, and Federal Express will bring a box to their door. Now, that's big! It's bold! It's outrageous! People will look at it and say, "What? Could this really be true?" It wakes people up, and that's what you have to do! **Your promise has to be big enough, bold enough, and unique enough that it just cuts through all the clutter out there, snaps people up, and gets their attention.**

This stratagem gets people into your letter, especially if you're writing a long-form sales letter where you want them to take a considerable amount of time to read your offer. **You make a big promise to them; you do something to get them to stop and pay attention.** This works on the Internet or by mail, but I'm thinking specifically about how, if you mail a sales letter to someone, they're probably opening their mail over their trashcan or close to their recycling bin or their shredder. You only have a few seconds to make an impression and get them to decide that your offer is worth paying any attention to. As they're flipping through their mail they see their water bill... and they put that aside. They know they've got to pay that. They see an ad for

Wal-Mart and, well, they really don't want to stop and pay attention to that, so that goes in the recycling bin. Then they get to your offer. The envelope looks promising, so they open it up and see a big headline, a big guarantee. And, of course, because you've done a good job of making sure that person is a good prospect for your offer, they see that outrageous headline on your sales letter and they stop. Maybe they were just planning on pitching it in the trash, **but they see your offer — your big, bold claim — and it stops them in their tracks.** They're looking for the big bold benefit you just promised them... and then you skip over it.

You don't reveal it right away; you jump right to something else. Pretty soon they've read to the bottom of the first page, still looking for information on that big bold promise you made them — so they turn to page 2. Soon they're on page 3, and they're into the letter, and maybe you *never* reveal the main reason or the main benefit or promise that you told them about on page 1. They have to buy your product to get that, or go to your website, or take whatever action you're trying to get them to take. **But by making that big, bold, outrageous claim or guarantee or promise in the headline, you got them to pay attention and at least take a look at your offer.** Not all of them will respond, of course, but you want them to at least take a look.

That's the purpose of Step 1. You tell them something amazing, something beyond belief, something revolutionary — something that's going to make them pay attention. **A headline that doesn't do any of those things is easily dismissed.** If someone's opening their mail over a trashcan, they're probably going to discard any message that doesn't jump out at them or make them pay attention. There's a huge difference between a bland, boring headline one that attracts people and one that makes them stop and pay attention.

For example: If you have a product for the diet industry, i.e.

for people who are looking for a miracle weight-loss plan, you want your headline to make some outrageous statement about how much weight they can lose and how easy it's going to be. Of course, you have to be strictly truthful here; you can't just make your statement up. **It has to be a factual, legitimate headline.** It can't be just something you make up to get people to stop and pay attention, or else they'll come to find out that your offer is insincere. But still, you want the headline that you're making to make some kind of a crazy, almost unbelievable, claim so that they have to read to figure out what the heck you're talking about! **You've got to get them beyond page 1 and into your offer.**

It's the same way when you're marketing online. People are searching for whatever your offer is, and the headline they see when they visit your website has to get them to stop and pay attention, to keep reading instead of going elsewhere. **One of the big problems marketers experience online is the fact that people are looking for instant info.** If they get to your website, that's the very first, minimal step; it's almost like a pre-Step 1, really. Once they're there, you have to get them to stay rather than click onto something else. On the Internet it's so easy for someone to move on. **If your site doesn't look appealing, they head back to the search engine directory and find another link to click.**

So right away, they've got to see some kind of outrageous guarantee or promise or benefit in big bold typeface. Tell them something revolutionary; give them something wild! Make an outrageous claim—something to get them excited and make them interested. If you can't get their interest right away, they're going to move on to something else because they're busy, they're bored, or they're skeptical. They've got other things going on, so it's easy to say no. **That's why you've got to give them some kind of an outrageous statement, just to keep**

their interest and make them want to keep reading.

Again, most people are jaded. We doubt things, because we've seen all kinds of promises, many of them false. **So when something comes along that gets *you* excited, that should be kind of an acid test!** And this thing I told you about as an example earlier, which gives people the opportunity to sell a membership that lets other people save 30-70% off their grocery bill — I got excited about that one myself! I got so pumped up that I almost called up a couple of my key staff members on Sunday, which is something I *never* do. If something excites you like that and you're somewhat jaded or doubtful, then that's a pretty good test (as long as you're similar to your customers, as you should be).

STEP 2: You tell your prospects that what you have for them is a variation of something that's already making tons of money. This gives them something familiar to link to. It's a positioning concept. You're talking about something they already know about, and it makes it easier to understand and relate to the new thing you're trying to present. Now you're speaking their language.

The first time I remember ever using this six-step formula includes my best example of Step 2. This was back in 1993. Computer bulletin boards, which were the precursor of the Internet, were the hot thing. There were people who were advertising on up to 60,000 or more of these bulletin boards — absolutely free! This was a few years before the Worldwide Web came along and rushed the computer bulletin board industry.

We were among the very first people who started working with Bulletin Board Service (BBS) experts, like Alan R. Bechtold, to show our clients how they could advertise for free on thousands of boards. In trying to show them just how amazing and how revolutionary this really was, we gave them examples of traditional advertising; that was Step 2. We showed them what it cost for them to set up and run a classified ad in dozens of the national magazines they were already familiar with. And then, only then, were they ready to wake up to this valuable new solution. **Our strategy gave them something to link to, and gave what we were selling much more perceived value.**

What you want to do here is make a leap from the familiar to the unfamiliar. This is especially important if you're jumping into a new thing that there's little or no understanding of. Usually you want to avoid those things, because they're unlikely to be successful; as they say, the pioneers are the ones who get scalped. We've had friends who ventured into uncharted waters, basically inventing new things that really hadn't been heard of before. It's like swimming upstream, because you have to educate people on why they should even bother with the new product or service.

You probably remember the Segway, which debuted about ten years ago. **It was by no means the revolutionary new product that its manufacturers built it up to be, but the buzz really caught people's attention.** They had a code name for it, and had all these patents they'd been granted, and they were launching this brand new product that was going to revolutionize the world! They built it up so big, and then when they launched it they said, "Here it is… the Segway!" And what is it? A little two-wheeled scooter thing you stand on, and it's got a gyro sensor; by moving your body around you make the thing go forwards, backwards, turn sideways, or whatever. It goes a whopping 12 miles an hour. Well, it was pretty much a failure. Some police departments bought a bunch of them, and some malls bought them and used them for security guards and things like that; but generally, the general public had no use for them, despite the hype. **They tried to create something brand new that people didn't even really have any concept of or**

need for, and it flopped.

Step 2 is crucial when you've got something completely new. I don't know how they could have applied it with the Segway; but still, when you're trying to get someone to understand something they don't understand, **the best way to do that is to move them from something they "get" first and then build a bridge to the thing that they** *don't* **get, which is what you're trying to educate them on.** When something's brand new, you *must* start with the familiar if you have any hope of making money.

One of the things we're working on right now is educating local retail businesses on how to use affiliate programs. People understand online affiliate programs well enough; they've been around for a while. Well, knowing that, why aren't local retail businesses using affiliate programs to do things *offline* to help local people make money, or to provide better gifts, premiums, or discounts? So we're developing a program to help them do so. **This program uses the Step 2 strategy: We take something familiar — an Internet affiliate program — and move them from their understanding of that into how you could make affiliate programs work offline.** They already understand online affiliate programs, and this is just taking that offline. Again, you start with something they understand, and move it into the area that they don't. It helps them build a picture in their mind of what you're trying to do for them, or the benefit they're going to receive when they buy your product or buy your service. **Start with what they know and build upon it.**

Maybe you've built a better mousetrap. What you do is take the basic mousetrap design and say, "Here, you understand how this works. Well, I've built a better one; here's what it does, and here's why it's bigger and better, faster and cheaper." **Instead of going straight for what they don't know and having to educate them on that, you build parallels between**

something that's familiar to them. By doing that, you're a lot closer to the sale.

Remember, Step 1 is: It's got to be bold! It's got to be new! It's got to be revolutionary! **The problem with that is that if it's *too* new, people won't understand it.** Think about the Segway. People really didn't know what it was. They didn't understand it, so they were skeptical of it. Most still are. **People want new things, but they have to be linked with what they already know about.** If it's too new, they're going to freak out. They're going to go from being excited to being scared and nervous very quickly.

STEP 3: Go into all the problems with the original variation that you talked about in Step #2. In other words, talk about the bad stuff. Before you can reveal the good points, **give them an example of something that's already working, something they're already familiar with, and then enumerate the negatives.**

Going back to the computer bulletin boards, we were showing people how they could advertise on thousands of these bulletin boards, absolutely free. People got so excited about that. The promise was big; it was bold; it was audacious! Then we showed them in Step #2 that the program was connected with something they knew, but was better. We told them that if they wanted to run a classified ad with traditional space advertising, here's how much it would cost, and here's what they would have to go through. That's where Step 3 steps in. One of the advantages of BBS was that you could deliver information products without any hard physical costs. **There were all these money saving and labor saving advantages over the traditional way—but you couldn't appreciate those advantages until you got to see a clear example of how it was before.** So before you even explain what your new breakthrough is, start going through all of the problems, the headaches, the hassles, the high cost of what it would take to do something that they're already familiar with. Only then can you go on to the next steps.

When you introduce a product into the marketplace, one of the first things people want to know is, "Why do I need this? Why is this different than what's out there? Why is this better than what I already can get? What makes this worth me spending money on? What in the marketplace does this compare to?" **People are instantly going to make comparisons in their heads, and in most cases, they have the ability to find things to compare it to.** Even if your product is unique, there's probably something similar they could do with their money that might, in their minds, be a viable alternative. **You need to answer their concerns by playing up the differences between what used to be and what now is, with the way your product solves the problems and challenges that plague the original, the thing that they already understand. Then you talk about the solution you've created, and the benefits that result.**

Here's another quick example. We have a product where we take something that's existed for many years in the affiliate industry—the standard method of paying affiliate commissions—and rework it. Normally, when you're a website affiliate and you bring them a customer, they pay you if and only if that customer makes a purchase. Now, three things could happen here. One is that the person goes to the website, doesn't buy anything today, and you don't get anything for sending them there. Option 2 is that they make a purchase today, you get paid a commission for referring them, and they never return to the site. Option 3 is that the person becomes a lifelong customer of that website, buys lots of stuff on an ongoing basis, and you get *nothing* besides the original commission they paid you for the initial referral. **Our version essentially pays lifetime commissions. We feel you should be paid commission no**

matter how long a person does business with us.

We've created a new model here. **We've taken what's already very well known in the Internet marketing world and kicked it up a notch.** We tell people that we think there's a better way to pay affiliates; not only are you going to get paid a commission if the person buys something today, but even if they choose not to buy today, if they wait and then buy something six months from now, **you** *still* **brought them to us, so we're going to reward you.** Beyond that, even if they do buy something today, we're going to reward you for bringing them to us by paying you a commission every time that customer does any business with us. As long as we maintain a relationship with that client, we're going to continue paying you an affiliate commission, because you introduced them to us.

I think that's a good example of Step 3. **We take something well-understood, talk about the problems inherent with that model, and then show how we've improved on it.** By being a part of this new kind of affiliate program, you can set yourself up to get paid not only today but any time that person does business with us in the future. That's another example of how you can use Step 3 to build on Step 2.

STEP #4: Show them that your new discovery eliminates all or most of the problems that you gave them from your example of something they're already familiar with. This step gives them more of the good stuff, less of the bad stuff. It increases their desire and makes them want it even more. **Now, all of a sudden, they're hooked.** If you did it right, this leads to the next step, which I'll talk about momentarily.

First, let's go back to our affiliate program: the Guaranteed Money Discovery, as we're calling it. With Step #2, we talk about affiliate programs in general; we make people comfortable with the fact that they already know a lot about them. In Step #3, we provide examples of the problems that afflict affiliate programs. **Then, in Step #4, we start revealing our solution: an affiliate program that keeps on paying you for as long as people buy from us, for the life of our company.** Every time a sale is made, our affiliates get paid. Only when people understand how it works in a traditional way (Step #2), and then when they understand all of the problems that are associated with the traditional way (Step #3), are they fully ready for Step 4: the solution! You can only truly value or appreciate something, or even understand it properly, when you have something to compare it with. That's not just a marketing principle, it's a principle of life and business. **The more you have to compare it with, the more you're going to understand it. So that's when we provide them with our solution.**

People are always making comparisons. But when you get right down to it, our job as copywriters/marketers is to make those comparisons for them, since they're going to whether you do it or not. **You want to compare what you're selling against something that makes your deal look even better.** You never compare apples to apples; you compare apples to oranges. You always try to position your solution. You make whatever you sell much more appealing by what you choose to compare it with.

This is industry specific. You're talking about selling to your target marketplace, so you know what their problems are, and you've written your sales copy so you're pointing out their pain, the challenges and struggles they're experiencing on a daily basis; and then you give them examples of things they understand. Then you talk about all the problems, and hit 'em with your solution. **By this point, if you've done your job in the selling process, the pain they're experiencing is real.** You're not *causing* them pain; you're just pointing it out to them. **You've reminded them of the struggle they're already having.**

Consider the weight loss industry. If someone's struggling

to lose weight, **they're looking for a solution—not necessarily a particular product.** They're in pain, and want something that works for them. **If you're selling to the business opportunity market, you're probably selling to people who are looking for a solution to the pain caused by money woes.** They want to make more money, they want to have more financial independence, and they're struggling with that. Maybe they're up to their eyeballs in debt, and so there's serious pain there.

All throughout the first three steps of this formula the pain has been building up. **Because Step 4 demonstrates how your discovery eliminates all their problems, this increases their desire.** It makes them want your product and, at this point, they're feeling a little relief, because they know there's a solution on the horizon. All they have to do is follow the advice you're getting ready to give them. There's no way they're going to stop reading, because they want the benefit you promised them under Step 1. **They want the relief from the pain.** Now, it may take you a while to get to that point, because you've got to cover a lot of examples in the previous steps. **You want to make it agonizingly real for them.** Many of our sales letters are 24, 36, even 48 pages long. People often say, "My goodness! Is anybody going to read 24 to 36 pages?" and the answer is: "If they're qualified prospects, sure they are." And even those who don't read the entire letter will skim it. **In fact, we write the letters to be skimmed, not necessarily read.** The point is, it takes time to build your case. The examples just help to make it real, so people can internalize it and personalize it.

STEP #5: Show your prospect a brief "sizzle" example of what your new discovery can do for them. Give them a glimpse of the greatest benefit. **That ties in with the headline you gave them in the beginning.** Take this BBS example I've been using. In Step #5, we provided a sample of how they could advertise free on computer bulletin boards, and kept pointing back to the examples we'd already used—things they understood, and how much those older strategies would cost them in time, money, and effort. We sold millions and millions of dollars worth of product, and then took a variation of that sales letter to sell websites, too. **We probably rewrote that sales letter for 10 years and reused it in various forms.**

And keep in mind: You do have to go through these steps in the proper sequence. If you were just to go from Step 1 to Step 5, you wouldn't make nearly as many sales. You have to make sure you have the intervening steps in place. **That's what we call the "build up," and it's absolutely crucial.** You've got to introduce the problem, and make the pain real—so that Steps 4 and 5 really hit home. If you tried to skip Steps 2 and 3, you'd be shooting yourself in the foot. **You can't skip around; the process is a progression from one to the other, in order.**

It helps them develop an affinity with you; otherwise, there's no reason why they would even give you the time of day, much less stop and open your envelope. **By the time you get to Step 5, though, they're feeling good about you. Every other step along the way is intended to move the customer from cold prospect status to someone who's willing to respond to your offer:** from a point where they don't know you, don't trust you, have no reason why they would want to stop and give you anything... to a point where they actually *want* what you're offering enough to take a chance on someone they don't really know anything about. You need to get the point where they're willing to put their credit card number down on the form and drop it in the mail, or fax it, or go online and give you their order.

By now, they've seen themselves using your product, and you want to show them what their life will look like with the benefits they'll receive. If you're selling a business opportunity, the flash and sizzle could be their new lifestyle after they've received the benefits... *after* they've purchased your product. If it's in the health industry, you're showing them what life will be like when they're receiving the benefits or have the result you promised them in your headline. If they're a single male, they may imagine themselves with six-pack abs and toned muscles on the beach, with women admiring them. If it's the ladies you're targeting, they could envision themselves being stared at by guys as they're wearing their bikini and lying out in the sun. **The benefit is no longer an abstract idea; now they're living it in their mind.** But this is just a brief thing: You want to leave them hanging on that thought, and then move on to the next step. But this step is important, because it makes them visualize themselves receiving those benefits you promised them. I hope you can see how all of this does flow together. It really is a logical process, one that makes a lot of common sense. And once you're aware of it, you'll see how other people are using variations on a theme here.

STEP #6 is the money step, otherwise known as the close. This is where you tell them how hard it would be for them to figure all this out on their own—how much time, work, and money that it took for you to do so. Then you show them how they can get everything put together for them, ready to go, just by sending you their money. If you set it up right, it makes the close very natural; each steps leads inexorably to the next. **You brought up the problem, you agitated it, you made it real, you offered a solution, and now they want what you have.** If they were to do it on their own, it would be very difficult. **So they're ready to give you their money, because you've put it all together for them.**

With the BBS example, we made a bold promise, built it up by showing how difficult ordinary advertising was and how simple BBS advertising was, made them feel the pain, and showed them the solution. All of a sudden, they just gave us their money! Within six months, we brought in over 2.5 million in sales. **The close ought to be like that: a very natural thing.** If you've set it up right and built it up properly, when it comes time for the close people see so much value, so much advantage… and they see that the promise you made them in Step #1 was absolutely true. **They go from being skeptical and jaded to being so excited they're ready to give you their money… and that's Step #6.**

Many people think selling is basically twisting people's arms, that you almost have to con people out of their money. **No, you've got to do something to get them to give up their money willingly.** Selling has a bad rap because of coercive tactics; so some people shy away from the close, which is a big mistake. It's important to remember that if you've targeted the right person — someone who's looking for the kind of benefits your product or service delivers — then you'd be doing them a disservice not to offer your solution to them. So the close should be a natural part of the process; it should be a logical next step. **The rest of the process is pointless if you don't go for the close.**

You've made the big, bold, outrageous statement. You've made them stop and pay attention to your offer. You've shown them why they're in pain. You've pointed out the problems and challenges they're facing, and ultimately you reveal why your product or service solves that pain they're having. **When you do those things in order, that person is going to be ready to buy.** Now, that doesn't mean that everybody *will* buy; in fact, most of the time, most people don't. As I've mentioned, in Direct Response you can make good money even with bad numbers. In some cases, as many as 95 out of 100 can say "no" and you still can make good money in Direct-Response Marketing. **So don't get too hung up on how many people say "no" versus how many people say "yes."**

The point I'm trying to make is that if you do follow this

process properly, assuming you've targeted the right kind of prospect, at the very least they're going to say, "I see myself using this product. I see myself getting the benefit." Some will buy, because this process is a progression that leads naturally to the sale, as long as you've chosen the right kinds of buyers. **When they get to the point where you make them an irresistible offer, it's going to be difficult for them to say no, because they've already visualized themselves receiving the benefits your product or service delivers.** Once they get to that place where they see themselves having lost the weight, or they see themselves as a millionaire, they don't want to go back. They don't want to be in pain anymore. **Your product is offering them the ultimate opportunity to alleviate that pain.** It's saying, "All you have to do now is buy my magic solution in a bottle," or whatever the case may be. You're offering them a final solution to their pain.

If you've done everything right you'll get the biggest percentage of your prospects to say "yes" to your offer. At least give it a try! This is a very simple formula. It's something you can easily learn the basics of, but that you can take a lifetime to master. **You'll eventually find success by using this formula and keeping these six points in mind.** It's a great formula, and I'm glad that I was able to share it with you.

And by the way, I'd love to see your sales letters! If you're using this formula for writing your own sales copy, send it in to us and let us take a look at it. **We'll offer tips and strategies on how to make it better.** This formula really can make you millions of dollars—and I'm dead serious about that. I can't guarantee that you will, but I know that you *can*, because these are the same things that we and a lot of other people are doing.

So go out there and do it!

The Best Secret Ever

Now I'm going to tell you about the fastest, easiest, simplest, cheapest, and most effective marketing method you can use. I've outlined this process many times in other books, talks, seminars, audio products, and workshops, so it may not be new to you at all. If you've been around the marketing world for a while, you've probably heard about it already. Maybe some of you are *using* it already. I hope you are.

But not everyone has heard of this secret, and even if you have, I think it's a good idea to go over it again, because it's so important. **And it's so simple; yet even within that simplicity there's a hidden complexity, so it can get extremely advanced, too.** In this chapter, I'll talk about some of the complexities involved, and help you get an overall well-rounded view of this strategy's strengths and weaknesses, not to mention its easy parts and difficult parts.

I realize that some people are using this method already and aren't getting very good results from it. I know some of them. Others have used it and haven't gotten *any* positive results from it. These people think this strategy doesn't work at all—and they're sadly mistaken. This marketing method not only works, but earns people millions of dollars, possibly billions, every single year. Furthermore, it requires less risk than any other marketing method I know of.

So here it is (drum roll please): **Two-step marketing!**

It's simplicity itself. **In the first step, you pull in the largest possible group of the most highly qualified prospects for the product or service you offer.** You get them to raise their hand and take an initial action, usually a small action. **In Step #2, you follow-up with those people.** Your goal is to get the largest possible number of those hot prospects to buy what you're selling. **It's all about generating leads and closing those leads. That's all there is to is.**

I expect that some readers will now either skip this chapter altogether or close the book and tune out. Maybe they've heard of two-step marketing before, and already have it figured out and are making a lot of money. If that's the case, maybe you don't need this chapter. But I still think it's better to tune in to what I've saying here, whether you know all about two-step marketing or not. But the question I would ask is, if you're already familiar with the subject, how much money are you making? If you're about ready to tune us out because you think you've heard it before... well, there must be some reason. If you're already successful through using this strategy, that's understandable.

But if you're not and you're still inclined to tune it out, then I'd challenge you to stop. There's got to be some reason why you're not already using this strategy. Maybe you've never taken the time to develop a two-step marketing system. Maybe it's been too complicated for you to figure out, or there have been some missing pieces, or something just hasn't clicked. If that's the case, hopefully this chapter will give you another opportunity to put two-step marketing into practice in your business, instead of just knowing about it. **It's one thing to have the knowledge; it's another thing to actually be implementing these strategies.**

So if you've heard a little bit about it, but you've just never done it, then I hope this chapter reaches you in a new way, and gives you a fresh perspective on the subject. Maybe we'll share some ideas that you haven't thought about, or a way to implement two-step marketing for your business that you haven't given thought to yet. That would be our goal for you today, if you're already familiar with two-step marketing.

But maybe this is new to you. Maybe you're hearing about this for the first time. Maybe you've got a local retail business that you advertise, and all you've ever done is brand awareness. Maybe all you've ever done is focus on blasting as many ads out there as possible, in different media, hoping that some of it sticks and that you do enough business to survive. If that's you, then I think this discussion will astound you. I think it will shock you and amaze you—in good ways, of course! I hope it provides a fresh perspective on the way you can drive people to your business and generate customers. **When done right, this really can be the safest and most profitable way to make money for your business—no matter what business you're in.**

So whether you know a little bit about two-step marketing or this is a brand new concept, I think there's something here for you. There's a caveat, though! **Remember, knowledge is only worthwhile when it's applied.** The secrets I'll share with you in this chapter will be good information, but it will *only* be information until you put it to use. **And no matter where you are in your business—whether you're a rookie or seasoned veteran—I think you'll find these strategies to be exactly what you're looking for.**

Have you ever heard the word **"internalization"? That's a fancy word that means that there's a difference between intellectually knowing something and knowing it at the instinctual, gut level.** You can take a mentally challenged person with a double digit IQ, and you can teach them 10 of the smartest things that you've ever learned in your life. You can have them memorize it, so that you can say, "What's Number Four?" and they'll spit it out for you. They might even make it sound like they know what they're talking about. But they still don't understand any of it; they're just a human parrot. They've never internalized it.

You can take the world's laziest person and do the same. Let's say they're really smart, but they have that regrettable illness known as "Motivational Deficit Disorder " (they're flat-out lazy) and they really don't want to learn anything. Well, you can get them to memorize those 10 smartest things you've ever learned and, sure enough, they can commit to the memory process. It's pretty simple. But that doesn't mean that they'll understand it, even if they're pretty sure they do. *The only way to understand something is to actually apply it, learn it, and become familiar with all aspects of it.*

That's part of the way that we deepen our understanding of anything: We learn the various pros and cons, the pluses and the minuses, all the little nuances, everything from the simplest of things to the most complex. When you've got a good, firm grasp of all of that, only then can you achieve this thing called "wisdom." **And that's what wisdom is: applied knowledge.** So look, even if you've heard about this form of marketing before, even if you're using it and think you know it all... think again. You don't. There are all kinds of nuances here. It's like the game of chess, where there are only six different types of pieces: King, Queen, Knight, Bishop, Rook (a.k.a. Castle), and Pawn. They move across red and black squares. Each piece can only move in certain constrained ways or directions. It's a pretty simple game, when it comes to the basic rules; and yet you can spend your entire life studying it, learning it, and always be getting better at it. This works the same exact same way.

I've mentioned before that we started with a few

hundred dollars and turned it into over $114 million—and two-step marketing has been responsible for 95% of that. We started our company in the late 1980s. By the 1990s, we were fairly good at some aspects of the game. And then the millennium came; and in that decade we got a lot better at other aspects of this process. We're still learning—but we do know enough to teach the process, and as they say, teaching anything can hone your edge even more.

So let's look at Step #1 again: creating an offer that you can use to attract a highly qualified prospect. **The goal is to attract the largest number of those people, but you just start with one. To attract that person, you have to know and understand them from the inside out.** So: Who is your average prospect? What do they want more than anything else? What are they searching for in all of the products and services that are similar to the ones you offer? **You want to create something that has a lot of perceived value,** so that by the time you're done making that offer, the cost pales by comparison with the potential benefits. **What you're offering looks *huge*, and the amount of money you're asking for looks small—even if you're asking for thousands of dollars.**

The secret is that you don't try to sell them too much too fast, at least at first. **All you're trying to do in Step #1 is create something that's similar to what you're trying to sell them on the back-end.** That's important: that your front-end is "married" or related closely to what you're selling on the back-end. **You're just trying to get them to take a small step.** Our million-dollars-a-month strategy starts with a $10 book. For ten bucks, they can get a little book that explains our secret, so we're not asking them for too much too fast. But we *are* asking them for something that pre-qualifies them; otherwise you'll get a whole bunch of people to raise their hand, and few or none will buy in the second step. We've had those problems before; it happens to the best of us. *Those* are the problems that cause a lot of people to say, "Hey, I tried two-step marketing and it doesn't work!" Well, you didn't pre-qualify enough!

You've got to get your hooks into them right away, because there's so much competition these days—so many people yelling and screaming at them already, so many marketers trying to hype it up. Everybody is trying to sell you something, and the racket is terrible. **So you've got to do something to cut through the clutter, something that separates you from the crowd, something that grips people.** That's what I mean when I say "get your hooks into them." To do that, **your offer has to be unique.** If you're selling the same old crap everybody else is selling, and you've got no way to differentiate it from everything else, then you're going to be severely handicapped.

What you're doing is making it easy for them to buy the very first time. That's what we're doing with this million-a-month deal. It costs $10. Everybody has $10! **And it's got a No-Risk Guarantee attached to it, too.** So if they give us their $10 and they're not happy, we don't want their money. In fact, we let them just keep the book; all they have to do is ask for their $10 back. **We're making it *easy* for them to buy the first time.** We'd like to cover our advertising costs in the process, but as long as we pre-qualify and get the best prospective buyers to raise their hands, we're happy.

Sell them a low-ticket item. Right now we're selling this deal for $10, but for years we've had other low-priced offers that range anywhere from $29 up to $129. **Again, it goes back to that whole thing where you're not trying to do too much too fast.** You're trying to sneak it up on them a little, making it easy for them to buy the first time. **You do want to pre-qualify, but if you put too many hurdles out in front of them, you'll get far fewer people to raise their hand...** and that will affect your numbers on the back-end when you convert those people. There are fewer coming in at the top of the funnel, so there are fewer that come out at the bottom, too.

You have to educate people. With our million-a-month strategy, we have a Special Report that goes with the book in which we tell them about the nine main problems associated with things similar to what we're offering. Then we show them how our solution solves each of those problems, so we're educating people on all the reasons they should be giving us their money. You need to do the same: **Show them all the reasons why what you're offering is superior to all the other, similar items that other people are pitching them all day long.**

The real power of two-step marketing is that most people feel that they're the ones who came to you, instead of vice versa. They feel they're the ones who sought you out. This isn't really true, of course — since after all, you drew them in with your front-end offer. But see, they don't feel that way, because they're bombarded with all this other advertising. They've got all these other people pitching them, but they choose very few. So they may see a hundred ads or get a hundred Direct Mail packages a month, but they only choose to respond to a couple of them. **In their mind, therefore, they're the ones who sought you out. And that's a powerful, powerful thing.**

How does two-step marketing differ from the one-step, traditional variety? **Well, most people just go for the sale right away.** They may do nothing but image awareness or Yellow Page advertising, which is where you just tell people that you exist. Think about the traditional Yellow Page ad. Usually, it has the name of the company at the top, and that may tell you a little about what they do. Other than the company name, they might have the hours of operation and their phone number and address, along with, maybe, some catch phrase. **But there's certainly**

nothing that would make anyone want to visit them or go into their store, other than the fact that they need that type of product.

And in fact, a lot of local retail businesses are need-based; for example, plumbers. When you need one, you usually just pick up the Yellow Pages and call the first one on the list. There are many, many companies like that: they feel that people are going to find *them* when they need them, and that's about all there is to their ads. **They're not going to aggressively go after any business. Similarly, some people do Direct-Response Marketing using a one-step approach.** They've got an offer they send out in a sales letter, or they place an ad somewhere. They've got a list of people they think might be interested, so they just show them the offer. Hopefully, if the offer is a good one and it's reaching the right kinds of prospects, a percentage of those people who receive that offer will respond. **But they never go any further than that—they never actively pursue their prospects.**

With a two-step marketing approach, instead of just going straight out for the business, **you focus on attracting the highest qualified prospect first.** Don't try to make the sale right away—although, in some cases, your first step *is* a small sale; I've discussed the book we're selling for $10. So, in some cases, you *are* selling something on the front end, **but that something you're selling isn't the main product or service you're trying to get people to buy.** In other cases, your offer might be to give away a free report, although that's not very creative these days. It's better to give away a CD or a DVD; or maybe, to get the great free package you're sending them, all they have to do is include five or ten dollars to cover shipping and handling.

Now, people tend to think that if you're charging money for shipping and handling, that's not really a free offer. But five or ten bucks may not even cut it, when you consider that you have to pay for the cost of the materials to produce the free product, plus the cost of shipping— especially if you ship by, say, priority mail. **These days it's about five dollars just for the raw shipping charge alone, let alone if you do it UPS or FedEx or use any special packaging.**

So don't be afraid to charge a few bucks in postage for something that's otherwise free. If you've ever watched infomercials on TV, you'll notice that they regularly charge around $10 for shipping and handling, or postage and processing, or whatever they call it. **That's standard, so if you've got something of value that you're giving away for free, don't have any problem at all telling people that your package *is* absolutely free, but that it requires a shipping fee.** Don't expect people to be upset with you. Not only is this pretty commonplace, **it's just another way to qualify people.** If they don't even want to pay a piddling shipping fee for something that's otherwise free, then will they ever be willing to pay for what you're offering on the back end?

Now, when generating your list of prospects, you'll have to face a real balancing act. While you want the highest possible count, you also want them to be the best and most qualified prospects. **Typically, the more you qualify a prospect, the fewer prospects you get.** For example, in the past we've had offers where we tell people right up front that if they respond, they're going to receive an offer that costs them about as much as a good used car. Now, obviously, something like that's going to cut down on the number of people who respond to your initial offer. **So it's a balancing act.** We want as many prospects as we can get, because marketing is always a numbers game at some level. You have to have a pool of people to sell to, people who have requested information from you under this two-step model, but you don't want them to be tire kickers; you want them to buy. **So the other problem you have, sometimes, is when you're trying too hard to make it easy for people to say yes to your initial offer.** You end up attracting a large number of people, but they're not very qualified, and a non-qualified prospect usually turns into a non-buyer.

That's where the trick comes in when you're doing two-step marketing. **Under Step 1, the game is trying to figure out the balance — determining exactly how to bring in the most qualified prospects, in the biggest numbers.** This game can drive you nuts, but it's supremely profitable if you can get it right. In the course of your attempt to do that, you create a great offer. **You don't try to tell them too much, but you do want to tell them enough to make them want what you have, and you want them to understand that you're going to be trying to sell them something else.** You don't want to trick people; you never want to sell them a deal where Part A works only if you spend more money on Part B. That's called a "bait-and-switch," and it's immoral.

Here's another quick example. We have an offer where we give people something for $39 on the front end; over the years, the price has varied from about $20-40. When they respond to that, we make them an offer to get more of it as well as other features, other benefits, other free gifts, and things like that. **Still, what they spend the $20-40 on works completely and separately from what we're trying to get them to also purchase.** They're similar; they can work together. But neither is required for the other to work.

So, you want to have them be able to use what you're selling them in the first place. You can't ever make them buy one thing upfront and then sneak something else in behind it that they weren't aware of. Your sales will suffer. **Just make sure what you sell them initially works and is fully functional... unless, of course, it's just a written report.** Otherwise, if you sell them something that's supposed to be a workable working product under the first step, make sure it really does do what you say it's going to do.

You should also make it easy for them to respond to your first offer. Make sure they can fax it in, mail it in, phone it in, or visit a website and order online. Again, you should still qualify them. You don't want to make it *too* easy, because you don't want to attract the wrong kinds of people. **By qualifying them and telling them a little more about what they're going to find out when they respond, or setting them up to know that you're going to be trying to make an additional sale, you end up avoiding the tire kickers and only get the people most likely to be interested in your product or service.**

Let's say that you've made them an offer to get an audio CD, and you've told them all about what they're going to discover when they hear this CD. They had to send $5 to help with shipping and handling along with their order form. Now they're waiting on you. You've sold or given them something they're anticipating, even if it's just an instant download. **When they get your other sales material, at that point the relationship has gone from them being just a prospect to them being a customer.** They're doing business with you in some fashion. **They're beginning to bond to you.**

That's an important benefit of two-step marketing over one-step marketing, because with one-step marketing you just send your offer out and hope people respond. And certainly some will, if your offer's a good one. **But in a two-step marketing situation, you have the ability to speak to them differently because they responded to an initial offer and you sent them something.** That low-priced (or free) entry point is there to build a bond with someone who doesn't know you or trust you until they respond to that offer and get your widget, download, or gift. **Later, you can ask them for a big-ticket purchase.**

Your inexpensive front-end item may be a basic version of your main package, or an information product that gives people all the information and resources they need to do it all themselves. **It's still a valuable product.** You can sell it for a few dollars—whatever you deem its value to be. **But you can also inform them that instead of doing it all themselves, they could just buy your Premium Package, where you do all these things for them.** That would be one example where you sell a low-priced thing first that introduces your audience to your main product. In order to do this right, you really need to get a good, solid understanding of what their goal is under Step 1. It's not just about generating leads; it**'s about generating leads that are the most likely to want to become paying customers.** And ideally, beyond that, it's not just about a one-time sale. **It's about setting up a lifetime of sales—a relationship that lasts months or years.**

When you're just getting started with this concept, study other people who are using two-step marketing effectively. This can help you more than anything else. We call it "getting on the other side of the cash register." **It's where you stop thinking like a consumer and start thinking like a marketer.** Every time you see a solicitation that's part of a two-step campaign, be aware of it. Send away for it—even if you're just doing so for research. We do that all the time; **we're constantly spying on the competition.** We're constantly sending away for things —even from people who aren't our competitors, but just other marketers doing great things. It's fun; and again, you've got to make a game out of it. You're a detective here, and you're trying to hunt down and snoop and spy on all these people who are making millions of dollars, trying to get their best-kept secrets. **Then you utilize some of their best ideas in your own marketing.**

Now, let's talk a bit more about this concept where the

prospect feels that they're coming to you rather than you going to them. In a way, it's sort of like the dating world. I've had attractive female friends, and they've told me how much of a turnoff it is when these guys are always chasing them and hitting on them constantly. But generally, whoever is being chased has all the power. **In a two-step marketing situation, that would be you; and yet, to the prospect it feels like** *they* **have the power. They feel like they've chosen** *you.* The truth is, all the power is on your side; and you do have to realize that.

Earlier, I talked about the marriage of the front-end and the back-end. **That's where what you're selling on the back-end is strongly related to what you're selling or otherwise offering on the front-end.** We give people a small amount of something, and then try to sell them a larger amount. In some ways it's like going to the grocery store, where they have those people who pass out samples of food. Take Mrs. Fields—they've built a multimillion dollar enterprise on free cookies! You're walking along, you grab a sample of their cookies, you start walking, you eat a bite, and then all of a sudden you turn around and run right back there to buy a dozen cookies. Brilliant!

We've made millions of dollars with this concept, by the way. For example, we've sold millions of dollars worth of Master Distributorships by first selling a basic distributorship for a small amount, and then upselling them on the second step to the Master Distributorships. The front-end and the back-end are very closely tied together. **If they're happy with what they got from you on the front-end, they're likely to purchase the back-end product. Now, you don't want them to be** *too* **happy, of course! You don't want to satiate them on the front end.** After somebody eats a great big meal, are they hungry after that? No, they're not. **So you always leave them wanting more, but you definitely don't want to disappoint them on the first step.**

You've got to think about all of this as an enjoyable endeavor, not a serious one, although sometimes you should get serious about it. After all, when you play a game, sometimes you concentrate very, very hard; you *do* take it seriously. But at the same time, it's still a game. You try to have fun with it. You try to be creative with it.

So in Step #1 you draw them in—and **then in Step #2 you slam-dunk them!** You bring out the big guns. Now you've got their attention and interest. **You're now in the position to show them how you can give them whatever it is they desire with the product or service that you're offering.** And let me be clear: When I say "Step #2," this may just be the first of a number of steps in which you pursue relentlessly. As I've mentioned in previous chapters, **we've had offers in which we had dozens of different follow-up pieces alone, including stuff besides Direct Mail.** One summer, during a four-month period, we had 32 different follow-up pieces—but it was still a two-step campaign.

So think about this as salesmanship! When you've got a hot prospect and you want them to do something, are you going to listen when they say no? Are you just going to give up? Not if you're any good, you're not! **The best salespeople are** *relentless.* They don't take no for an answer. If you say "no" to them, they'll say, "Oh, that's fine. I understand," and then they'll just take another angle and come right back at you. They're just not going to give up! **You've got to do that with your second step, too. Be relentless with your follow-up.** Match the second step to your first. Have a marriage there between the two steps. Keep your prospects happy, but not too happy. Because, again, if somebody eats a great big meal, are they really going to want any dessert? No. And dessert is where you make all your money.

So even though we talk about them as being two different things, the two steps are very closely related,

because you can't have one without the other. They go together like peanut butter and jelly. Once you have the list of people who have raised their hands under Step 1, **your goal is to do everything in your power to get them to take the action you want them to take.** In this case it's to give you their money for the product or service you're offering. If you've done a good job of setting up your offer and deciding what your price point is, then you're convinced that the offer you're making to them is solid. You're convinced that it's worth every penny you're asking — that their money is better served in your pocket and your product or service is better served by being with them.

Once you've done all of that, it's your duty and responsibility to make as many sales as possible. The worst position you can be in is to not be confident about what you're selling. If you're in such a position, your sales are going to suffer because of your lack of confidence. So you've got to start with that frame of mind that your product or service *does* deliver the value you said it would, that it's well worth the money you're asking, and that your prospects would be foolish not to exchange their money for it. With that knowledge, go after that business as much as possible, and give them every opportunity to respond to your offer.

Even if they've got this basic concept down, most people who use two-step marketing still give up way too early on their prospects. They might send out an offer or call the prospect up once and try to sell them over the phone, but that's about it. And if the prospects don't respond, then well, better luck next time. No! **If you've built up a list of good qualified prospects, you need to keep reminding them that *they still haven't done business with you.*** You have their attention, you have their interest, they have requested something from you, so it's time to follow-up with them relentlessly!

There are only **three reasons** why you should stop

following up with them on a particular offer. **The first, best-case scenario is that they buy.** Now there's no need to follow up with them. The second is that they tell you, "Stop mailing me stuff! I'm done with you. **I don't want to be a part of your customer list anymore!"** Some people will tell you, "Remove me from your mailing list," and you have to oblige. That does happen; it's a reality of business. **The third option is that it no longer becomes profitable to continue to mail follow-up with your prospects.**

Here's how it usually works. The first day you do your follow-up marketing, you get a certain number of sales; generally the highest number of responses possible. Then, on the following days, the number drops lower and lower, partly because you're making sales and the people who are responding are being purged from that list. Some of your prospects are purged because they never respond, or tell you to remove them. **And so your pool of prospects continues to decrease as you do your follow-up marketing.**

The number of sales keeps dropping as you spend more money following up with your prospects. At some point, that number of sales dips below the profitability line—that is, it becomes no longer profitable to follow-up with them. **Only you can figure out where the profitability line is; that's where you should stop, because if you continue, you'll lose money.** That's a good time to start thinking about wrapping it up—though most people don't wait until then to wrap it up. They quite much earlier in the process, while profits are still coming in from that follow-up.

So continue following up with your prospects; continue reminding them that they still haven't done business with you, until they either buy, tell you to stop following up with them, or it no longer becomes profitable to continue. Then you can stop. **And don't get tired of finding new, creative ways to remind**

them that they haven't bought from you. That's what Step 2 is: just continuously giving them another opportunity to buy. Because if you don't give them an opportunity to buy, guess what? They won't. **And here's the kicker: Even if those people don't buy from you on one offer, you should still keep them on your list as long as they're qualified to be there, so you can keep going back to them with additional two-step offers.** Build a relationship with them. Let them know a little about you. Win their trust and respect, and keep going back to the same well until it's dry. **Your mailing list is gold, if you know what to do with it!**

Earlier, I mentioned what you can do if your sales come too easy. One way to fix that is to raise your prices a little bit, or try to expand your offer otherwise. Maybe you've got something that's really magical, that can make you millions of dollars a year if you tap into it. If you're aggressive enough and you're still not getting enough conversion, if you're generating a ton of leads but not closing enough of them... **there are plenty of things that you can do to try to get them to qualify themselves even more.** It's sort of the reverse of what I said at first. **Instead of trying to expand and see how many more people you can reach, you're trying to do things to close the funnel just a bit so that fewer people are coming through the top... but those that do are better qualified.**

In the end, all this can get very complicated. I've touched on a few advanced techniques here. Hopefully, I've convinced you just how complicated this type of marketing can be; there are many different potential moves you can make within these two steps. **I also want you to realize that you need to keep going back to the basics.** Any time you're confused or frustrated—basics. Remember how simple it is. **We're talking about dollars spent versus dollars made, minus the cost to generate those dollars.** That's all business is, really. Your primary focus shouldn't be worrying about what stuff costs you; **worry instead about what it takes to make an effective sale.**

You know, some people these days are blown away by circumstance. **As I'm writing this, we're in an economic downturn; times are pretty tough.** So some people are perplexed when they hear that we're selling items for thousands of dollars right now, because they didn't think you could do that in a market like this one. **Well, you can, as long as you do a complete and thorough job of selling. That's what a good two-step campaign does.** You're only looking for the people who are well qualified, not people who are broke! If you want to sell something for thousands of dollars, you'd better make sure that people have money to spend.

We like to tell people flat out, "Look, this is going to cost you about the same amount you'd spend for a weekend in Las Vegas." Or we use the used car analogy: "This will cost about as much as a good used car." **Either way is we're saying, "If you haven't got the money, then please don't waste our time or yours."** That's one way to pre-qualify, but there are plenty of others. You can ask people to only mail the order form in, if you do business by mail. There's no option to go online, which makes it harder for them to respond. **Just by making it a bit more difficult, you raise the barrier so that fewer people will respond.** We've also had prospects call and listen to a recorded message 15 minutes long. There was no cost or obligation to get the package; we didn't even charge postage. It was just a matter of them listening to the message. **If someone is willing to sit through a long message and then leave their name and address, they're a qualified prospect.**

Those are some of the ways you can manage the size of your list, if it's getting too unruly or too big. **Remember: you only want to do this after you've examined the numbers, because you want as big a list as possible as long as your**

conversion rate is good... which is where Step 2 comes in.
When you're able to convert those prospects into buyers, you're
golden. If that's not going well for you, then change your Step 1
offer and make it harder for them to respond. **You'll bring in
less leads, but they'll probably be more qualified—which is
the entire point.**

On the flipside, if you're converting them too easily and
everybody is buying, maybe you've done too good a job of
qualifying them on Step 1. **Maybe you could be making more
money by bringing in people who need some more selling.**
Maybe they need someone to talk to them, a salesperson on the
other end of the line helping them make a buying decision. Or
maybe you need to send them more follow-up mail. **Sure, they
may be harder to get, but there are more of them out there.**
So if you're closing all your sales, consider opening the funnel
up a little bit more and bring in even *more* leads.

**In other words, you can monitor your front-end (Step 1)
and your back-end (Step 2) response rate, and you can keep
an eye on that and adjust accordingly as you work to hit
your goals.** I talked earlier about our goal of a million dollars a
month. One of the things we have to do is monitor both our lead
counts and our back-end Step 2 conversions very closely—
because any adjustment, even a small one, in the response rate
can throw off our numbers. **We pay very close attention to the
number of people under Step 1 who say yes to our initial
offer for the $10 book, and the number of those people who
respond to our Step 2 back-end offer.** In watching those
numbers really closely, we can know whether we're doing a
good enough job bringing in the right number of prospects.

**Once you've pre-qualified people with Step 1, don't be
stingy. Spend money to convert those sales!** When I look back
at the times when our company has made the most money, it's
been when we were spending a lot of money on the follow-ups.

We weren't worried about cost; we were worried about doing a complete and effective job of selling.

I promised to show you just how easy it can be to make a million a month. We're looking at just four numbers. The first is the million dollars a month; then we work backwards. On average, our company mails, 40,000 pieces a week for new customer acquisition—that is, to people we've never done business with. We're looking for a 5% response on the front end. That is, for every 1,000 pieces we mail, we want 50 of those people to raise their hands. And then we're looking for a 5% conversion rate: that is, we want those people to make a $2,500 average purchase. And notice I said "average purchase." You have to factor that average in because there *will* be problems. You may have to sell something for $1,000 more than that to get an average sale of $2,500. In any case, all that works out to $1,000,000 a month. **There are only four numbers to play with. We need 5% to respond on the front-end, and 5% on the back-end—mailing 40,000 pieces a week on a $2,500 average sale.**

It's simple! It's fun! It's challenging! And yes, it's frustrating sometimes. It's stressful sometimes. **It's *confusing* sometimes. But show me anything in life that's worthwhile where there's not a tremendous price to pay.** And anybody who expects to bring in a million a month with no amount of headaches and hassles and work... well, you're just living a fantasy as far as I'm concerned. **You've got to be willing to put in the time and go through the effort and energy. Do that, and potentially, millions of dollars are your reward.**

Rule Fourteen:

Take Massive Action!

Life is always changing. Business is always changing. Your market is always changing. One secret to staying on top of these changes, and staying at the top of your game, is taking massive action. **You should always take massive action against your challenges, so that you can overcome them as quickly and as effectively as possible.**

Of course, that begs the question: what *is* massive action? **In my opinion, it's a willingness to go out there and move forward at all times, under all circumstances.** You don't have to have all the answers from the very beginning; you don't even have to have everything figured out. What *is* required is that you spend a little time trying to determine what your best strategies are, then get out there and do four or five things at once to find out what works best — and then do more of *that*. **I know it sounds simple, and it *is* simple, but that doesn't mean it's always easy to do.**

You see, so many people become vapor-locked. They become trapped and get confused. They spend too much time trying to figure out what to do, and then they don't get anything done, because the more they worry, the more confused they get. **Well, the recipe for confusion is *action*.** Just go out there and try to determine what your best strategies and ideas are so that you don't become immobilized. Face into the challenge and move forward. It should go without saying that a little frustration will come with any challenge, because at first, you won't always know what the best thing to do might be. But then again, you can use the energy of that frustration to solve the challenge itself. **The concept of massive action invokes thoughts of doing big things, and that's really what it's about.** You can't take massive action by sitting back and relaxing; you've got to be out there, pushing. You've got to be aggressive to succeed in marketing, and that's one of the themes this book series is based on. **In our lexicon, ruthless is a synonym for aggressive, not heartless.**

You've got to be aggressive in marketing, and massive action goes hand in hand with that. Think about real-life examples of massive action you've witnessed: in sports, for example. Consider the athletes who make it to the big leagues; they're very toned, very athletic people, because they've taken massive action to get there. If those people had decided back when they were trying to become professional athletes that they *weren't* going to take massive action to reach the pinnacles of their sports, they wouldn't have gotten where they are today. Take a tennis player like Serena Williams, or football player Peyton Manning — someone who, throughout their career, has been regarded as being a peak performer, at the top of his or her game most of the time. These kind of people don't just stumble upon success. They get there by taking massive action to prepare themselves physically, mentally, and emotionally to play their game at the highest possible level.

In business, it's pretty much the same way. **You've got to get into the right mindset to take massive action — and then you've got to get out there and actually do it!** Massive action means throwing yourself out there with all you've got, with all your being, and not being too worried about where you're going until you're on your way. Too many people try to plan out their businesses in meticulous detail, planning for all the possible things that could go wrong. **They worry too much about getting everything just perfect before they even start.** Again, that paralyzes a lot of people; it keeps them from actually getting out there and doing something because they're so focused on trying to prepare that they never actually do anything. **I call it *paralysis by analysis.*** You're so determined to analyze all the possible angles and try to get everything figured out that you can't move at all.

The strategy I'm presenting here is the same one you see on the classic Nike commercials: ***Just Do It!*** Throw yourself full on into the project; just pour yourself into it. Take massive action and see what happens. **Analyze your results as you go, and tweak your strategies as necessary.** Yes, of course there's always game planning and strategizing that has to happen at the beginning and along the way; but you need to do most of that when you're already moving forward. **Don't think yourself to death, or you'll over-plan and you'll never achieve anything significant.**

At M.O.R.E., Inc., we take massive action each and every day, and the same is true of all the successful marketers I know. We do everything we can to make sure that we're giving each of our projects the maximum chance to succeed. **The idea is to be relentless: We never quit.** We try to be like a pit bull. Pit bulls are relentless — and when they take action, they're going to succeed or die trying. In this chapter, we're going to look at a few of our best pit-bullish, massive-action secrets.

Priority is Job One

If you don't know from the word "Go" what your most important priorities are, then you're lost before you've even started. **You should *always* invest the time necessary on those activities that are your priorities; that is, you should identify and focus on the few things that stand the greatest chance of making you the most money.** Everything else can be delegated to other people. I think that this is such a huge distinction, such an enormous idea, that it escapes most people. *You want to focus on what's going to make you the most money.* That's it. For many of us, it's writing copy and working on growing our businesses, so putting out new marketing campaigns is our top priority. Personally, I like to delegate everything else, because I've found that when I'm writing a new campaign that has the potential to make hundreds of thousands of dollars, I don't want to go to the mailbox or run to the bank. That's not going to make me any money; it's something that I can pay someone maybe $10 an hour to do. I can't afford to treat myself that way, because if I do, it's going to harm the company. If instead I focus on writing copy and developing new campaigns, products, and services, and servicing my customers at a higher level, that's going to make me a lot more than $10 an hour; ultimately, it can make me hundreds or even *thousands* of dollars an hour. Clearly, that's where my time is best spent. **The more I do that, the more I'm throwing fuel on the flame of my success.**

It takes effective delegation to get ahead. This is true not just in business, but in every area of your life. If you mow your own lawn, what are you doing? Maybe you're putting the neighbor kid out of a job. Besides, if you can hire that neighbor kid down the street to mow your lawn for fifteen bucks and instead you can take that same hour and you apply it to your business, you've just had a price arbitrage — meaning that your hour is more valuable than if you're mowing. Again, figure out what's most important and focus on that. Delegate everything else. The late, great Gary Halbert once said, "Here's what you should do. **Draw a circle, and put whatever you're the very best at and whatever makes you the most money inside that**

circle. Everything else should go outside that circle. Delegate everything outside that circle and focus on what's inside. If you do that, I'll guarantee you you're going to have phenomenal results. You have the potential to make millions of dollars doing that."

This is a very basic secret of marketing success — and it *is* a secret, as obvious as it seems, because so many people just don't think of it. One of the best books I ever read, more than 15 years ago now, was *The E-Myth* by Michael Gerber. One thing that Gerber talks about is how most business people want to do one of two things: they either want to wear all the hats in their business, so they're trying to do everything themselves, or they want to abdicate everything to other people. I've made both of those mistakes before, and I *still* make the second mistake sometimes. **But the first mistake is what plagues most small business owners. They really are trying to wear all the hats.** And let me point out here that just because I'm talking about massive action, doesn't mean you're supposed to move in 40 different directions. That's unproductive. You have to prioritize and do only whatever's the most profitable that you do best; that's the core of effective massive action. **Everything has to have a profitable purpose because that's what makes you the largest amount of money.** And why waste your time on anything else?

So many people say they don't have time to make money. And you know, it's a funny thing, time, because we've all got the exact same amount of it; we all have the same 24 hours a day to work with. Sure, there are some variables; some people sleep only a few hours a day, some much more. And yet some people find the time to do the important things, while others don't find the time to do much of anything. Some people are good at making excuses, and some people are good at making money — and usually, the two are mutually exclusive. **This concept of**

prioritizing is how people get more work done. Not everything within your business is important. Again, getting the mail from the post office, or processing checks and taking them to the bank — those are things that you could have someone else do for you. Now, maybe you're just getting started, and you like getting the checks in the mail yourself. That's not a bad thing; it's just that there's probably something else you could be doing that's more important. **If you find yourself not having the time to focus on your marketing, that means there are certain things that you need to delegate to other people.**

And if you're thinking right away *I don't want to hire employees*, well, don't worry about that. If you've got kids who could help you, give them a little bit of spending money on the side to help you out. Maybe you've got some friends or family who would be excited to help you as your business is growing. And if you have to pay somebody, you can outsource. **You can find people to do things as independent contractors, so you don't have to have them on staff, where you're paying benefits.** That way, you don't get bogged down in those details.

Focus on the things inside your circle. The most important things, the ones that make the most money, should go toward the center. The further you get away from the center of the circle, the less directly the things should have to do with you making money. And the further they are away, the more you need to think about those things. Is that something that you really should be doing? Now, certainly there are hobbies, things that aren't directly related to making money that you can do; I'm not suggesting that you spend 24 hours a day on business. Have some free time, but recognize that free time for what it is. Prioritize it in the scope of your goals and what you're trying to accomplish. Maybe you really like watching TV — so you watch TV six hours a day and you continue to say, "I just don't have any time to do any of my business." If that's the case, maybe you need to tone down your hobby, and only spend one or two hours a day watching television.

So focus on the things that could make you the most money, and on those things you need to take care of yourself. The rest can get delegated. That goes for everything; look at each task in regards to how it makes you money, prioritize, and decide which things you can let other people take care of. **Everything has a dollar value — and in many cases, your time is worth more money than it takes to pay someone else.**

Details Come Last

I use to have this next point hanging on a banner in our old conference center: **"Concepts first, details last."** Details *must* come last! First of all, you've really just got to figure out what you want to do. You don't have to figure out *how* you want to do it and get bogged down by all the details; **just go into motion.** The internal dialogue of most people when they think about something goes like this: "Hey, I want to develop a marketing campaign!" Then all this sort of stuff pops in their mind: "But I don't know enough about marketing. Where am I going to get the envelopes? What if I make a whole bunch of money, and I have to pay a lot in taxes? I don't have a good accountant. And where am I going to get the money to do this anyway?" **These are the kinds of details that can result in paralysis analysis. Focus on the concept itself.**

If you say, "My concept is to do a marketing campaign," and you know why you want to launch your business and make a lot of money, then you can sort out the details as they come up. **You have to take that leap of faith and go into action.** To quote Gary Halbert again, "Motion beats meditation." Just go for it — take massive action! As you take steps in the right direction, realize that while you don't know everything about how you're going to do it, **you still have to do it.** Have confidence in yourself, confidence that you're going to figure it out. **Tell yourself that you're going to learn new stuff as you go, and you're going to implement it.** That's how you move things into your comfort zone. If I know I want to create a marketing campaign, **the first thing I'm going to do is go as far as my knowledge will take me, and then learn whatever else I have to in order to succeed.**

Here's the liberating concept I want you to get: **you don't have to know exactly how it's going to come together, you only have to know what you want to do.** You can find the right resources, the right people to teach you, the right seminars to go to, the right books to read, the right vendors to assist you, the right mentors. **They're going to come into your life as you're taking action, as you're in motion, in flow.** When they do, you'll find that next step you need to take. If you happen to get stuck on a step, I want you to realize that there are tons of resources out there, plenty of people willing to teach you what you need to know and do to move forward. **Because here's the thing: whatever you're facing now is probably not unique.** Others have been where you are. Even though it may seem earth-shattering to you, other people have already created many successful marketing campaigns — and they're there to help you. That's why the concept should always come first, the details second. **The details can be filled in as you go, and there will always be someone there to support you.**

When I have an idea, I try it out. I don't always know exactly how I'm going to implement it, but that's part of the fun; that's part of my growth process as a marketer. As I try new and different things, I know I'm going to discover ways to pull things together. **As I do things that I didn't know how to do before, and the details come, I deal with them.** I gain more confidence, more faith in myself, by taking massive action and letting the details take care of themselves. I can delegate some of the details to people working with me, and I can send others to be dealt with by outsourcers. **Concepts first, details second: it's a liberating concept!** You don't have to know what you're going to do in order to do it. You just have to take action, and you'll find out as you go.

In many ways, you have to see marketing as a game, or a sport — and those aren't always fun to play. The people who become champions are the ones who work hardest and put the most into it. I recently read a biography about Arnold Schwarzenegger and the game he was playing to help to open up his career, which was the sport of bodybuilding. There were times when he lifted so much weight that he would just pass out. That's the degree to which he was pushing himself — and sure, in marketing that's mostly a metaphor. But you can't just be cautious all the time and lift the weights you *know* you can lift. **You have to be willing to make uncertainty your friend.** It doesn't always feel good, but the fact is, you *don't* have to have all the answers right off; **just figure things out as you go.** The concept, or the goal if you will, comes first.

Now, when you decide on that goal and dive right in, does that mean you'll succeed? Of course not. All business is calculated risk, since nobody knows what the future holds. We all know that we can get side-swiped by life — and business is just life accelerated. **But once you make a solid decision on your direction, it makes all the subsequent decisions easier.** I look at it like driving at night. As long as you have a good vehicle and you're on fairly good roads in fairly good weather, then you can have the blackest of all nights, where all you're really able to see is 75 to 100 yards ahead of you with your high-beams on, and you'll still be relatively safe — as long as you keep under the speed limit and don't outrun your headlights. Just keep on eye out on what's ahead. Try not to hit any deer as they cross the road, look out for potholes, and you'll be fine.

Your only other real option is to play it safe and do nothing — and for people like us, that's no option at all. **I've seen too many people get stuck trying to have everything figured out before they get started,** people who could have made their dreams come true if they had just taken a few careful, calculated risks. Sometimes that hesitancy comes from a person's need to work it all out in advance; sometimes it's due to control issues. In any case people have this tendency to want to have all the details, and we see this a lot when we create — not even in the creation stage, really, but in the embryonic stage when we have a new idea that we're cultivating.

We know that not every idea is going to be a million-dollar winner. We know that not every idea is even going to be *practical*, **but you don't want to kill an idea in its infancy.** Yet what often happens is that an idea will roll off someone's tongue, and the people around them will instantly shoot it down, explaining all the reasons why that idea won't work. Well, an idea in its infancy doesn't need to be shot down; it needs to be cultivated and considered thoroughly. **In other words, you have to spend some time thinking through all the reasons it could work.** Think about what you want that idea to turn into. How are you going to get it from a little baby idea to a full-grown idea? During the course of cultivating that idea, you may very well discover that it isn't reasonable to pursue it. That's fine. But you won't know that until you flesh it out and look at it from every angle. What's more, that scrutiny might result in a workable idea, or at least an aspect that can contribute to a workable idea.

The way you get there is by thinking of the concepts first and not worrying about the details until later. In the beginning, you think things through from a very abstract conceptual nature, where you're just focused on what we sometimes call a "brain dump." **This is where you're just writing down all kinds of**

ideas and letting the thoughts flow freely, not worrying about whether what you're saying is correct or not. **The ideas just come, and you get them all on paper.** Once they're out, you can go back and start filling in the blanks, and trying to think things through a little more clearly. But that comes later, after the conceptual phase. If you'll do that, you'll find that you end up having a lot more ideas. **Ideas flow more freely when you're not instantly shooting them down or trying to flesh them out immediately.**

Ultimately, you'll also come up with better ideas. Let's say you have to come up with 10 ideas before you have one that's really practical and comes to fruition. Well, you obviously need to get through those nine bad ideas before you got to the one that works. But if you're only focused on seeing the good ones, you don't get to the nine bad ones; you end up striking down every idea, so you never let the ideas flow enough to find the good one. **You've got to let ideas die on their own. Let them come through, and eventually they'll die out or take root.** The ones that take root are the ones that you end up making money on. Don't throw the baby out with the bath water.

The Real Meaning of Luck

I believe that if you work at it, you can create more luck than a lottery winner. As the saying goes, fortune favors the prepared: the harder and smarter you work, the luckier you get. **In other words, you create your own luck. By my definition,** *luck is where preparation meets opportunity.*

Let me give you an example. Back in the early 1990s, when we were just starting to have some real success here at M.O.R.E., Inc., they hadn't really developed the World Wide Web yet, and Yahoo and Google weren't even on the radar. But they were in the air — and if we'd been prepared at that time and had seen the opportunity, we could have created something like Yahoo or Google and raked in a fortune. But we didn't.

Now, a lot of times, people on the outside of a success story will say, "Look at these guys — they're billionaires now. They're so lucky!" But they've got it completely backwards. Those Sergey Brins and Larry Pages got "lucky" because their preparation met opportunity. The guys who started Google are multi-billionaires now, and they're barely in their mid-30s. But they were preparing themselves all along, learning computer science and techniques for searching the Internet and all the other things necessary to build a better search engine. When they went public they made a fortune, because their search engine was the best of its kind. The rest is history. Their preparation met opportunity in a big way.

The harder you work, the luckier you get. If you want to be really lucky — and really successful — you'll need to work like a dog, going all out. I realize that for some of you reading this, that statement will pretty much be it for you. You're going to give up. But if you relish a challenge, it's not going to stop you. You'll keep on working hard, so that someday, all those envious people on the outside will look in at you and say, "You know what? They just got lucky." **Think of it as justification for all your hard work,** because you know what? **Successful entrepreneurs didn't just get lucky,** *they took massive action and went for it as hard as they could.* They put their dreams on the line, they stared failure in the face, and they beat it.

This idea that successful entrepreneurs are lucky is just nonsense. In this world, we're all self-made, from the meanest beggar to the richest tycoon, though only the most successful people will actually admit that. **If you want to be lucky, if you want to be very successful, work hard.** Take massive action as often as you can. Thomas Edison, the great inventor, once said, "If you want to be twice as successful, double your rate of failure." Babe Ruth struck out much more often than he hit home runs. **Just burn through all the bad ideas; try them out, and if they don't work, move on.**

According to statistics, as many 9 out of 10 businesses fail. Most people sitting on the sidelines look at that statement and say, "Wow, it's pretty risky to be an entrepreneur." But so what if 90% of businesses fail? Here's what I say to that: I'm going to stack the odds in my favor by starting *10* businesses. If 9 out of 10 really do fail, then I should have at least one successful business. And that's all I need: one successful business. Sure, it can be painful, even horrible, to crash and burn when your business fails. But you just pick yourself up, dust yourself off and get back at it. Never quit; keep the faith. **Think of it this way: if your first business fails and you quit, you'll never be where you want to be.** You'll be working some job, living in the rat race, having the Monday Morning Blues over and over. But in the back of your mind, there'll be that nagging question, wondering *what if* — what if you'd gone for it? What if you'd made it happen?

So keep working hard on your business, so you can improve your luck. **The average person has more opportunity now than ever before, thanks to the incredible, innovative modern technologies of communication and distribution.** People can go from rags to riches more easily than ever — it's happening more and more, even though the government doesn't want you to realize that somebody can be born in poverty and end up a multi-millionaire, or perhaps even a billionaire. I'm living proof of that. Early on, my wife and I struggled for a number of years, and we had a bunch of friends and family who just laughed when we told them that we were going to get rich. We were sending away for all kinds of get-rich programs, and they thought that was the funniest damned thing they ever heard in their life. They made jokes about us, they criticized us, and they thought we were delusional and needed professional help.

But we refused to quit. Eventually, when we found a few good ideas, took massive action, and *did* make our millions of dollars, those same people who laughed at us and criticized us started to talk about how lucky we were. **I think it's so amusing, the way people always attribute it to luck whenever someone becomes successful.** Nobody ever makes it on their own ability, right? No matter what the situation is, people who are successful *must* have gotten there out of luck. I think people say that just to make themselves feel better, better because if it's not luck, then obviously they lack something the other person has. If it's just happenstance, then it's easier to write it off. If you can do that, it absolves you of your responsibility to make something of yourself. Because if it's not luck, then maybe it's a formula — which means that you *could* make it work if you were willing to do what it takes. No one wants to admit that they aren't, so luck takes that responsibility out of their hands.

It's the same way across all forms of success. Saying someone succeeded through luck makes it so that you don't have to worry about it. Anybody could've been as successful as Bill Gates — it's just that he did it, and we didn't. Anybody could've gotten as rich as Jeff Bezos of Amazon — except he did, and we didn't. Anybody could've done all those things, but a few people did, and most people are sitting there are calling it luck. **But those of us in the know realize that there's no such thing as luck in the business world; you create your own luck.** There are some rare exceptions, but by and large, it's the things we do, the ways we think, and the actions we take that create our lives and determine whether or not we're successful. **We all make ourselves into whatever we are.**

I would encourage you to think deeply about that. Think about luck, and how many times you've either attributed or been inclined to attribute someone's success to luck. It's a natural tendency to say that someone got lucky, but I'd encourage you to try to get that out of your vocabulary. **Be honest and admit that it *wasn't* luck in most cases.** Of course if you're talking about someone who played the lottery and hit the lucky numbers, sure, that's luck. But if you're talking about people who succeed in business, get that word "luck" out of your vocabulary. Read their biographies and autobiographies. Watch what they're doing and figure out what they did, because chances are, you can apply that to your business. There's little chance that someone could repeat exactly what Google did, but maybe you could be the next best thing, or even replace Google a few years down the road. **As technology advances, as people innovate, you're going to see new things come around.** Google may be around forever, but there *will* be something new eventually.

Many of these businesses only last a few years, and yet their founders make millions, if not tens or hundreds of millions, of dollars, in a short period of time by creating their own luck. **It's all in seeing the opportunity and then seizing the day, by being in the right place at the right time to take advantage of opportunities as they arise.** People who are great at making excuses will never, ever become rich. It's all about taking responsibility for your own luck.

A Tight Deadline is a Marketer's Best Friend

The deadline might just be the single greatest productivity tool ever invented. Think about it: if there were no deadlines, what would get done? Possibly a fraction of what *does* get done. If you didn't have to file your taxes on April 15, when do you think you'd get around to filing them? You see it every year — people furiously scrambling at the last minute to get their taxes in, running to the post office at midnight so they won't be late. Deadlines motivate people; it's just human nature. **A deadline forces you to move ahead, make decisions, and**

get things done a lot faster, so keep those deadlines tight.

I like to set a deadline for everything I do, meaning that
if I have a project I'm working on, a sales letter to get done, I
want to be sure I get it out by a certain date. **Without a
deadline, you might work on a sales letter for months,** rather
than take the necessary action to get it out to your prospects. You
might tweak it to death, going back to it and revising and re-
writing it. But once you establish a deadline and say, "Hey, this
is the mail date. This is when this thing is going out!" then you
have a firm, fixed date when you have to get it done.

So set yourself a comfortable deadline. Decide whether you
can get the project done in a week, or however long you expect
it to take; and then, if you want to to make yourself massively
productive, shorten that deadline a little bit and do the best job
you can in the time you've allotted. That's the real secret to
using deadlines effectively. **If you think it might take you five
days to knock out a sales letter, shrink it down to maybe
three or four days.** Commit to that deadline — even if it's self
appointed. **Treat that deadline as an appointment that you
just never violate with yourself.** That way, you're forced to be
productive, because you have that deadline and really respect it.
If you've promised yourself to have a mailing out on a certain
date, that means you have to rent the list, get your stuff to the
printer and to the letter shop ahead of time, and make sure it all
gets out there in the mail.

What I recommend here is not just a self-imposed deadline,
which is excellent, **but also an outer deadline — that is, one
that others can hold you accountable for.** You might
communicate your deadlines to employees or others by saying,
"Hey, I've got a deadline where I'm going to do this by then."
That will force you into maximal productivity as the deadline
bears down on you. You knock out your sales letter or campaign
in time so you're able to look the people you promised the

deadline to in the eye and say, "I did it! I met the deadline." It's nice to be able to meet the deadline for yourself, but you also want to be able to tell others, "Hey, I'm doing what I said I was going to do." So figure out what's comfortable and then ratchet it up a notch. Make the deadlines tight — within reason. **The tighter the deadlines, the more productive you'll be.** I think that quite often, it's in the final days or hours, just before the deadline, when the inspiration hits. Everything comes together, and suddenly you can finish up that sales letter and get it before the deadline. So if you've never set deadlines at all, start setting them — and then hold yourself firmly accountable to them.

Here's a quick example. My friend and colleague Kent Sayre once had a project he was really lagging on, so he set himself a self-imposed deadline. At the time, he didn't know about committing this deadline to other people, or tying up resources so that there would be consequences if he didn't meet the deadline. So here's what he did: Kent went to the store, bought a can of dog food and set it on his desk, and said to himself, "Kent, if you don't meet this deadline, you're going to eat that can of dog food." Well, Kent didn't want to eat that dog food! Because he knew he had to get the sales letter done by the deadline, lo and behold, that's exactly what he did. He got so motivated he just knocked the sales letter out and got it in the mail. He never had to use that aggressive motivational trick ever again — but it worked, didn't it? He had consequences for not meeting the deadline, and that's critical, too.

Sometimes, you just have to find ways to make yourself do what you know you *need* to do. I like Kent's idea, but it's something we've never tried here at M.O.R.E., Inc. We have another way of motivating ourselves. **See, we do a lot of what we call two-step marketing; and one reason we do it is because that's what makes us the most money.** Everybody in the business knows that when you get people to raise their

333

hands, to request more information, you're able to separate the smaller group of more-qualified prospects from the larger group of less-qualified prospects. What we don't tell people is that a lot of times, we do two-step campaigns as a way of setting those deadlines for ourselves. You see, if there's one thing that I hate more than anything else, it's seeing leads pile up where we don't have lead fulfillment put together and out the door. Every day those leads just sit there, it drives me crazier and crazier. I just can't take it — I hate it! And so we'll do things to generate a bunch of leads — and we won't have the lead fulfillment package done yet. Nobody knows that but us. Then, as soon as the first lead comes in, every day that lead sits there and they don't get a fulfillment package, I just go crazy. **Soon I just can't take it anymore — it's too painful for me, and I work harder than I normally would in order to fulfill that order.**

That's just one thing that we do. We also have meetings every week where we schedule things in advance. **We have dates set; we don't always know what we're going to do, but we do know that the most important thing is to schedule the mailing, to get the date set in stone.** Everybody's got a dream and some people have goals, but those goals are really just dreams until you put a deadline on them. **That's all a goal is: a dream with a deadline.** So you've got to have those due dates. You've got to stay organized, and you've got to find ways to put leverage on yourself. Our two-step marketing process is one way that we put leverage on ourselves, and I believe it would work well for just about anyone. **It's an effective way of making us do what we know we need to do, so that we always have more projects than we can comfortably handle, and we're always working hard.**

We're Kansas City Chiefs fans where we live; our enemies are the Denver Broncos. But there was a quarterback that used to play for the Denver Broncos who I secretly admired, even though I'm supposed to not like the Broncos. His name is John Elway. It was so amazing to watch him play, and I'd watch every chance I got. In the fourth quarter, if the Broncos were behind, nobody worried when Elway was the quarterback, because in the last two minutes of the game he came alive. And you wondered, "Where was this guy the rest of the game?" All of a sudden, he's doing amazing things! It was incredible, what this man was able to do! He drove fear into the heart of every team that ever played the Broncos, because in the last quarter, that man would really take off — especially if they were losing and his back was against the wall. **So you can see this deadline concept in sports, too.**

I know a lot of people who are dabblers — and I can be one of them. Sometimes I have my hand in multiple projects, or I've got ideas for projects or programs. So I'll write some sales copy; but it doesn't get done; it's just something I tinker with a little. **I've found that a deadline is a great way to force myself to get things done. You can use the two-step method, if that works for you; or you can tie up resources and force yourself to do it.** Let's say you've promised your clients a seminar; go ahead book the hotel for the day of the event, and that will force you to develop and promote it, because you've got to put butts in seats at the event. There are lots of things you can do to put a deadline on yourself. You can even make yourself eat dog food if you fail!

In any case, I encourage you to verbalize your deadline with people, and maybe even your customers. Or maybe you just verbalize it with your staff, or a spouse, or a business partner; but if you do verbalize it, you make it real, and someone else is there to hold you accountable to that deadline. **If you just decide in your own mind that you're going to do something, you might not do it.** Let's say that by this Friday, you're going to have a certain sales letter done. Well, who's going to know if you miss that deadline? Only you, if you haven't told anyone. And if that's the case, you'll lie to yourself and come up with excuses for why you missed the deadline. But if you commit to someone else that you're going to meet that deadline, then they can hold you accountable for it. It doesn't take much; if nothing else, just call someone you know and trust, someone you respect, and tell them, "Hey, I've got a deadline. Here's what I'm trying to do. **Will you call me tomorrow and make sure I've done something toward that deadline?** Will you call me two days from now and make sure that I'm on track, and will you call me three days from now? Every day, will you call me at this time and just say, 'Hey how's it going? Are you on track?'" Maybe they can just send you an email. **The point is, have them do something to communicate with you and remind you of your deadline.**

Stick to that, and you'll get more things done — and **you'll find yourself being more productive than you ever were before you made those deadlines.** A deadline doesn't have to be real, incidentally; it can be made up. Even if there's no pressing need to finish something, you can still make up a fake deadline that turns out to be real because you've imposed it on yourself. **It doesn't have to be tied to something that's really happening.**

I think this is an excellent final strategy for our chapter on taking massive action. If you'll take it to heart and put it into play, along with the other strategies I've discussed here, then I guarantee you'll move forward and get things done.

RULE FIFTEEN:

Fifty in Fifty

This final Marketing Rule is to <u>always</u> **strive to give your customers <u>more</u> than they expect.** So that is what I doing with this last chapter!

I'm known as America's "Blue Jeans Millionaire" for a good reason. I'm an average guy who started with absolutely nothing. I was dead broke for a number of years, searching for a way to make a lot of money, trying one thing after another and failing every step of the way. Ultimately, I discovered some great marketing secrets, and gathered in some superb people to help me. **Thanks to all the help I got from those people, and the marketing secrets they taught me along the way, I've been able to generate millions of dollars over the past two decades or so.**

Now, I'm not trying to brag here. **I'm telling you this because I want to emphasize that if *I* can make millions of dollars, anybody can.** There's nothing special about me. I'm the most average guy around. If you had me in a lineup and tried to pick the millionaire out of that lineup, you would never pick me. And yet, here I am—having earned more than $114 million in less than 21 years. **I just want to remind you that *anybody* can make millions of dollars if they want to bad enough**—if you're willing to do whatever it takes, if you surround yourself with the best people, if you don't give up, and if you learn and practice some great business tips, tricks, and strategies along the way.

With that in mind, I recently turned 50 years of age, and I wrote a book called *50 in 50*. **It contains the 50 greatest secrets I've learned in my first 50 years of life, and how they can be vital to your success.** I didn't start my first business until I was 25. By that time, I'd already tried and failed at a number of things. I started my first "official" business in December 1985. Since then, I've managed to learn a lot of great stuff—and in this chapter, **I'll briefly cover all 50 that I covered in my book.** So let's just jump right in there!

SECRET #1: There are only three ways to build a business: **1)** You can get more customers, **2)** You can sell more high-ticket items for bigger profits, or **3)** You can sell more often to your customers. No matter how complicated business gets, there are only these three ways to build a business. They work for every business there is. If you get confused, keep bringing it back to these basics, and that'll take all the confusion out of it.

SECRET #2: Selling is the art of proving that what you have to offer is worth far, far more than the money that the customer must give up in return. Enough said.

SECRET #3: Create irresistible offers! Back in 1977, I wrote: "I want to create offers that are like heads of fresh lettuce thrown into a pen of starving rabbits." That's the kind of thing you're looking for here. **Create offers that are so exciting that people just can't help but give you their money, because of all the value that you've created for them.** The best way to learn how to do that is to study how other people are doing it themselves. There are plenty of examples of how other people are already creating great offers that get people excited, that get them fired up, that get them to give their money in exchange for those products and services.

SECRET #4: Think on paper. The very act of putting your ideas on paper forces you to think. Whenever you're confused or frustrated, just start writing things down. **Whenever you're excited, start writing things down.** Start putting your thoughts on paper. It will help you reach a higher part of who you are.

SECRET #5: Blur the lines between your work and play. Making money is *not* a serious thing; it's a game. Now, you should play it with your whole heart and soul, but it's still just a game. So have fun with it! It's an adventure. **It's not something you should drive yourself crazy with; it should be fun and challenging and rewarding.**

SECRET #6: The power of the Five A.M. Club. Force yourself to get out of bed before you want to, put on a big pot of strong black coffee, pull out some paper and pens, and start writing. **Ideas will come to you and through you that you would have never discovered if you had stayed in bed.** There's a magic at work here that's hard to explain, but you've got to experience it before you can actually believe it. I've been getting up every morning at five A.M. for years.

SECRET #7: "Less is more." That's a Robert Browning quote from hundreds of years ago. **It's far better to be a master at two or three things than to be average at doing a whole bunch of things.** Mastery is what we're all after here!

SECRET #8: The real business is between our ears and in our hearts, *not in the office.* Russ von Hoelscher first told me that when I was going through some tough times back in the early 1990s. It was one of our very first business crises, and I was talking to him on the telephone one day about the future of the business, and things didn't look good. Russ just told me, "T.J., just remember, the real business is between your ears and in your heart. It's not in the office." **So it's not in your physical location; it's something that you carry with you at all times.**

SECRET #9: A strong risk-reversal offer takes a lot of courage, but can make you super rich. A risk-reversal offer is one where you're taking all of the risk; the people you're asking to respond don't have any at all. **If they don't like what you're offering, they can send it back for a full refund, losing nothing in the process.** That's part of what you do to create irresistible offers.

SECRET #10: I have a lot of competition, but ZERO competitors! This is a quote from Kerry Thomas, who runs my best friend's pest control company. One day when I was working with him, we were talking about the fact that they had over 100 competitors right there in Wichita, Kansas, which is a fairly small city. Terry said, very matter of factly, "Look, we've got a lot of competition, but we've got *zero* competitors!" That was so brilliant! I wrote it down that night, and I've never forgotten it.

So many people focus on and worry about the competition. **Well, competition is a good thing. It means that a market for what you're selling is well established —and there's always room for one more, assuming that you deliberately differentiate yourselves from all the rest.** You're going to find some way to do it better than the rest of them do it. So remember that quote from Kerry: "I have a lot of competition, but *zero* competitors." There's an attitude to that quote. Kerry isn't an overly egotistical guy, but he believes in what he does. He believes in his company, and so do the people he works with—or they leave. You either adopt that attitude or you don't make it in that company.

SECRET #11: Test new ideas, but never stray too far from the winning formulas that have been proven to be the most successful in your marketplace. Some things work better than others, and in every market, there are common denominators you need to recognize. **The more you study the competition, and the more you subject yourself to all the**

things that they're doing, the more you're going to find out what works best. Don't stray far from those formulas, because they're proven to make money! The time to start testing more radical things is when you've got a lot of money in the bank.

So in the beginning, stick close to what other successful people are doing. It sounds like common sense, and yet so many entrepreneurs want to be independent. They want to try all their own ideas first... and a lot of their ideas don't necessarily work in the marketplace. They haven't been proven, so you stick with what *is* proven.

SECRET #12: All this talk about retirement is nonsense. Work gives our life purpose, meaning, and structure. Stop telling me to take it easy—I'll have *eternity* to take it easy! I want to live fully. Retirement is simply a bad idea. For most people it doesn't work at all. They retire, and then they die. What we need to do is to pace ourselves and push ourselves. We need to be in the flow of life, in the flow of business, and that's one of the reasons business is so great. It keeps you moving. I feel sorry for people who just do it for the money. Their real passions are all the things that they do *off* the job. Well, if they don't enjoy what they're doing, they should either quit or learn *how* to enjoy what they're doing. I watched my Dad and my step-dad both die a lot younger than they had to because they retired. They got out of the flow of life... and pretty soon they were dead. It doesn't have to be that way. Some of the people who live the longest are the ones that are most active, the ones who are involved in as many things as possible... and that's what a good business can do for you!

SECRET #13: The question all marketers *must* constantly ask is, "What's next?" There's always got to be something next. Customers are addicted to the new, and so you've got to give it to them. Always be looking for what's next. Always have a bunch of projects waiting for you. As I'm

341

writing this, I've got six or seven different projects planned. They're hanging up on Post-It notes with all of my goals, which are also on Post-It notes. Every morning when I'm on the treadmill, I can look over there and see those notes, each representing a certain project that we're working on. You should always have things that you're working on, constantly. Is it stressful? It can be. It can be frustrating, too. **But it's also a necessary thing, because it keeps you busy, keeps you moving.** You can pace yourself, but do force yourself at the same time.

SECRET #14: Jump and the net will appear! Make the commitment first. Set the deadline. Run the ad, and then scramble to put the fulfillment together. **Make big, bold promises to customers and then scramble to fulfill on those promises.** Do whatever you can to force yourself to do more.

SECRET #15: Salespeople get paid to hear the word "no." Accept that. **In any case, a "no" doesn't mean "no" to the aggressive salesperson who wants the sale—and you've got to be aggressive in this day and age.** Most people give up way too soon. The marketers who are doing the very best, those who are making the most money, are the most aggressive ones— the people who refuse to give up. They do the most relentless follow-up. **You've got to keep that pressure on, assuming you're dealing with good, qualified prospects and you've got a great offer for them that really can deliver the goods.** Just because they say "no" seven times doesn't mean they're going to say "no" the eighth or ninth time. **If they're highly qualified, you'll eventually get them to see things your way.** It takes persistence; it takes a certain amount of relentlessness. But those who do the most follow-up marketing are the ones that make the most money.

SECRET #16: Take good care of the people who take good care of you. Again, this sounds like common sense, and yet we often end up taking for granted the people who help us the most. **We don't show them enough appreciation, we're critical of them, and we don't pay enough attention to them.** You have to take good care of the people who take good care of you. It's a simple thing. Most people would agree, but ask them what they're doing to accomplish that, and they can't tell you much. **Don't make that mistake!**

SECRET #17: **Your best work is still out there.** You always have to believe that. **No matter how far you've gone, you always have to believe that there's something else out there for you that's even better.** A good friend of mine once told me that his dad told *him* that the secret of happiness is to always have something to look forward to. I believe that. Have something to look forward to, to get excited about. Always believe that your best is still out there.

SECRET #18: **It's better to strengthen your back than to lighten your load.** You've got to run towards the things that most people are trying to run away from: setbacks, adversities, responsibilities, obligations, pressures, commitments. **When you face those things head-on, you'll find that they're often the stepping stones to your ultimate success.** Everybody secretly wants the easy life, but truly, it's better to strengthen your back than to lighten the load. You don't want to drive yourself crazy, or stress yourself to the breaking point; remember, pace yourself but push yourself. **The more you *do* push yourself, the stronger you're going to get. The stronger you get, the more success you can handle.** You're going to do the things that most people couldn't possibly do, because you've developed an inner strength that they haven't.

SECRET #19: **All growth comes from consciously living outside of your comfort zone.** This is related to Secret #18. If you're not regularly doing things that scare you just a little (or a lot), you're not growing. **There always should be a certain sense of fear in your life.** As I mentioned in the previous section,

10 or 12 years ago I lost over $100,000 on a certain business situation I got involved in. One of the reasons I lost all of that money is because I was overly confident. I had a tremendous ego. Not that I don't have one now; to some extent, I think that's healthy. But you know, I wasn't scared at all. I was overly confident. I thought that I could come in and do some big things and make some bigger things happen... and ultimately I ended up losing a lot of money. More recently, I went into something similar, and though at that time I was dealing with a lot of doubt, a lot of confusion, a lot of fear, I didn't let it stop me. **I think it's a good thing to live beyond your comfort zone.**

Don't wish that things were easier, wish that you were better. Always push yourself. If you're not always just a little bit scared about something you're working on, that just means you're doing the same thing over and over, and you're still living in your comfort zone. **All growth comes *outside* of that comfort zone.**

SECRET #20: More business problems are created by indecision than bad decisions. You've got to go ahead and take massive action. You've got to try many different things, and fail, and learn from your mistakes while you're daring big and failing again. **It's not really failing, you see, unless you just give up and quit.** Fear holds people back in most things. It stops them from getting all the things that they could and should have. Mostly, they're afraid of failing; **but they should take some of that fear and start doing more planning, start thinking things through.** That's why I talk about getting up at five o'clock every morning and putting on that pot of coffee, getting a little caffeinated, and starting to write all of your ideas down. **Take some of that fear and begin thinking about ways you can overcome the obstacles in your way.** Then decide you're just going to keep moving forward, no matter what... that you're going to continue to stretch yourself.

SECRET #21: Spend *more* money to close more sales.
As long as your percentage of conversion is going up, you
simply can't spend too much money if **a)** you're spending the
money on super-qualified prospects, or **b)** if you're selling big-
ticket items with good profit margins. **Everybody's worried
about spending too much money, and yet most people don't
spend *nearly* as much money as they should on their
conversions.** We talked about relentless follow-up marketing. It
costs money to do that. But as long as you're dealing with good,
qualified prospects, as long as you've got good profit margins...
well, you almost *can't* spend enough money. You've got to stay
after these people! **If they express an interest, especially if
they spent some money initially, you can usually assume
they're really good prospects for larger ticket items.** But
you've got to be willing to spend as much money as you can on
the marketing to convert the largest amount of sales.

SECRET #22: Most marketers are weak. That's not a
judgment, just an observation. **And here's why they're weak:
they give up way too soon.** They're too worried about
offending the prospects or customers, or simply don't realize
that there's a great deal more money lying on the table that could
be theirs. If they went after it more aggressively and stayed after
it, they would ultimately get that money. Now, we tell you not to
worry too much about the competition, but you *should* be
focused on them at some level. **You should know what they're
doing; you should know their strengths and weaknesses.** And
I'm telling you, most competitors are weak in the sense that they
give up way too soon. **They leave a lot of money on the table,**
and any aggressive marketer who wants to come along after
them... well, all that money is theirs for the taking.

**SECRET #23: Your business is like a bicycle—either you
keep it moving, or you fall down.** Get that visual in your head!
If you're on a bicycle, you can coast a little if the weather and

road conditions are right. You can lift up your arms and just roll downhill and enjoy the ride. But the bottom line is, you've got to keep pedaling at some level. **You have to keep it moving... because if it doesn't stay in motion, it's going to fall. That's how a business is, too.** So don't rest on your laurels. **Keep searching for your next big winner.** Keep finding better ways to sell your customers and prospects what you know they want the most. We're all in business to serve customers, to find out what their biggest desires are, and then fulfill on those desires through the products and services we develop.

SECRET #24: Create as many "businesses within your business" as you possibly can. It will make things fun and interesting. **You'll be able to work with other people.** There are all kinds of different things that you can do to create anywhere from three to seven different smaller "businesses" within the business—even if it's just with joint venture partners, where you're working with other people who have related products and services, and they want to go out to your mailing list.

SECRET #25: Get your best offer in front of more people and follow up like crazy! You know, if I had to stop right here and now with my secrets, this would be enough. **If this was the only secret I could give you, a singular formula for success, this is it.** What's your best offer? It's all the things you're offering to give to people in exchange for the money you're asking for in return. What is it that makes an offer special? How can you create better, more exciting offers to attract more qualified prospects? **Answer those questions, then follow up like crazy and be relentless in that follow-up!**

SECRET #26: The best product does not always win, but the best marketing always does! This is a sore spot with many newcomers. They think that if they have the best product or service, somehow that's going to be their gateway into the marketplace, that somehow it's going to be enough. **That's a**

delusion. They get upset when they find out that in many cases, the companies making the most money in their marketplaces are *not* delivering the best-quality products and services. **They're just doing the best job of marketing.** People feel that's unfair, and some spend a lot of time whining and crying about it. **Instead, they should get better at marketing.**

And what *is* marketing, anyway? If you ask a hundred different marketing experts you'll get a hundred different answers. But I think every one of them could agree with this: **Marketing is everything you do to attract and retain the best qualified customers, the best people in the marketplace for the types of products and services you sell.** The companies that do the best job of marketing don't always have the best products or services in their marketplace, but they're doing the most consistent job of attracting and retaining the largest percentage of the most qualified buyers.

SECRET #27: All business is show business! In the end, people want to be entertained a little. People want things that are exciting! **They want things that are new! They want things that are different! That's part of the "performance" aspect of business.** It really is a performance at some level, where you're always giving people what they want and you're mixing it up a little.

SECRET #28: Your best customers are like fires. They go out if unattended. The key word here is "relationships." The better people feel about you, the more money they're going to give you. A good metaphor for this is to remember that a fire never dies as long as you keep feeding it. **Your communication and relationship with your customers is the fuel for their fire.** You've got to keep feeding them. You can't just wait for them to call or come to you; **you've got to make a sincere effort to deepen those relationships in some way.** Now, that's easier to do with some businesses than with others—and yet, all of us are in the relationship business. **We're out to serve customers and give them more of what we know that they want and value the most.**

SECRET #29: Many people think nothing of spending $60,000 to put their son or daughter through college for four to six years so they can become a nameless, faceless, middle manager and make enough money to drive a nice car and live in an upper middle class neighborhood. **Yet these same people will freak out when you ask them to cough up $3,000 for a marketing seminar that's designed to show them how to make millions of dollars!** Why is this? It's something that's always perplexed me. They have their priorities screwed up, as far as I'm concerned. Just good food for thought.

SECRET #30: What are you willing to do? "Willing" is the important word here. It implies a positive attitude. What are you *willing* to do? **So many people want all of the best things that life has to offer, but they're not willing to do a whole lot to get those things.** So willingness is very important.

SECRET #31: Rock star or brain surgeon? Your time is your most precious commodity. So why would you want to sell it for any amount of money? Don't do this! **Find as many ways as you can to make money that have little or even nothing to do with the amount of time that you put into them.** Now, that seems like a fantasy to most people. They're getting paid for the hours they work. **And yet the world's richest people don't trade time for money.** I like to use the metaphor of the rock star here; some are worth a hundred million bucks, and that worth isn't based on the absolute amount of time they spend working. On the other hand, a brain surgeon gets paid *huge* money, but if he is not performing any surgeries he's not getting paid those big bucks. So what would you rather be? **Think about a situation where the money you make comes from the sale of a product or service.** You're not selling your time. You can sell far more of those products or services than you can hours or minutes. Look in the marketplace for specific examples. **Get on the other side of the cash register.** See how other companies are doing it; the more you do that, in an objective manner, the more common denominators you'll see.

SECRET #32: What is the best way to deepen your relationship with your customers? The answer: **hold seminars, teleseminars, workshops, and other training events** that bond with them by showing them that you care and really do want to help them. You can do all this through the careful creation of all kinds of information products sold or sent to them. **Let people get to know *you* and who you are. Don't play games with them.** Don't try to be anything you're not. Just try to help them. Try to give them everything you possibly can that will help them get what they really want.

If you hold these events, even the customers that don't show up will realize you really do want to help them—or at least they're going to sense your desire to help them. Why else would you be inviting them to all of these events? You've got nothing to hide. Those that do come to those events are going to get a sense of who you are. **They're going to bond to you. They're going to feel that relationship, which is what people really want: relationships with others who are committed to helping them get what they want.**

SECRET #33: The only three ways to make money: 1) Sell your time for money, charging by the hour and trading your life for a paycheck. That's how most people do it. **2)** Sell some type of product or service. Your money then comes from the sale of the product or service, not the time or work that it takes to sell it. **3) Leverage your money to makes you more money without direct effort.** All of the world's richest people make most of their money with this third method. You need to do that too.

You know, rock stars go out on the road. They work hard. But they also make money on their album sales. They get royalties for the songs that they write or co-write. **That's passive income.** The more you can do to make money passively, the more you're going to be tapping into the highest way of making money.

SECRET #34: The nine major marketing mistakes and how to avoid them:

1. *No focus.* Your list of prospects is of primary importance. You've got to hone in on one specific highly-qualified prospect and know them in the most intimate way. So who are you trying to reach? A lot of companies have no focus. Their marketing messages are too bland, and they ultimately do a poor job of attracting people.

2. *There's no compelling offer.* You've got to have something hot to get people to take action right now. There's got to be a reason why they have to buy right now; and you create all that when you create your offer.

3. *No deadline.* The more urgency that you can build into your offer, the higher your response rate will be. You've got to have a deadline and tell people why that deadline is there.

4. *No testimonials.* What other people say about you is more important than what you say about yourself.

5. *No measurement of results.* The only thing that counts is return on investment: ROI. You've got to know your numbers. Don't get hung up on response rates. How much does something cost you? How much does it make you? That's the *only* thing that's important.

6. *No follow-up.* Most people are giving up way too soon. Eighty-two percent of all sales happen after the first follow-up. So keep following up! Be relentless! Assuming you've got good, qualified prospects, you almost can't do enough or spend too much money to try to get them to follow up. Several years ago, we had a very successful campaign where we had 32 different follow-ups. We also had a team of high-caliber salespeople who followed up on the phone with all those people. We put a lot of pressure on prospects, and that's what you *have* to do. If you've got something that can help people and you believe in what you're doing and know you can deliver the goods, then you're doing them a disservice by not trying to do everything you can to try to get them to make that purchase.

7. *Trying to be cute and funny.* Too many people try to use humor in their ad copy or their marketing message, and it just doesn't work. As Claude Hopkins said, "People don't buy from clowns."

8. *Bad copy.* It's the right words that make all of the difference.

9. *Too much reliance on one medium.* You've got to diversify and use different approaches to attract and sell to different kinds of customers.

Do the opposite of what most people are doing, and you won't make these mistakes—*and* you'll get the money they're not getting.

SECRET #35: "Business is always a struggle." One of my favorite quotes is from Herbert N. Casson, and it's on the wall near where I do all my work, so I can see it all of the time. Here it is: "Business is always a struggle. There are always obstacles and competitors. There is never an open road—except the wide road that leads to failure. **Every great success has always been achieved by fight. Every winner has scars.** Those who succeed are the efficient few. They are the few who have the ambition and willpower to develop themselves."

However often we may wish otherwise, you've got to fight for success, and develop yourself along the way. **You've got to work on yourself as much as you work on your business.** With so many people, when business is good they're okay. But when business gets bad, they just can't handle it. That's one of the reasons why so many companies just throw in the towel during economic downturns. **But all of life comes and goes; it's in flow constantly, with both good days and bad days. That's just part of life, and business is amplified life.** You get some of the good; you get some of the bad. You've got to be willing to take both. You've got to be willing to just get through it.

SECRET #36: Our greatest rock and roll model is the heavy metal band AC/DC. AC/DC has recorded nearly 20 albums. They've sold over 200,000,000 copies worldwide... and every one of their songs has the same three or four chords. That's it! They've got a trademark sound; and while they do vary it occasionally, it's rare for them to do so. Yet this band has fans all over the world. If they were ever to stop using those same three or four chords in every song, their fan base would quickly dry up.

The point I'm trying to make is this: **You've got to find your formula and, once you do, never stray from it. You can have variations on a theme. You _can_ do some new stuff.** And yes, I've talked about the importance of the new, and it's true that customers are addicted to it... but they're more interested in the veneer of newness rather than newness through and through. **Underneath that veneer is the same familiar old stuff they bought from you the first time, or the first few times, or the** first few dozen times.

SECRET #37: Hard work is good for your soul! Plus, it may keep you alive longer. And if it doesn't, it will surely add more life to your years while you're here. Here's a quote from David Ogilvy: **"Hard work never killed a man. Men die of boredom, psychological conflict, and disease. Indeed, the harder you work, the happier you'll be."** I'm pretty sure David is still alive. He's very old now, and he's proof of his quote. And here's another guy who lived to a ripe old age before he died: Edward DeRopp. He wrote a whole bunch of books, and some of them are kind of strange. Here's a quote from one of his books called *Warrior's Way*: **"Seek above all else a game worth playing, and play it as if your entire life and sanity depended on it. For it does!"** And remember, earlier in the chapter I pointed out that making money shouldn't a serious thing. It's a game you play. **Don't take it too seriously, but do play the game with all your heart.**

You know, for most people, work is just something they do for money, nothing more; everything they do that relates to work is all just to get a paycheck. Their passion isn't in it. Their heart's not in it. Their soul is not in it. They're just going through the motions. They live their entire lives that way, which makes this quote from Henry David Thoreau all the more poignant: **"Most people live lives of quiet desperation, and go to their graves with their song still in them that they were born to sing."** It's because they're just going through the motions. They've never learned that hard work is good for the soul. They've never put their whole selves into it. They've never sought a game worth playing.

SECRET #38: More problems = more action. So bring it on, baby! You get rich by consistently doing the things that other people cannot or will not do: taking huge risks, putting your neck on the line, facing tremendous struggles, backing yourself into a corner you have to fight your way out of, or tackling more than you can possibly handle. **The secret is to create a lot of problems that can spur you on big-time! So you're always biting off more than you can chew.** You're always getting involved in one more project than you can comfortable handle. You're always keeping that pressure on yourself.

Again, you don't want to make yourself miserable; quite the contrary. **You want that pressure to drive you and keep you moving forward.** That's part of the way you get the best work out of yourself. You demand more from yourself. **You** *expect* **more from yourself. You set bigger goals.** It's part of the way that you push yourself to where you can develop your skills and knowledge, and you can be the best you can possibly be. You're not going to do any of that without driving yourself. **Problems drive you.**

Again, most people run from all of this. They don't want a lot of adversity in their lives. And I'm here to tell you that those things are *good*. They're life-giving! **If they spur you into some positive action and you keep moving forward, they'll actually enhance your life.** They'll help you be more and do more; and then, ultimately, you'll *get* more!

SECRET #39: Delegate your weaknesses. Focus on your strengths. It takes a team to achieve; it really does. Hillary Clinton had that great little quote that everybody made fun of: "It takes a village to raise a child…" **But it** *does* **take a team if you want to make millions of dollars.** The more money you want to make, the more people you have to surround yourself with; and **you've got to find people who are good in the areas you're** *not* **good in.** That's what I mean by about delegating your weaknesses.

SECRET #40: The 10 main things that made us millions. This comes from the 10-year anniversary seminar we had in 1998. These 10 things were the most responsible for all the money we made in our first ten years of business, and I'd even go as far as to say within our first 20+ years now.

1. *We knew the market before we got started.* I was already buying all kinds of moneymaking opportunities before we ever started selling them to other people, so there was a familiarity with the marketplace.

2. *We had some previous business experience.* That helped tremendously. I started my first business in December 1985, and Eileen joined me later.

3. *Eileen and I formed a partnership of two very different people.* In my first business I went through two partners, and both were exactly like me. They were salespeople, and that's all they were. Now, I think salespeople are the greatest people on earth; but the strength of my partnership with Eileen has been phenomenal. There always has to be at least one salesperson in the partnership, or you don't have a business; but there has to be a manager, too. Eileen is my opposite in so many ways, especially when it comes to business.

4. *We fell in love with our business.*

5. *We focused on serving our customers,* really giving them what they truly needed and wanted.

6. *We got a lot of help from a lot of experts,* people who were professional marketing consultants and knew what they were doing.

7. *We developed a great staff.* Eileen stepped down from the business in 2001, and one of the best things I've

done since then is that I've held onto the staff she'd developed in our first 14 years.

8. *We learned the art and skill of developing products and offers.* It *is* an art, but it's also a skill; there's a lot of knowledge that goes with it. It takes a lot of practice. You never can learn enough. You never stop learning.

9. *We learned how to develop front-end and back-end marketing systems.* A front-end marketing system is designed to automatically attract new customers, and a back-end marketing system is designed to resell to those customers again and again.

10. *We always strive to give our customers more than they receive from our competitors.* Are we successful? Sometimes yes, sometimes no. But we always strive to be. That's within our control—that intention to be the best.

SECRET #41: Never fear objections. Don't hide. Be up front about the skepticism you know your prospects feel. **Bring up their biggest objections, then overcome them one by one.** You'll win their trust and their respect, and you'll get their money. The key here is the fact that the best prospects have major objections that must be faced head-on and not skated around. In fact, if they don't have a lot of objections, I think you should be just a little cautious.

SECRET #42: "The pain of discipline hurts less than the pain of regret." This is a quote I have hanging up on my wall. Look, discipline hurts. Forcing yourself to do what you know you have to do... well, sometimes your heart's in it, sometimes it's not. **When your heart's not in it, you've got to force yourself to do it, and that's painful.** And yet, that kind of pain hurts a lot less than the pain of regret. Discipline yourself.

SECRET #43: You've got to roll with the punches, and keep getting up every time you get knocked down. So many people want to make a lot of money, but they want everything to be easy. They've got this notion that it's all going to go smoothly. Sometimes it does, but sometimes you have to deal with a lot of problems. The more money you want to make, the more problems you've got to deal with. The bigger your company, the more problems you have. **The secret is just to keep getting back up and never give up.** Just keep moving forward. Fight. Always fight. Remember that quote from Herbert Casson that I talked about earlier: "All business is a struggle."

SECRET #44: Are all highly successful entrepreneurs a little crazy? Maybe. But one thing is certain: **Almost all tend to be very creative.** And, of course, the symptoms of creativity are directly related to insanity. **On creative side,** you have high energy, heightened senses, emotional expressiveness, risk-taking, spontaneity, single-mindedness, unusual perceptions, visions, big ideas, affluency of ideas, high standards, and a feeling of giftedness. **But on the flipside,** these balance out with mania, insomnia, mood disorder, erratic behavior, emotional volatility, impulsiveness, recklessness, obsessiveness, distortions of reality, hallucinations, grandiosity, flight of ideas, perfectionism, and narcissism.

The more you think about it, the more you'll realize that all great entrepreneurs definitely have the symptoms on the left hand of the chart, which are all the positive things that go with what it takes to be really creative. And then, sometimes, especially when they're younger, they've got personal problems from the right side too. **So all entrepreneurs are a little bit crazy.** In fact, one of my business associates recently told me, "You're crazy!" He meant it as a put-down, but I took it as a compliment! **I mean, the entrepreneurial way is that we're creative people, and we're always dreaming big dreams, and** we've got all these plans and ideas. *Of course* there's a certain amount of insanity that goes with all of that.

SECRET #45: Stop lowering your prices. Low prices are reserved for those who cannot market themselves effectively. **If you're competing on price, you haven't established enough value in the minds of your prospective customers.** It's up to you to prove without a doubt that the very best prospects in your market should be giving you *more* of their money. **Marketing is all about differentiation, but *you* have to create those perceptions of difference in the minds of the people you most want on your customer list.** The easiest thing to do is drop your price, but that's not marketing.

SECRET #46: Strive to be more human in all of your communications. Be real! Be raw! Be imperfect! Let them feel what you feel, and let them see the real person behind the words they're reading.

SECRET #47: Learn by doing. You can't let a simple thing like the fact that you've never done something or don't know how to do it stop you from trying. **The fact that entrepreneurs are willing to boldly step out and face the unknown and figure it all out as they go is one of the things that separates us from everybody else.**

SECRET #48: The front-end builds your list, but the back-end makes you rich. Again, the front-end is all the things you do to get new customers. That's essential; you've got to have some way to constantly bring in new customers. But it's your back-end that makes you rich. They're all of the people you sell to again and again.

SECRET #49: The #1 reason that the most solid businesses begin to decline is simply because they stop doing the things that took them to the top. They lose their edge. They lose their focus, their hunger. They lose the boldness and creativity they had when they were struggling on their way to the top! They become conservative and complacent. Now they're easy targets for the companies that are just like they once were.

SECRET #50: You can't kill an elephant with a BB gun. That's a great metaphor, because in marketing, people are always trying to get huge results with a small amount of effort and expense. That's the BB gun. P. T. Barnum used to say that most people want to catch a whale by using a little tiny minnow as bait. **But, folks, the more you want, the more you've got to be willing to do to get it.** It just makes common sense!

*****

Now, I'll admit I went through that list awfully quickly; but after all, I did write a whole book about these 50 things! **You can find that book on Amazon.com,** by the way: just type in my name and look for *"50 in 50."* **I've also got an additional 50 bonus secrets in that book, for a total of 100 different secrets.** I hope you'll go to Amazon and buy the book, and study what I teach in there. I realize that a lot of those ideas sound like common sense (because they are) and some are more important than others. **But when you take them collectively, you'll see that this is a great way to turning small amounts of money into a fortune.** So I *am* living proof that anybody in America can get rich, if they want to. I'm the most average guy around— but I've surrounded myself with extraordinary people and leveraged these secrets to build an enormous fortune.

I honestly believe that you can do the same. Take all of these tips and put them in play, and the answer won't be, "Will you get rich?" It will be, "How rich will you get, and when will you get it?" **All the money you're looking for is out there right now!**